The Captors' Narrative

THE CAPTORS' NARRATIVE

*Catholic Women and
Their Puritan Men on
the Early American Frontier*

WILLIAM HENRY FOSTER

Cornell University Press

ITHACA AND LONDON

Copyright © 2003 by William Henry Foster

All rights reserved. Except for brief quotations in a review, this book, or parts
thereof, must not be reproduced in any form without permission in writing
from the publisher. For information, address Cornell University Press,
Sage House, 512 East State Street, Ithaca, New York 14850.

First published 2003 by Cornell University Press

Printed in the United States of America

Library of Congress Cataloging-in-Publication Data

Foster, William Henry, 1963–
    The captors' narrative : Catholic women and their Puritan men on the
early American frontier / William Henry Foster.
        p. cm.
Includes bibliographical references (p.) and index.
    ISBN 0-8014-4059-9 (cloth : alk. paper)
    1. Sex role—Canada—History.   2. Slave labor—Canada—History.
3. Indian captivities—Canada.   4. Captivity narratives—New England—
History and criticism.   5. Catholic women—Canada—Social conditions.
6. Nuns—Canada—Social conditions.   7. Puritan men—Canada—Social
conditions.   8. Frontier and pioneer life—Canada.   9. Canada—History—
To 1763.   I. Title.
    HQ1075.5.C2F67 2003
    971.01′8—dc21   2002151455

Cornell University Press strives to use environmentally responsible suppliers
and materials to the fullest extent possible in the publishing of its books.
Such materials include vegetable-based, low-VOC inks and acid-free papers
that are recycled, totally chlorine-free, or partly composed of nonwood
fibers. For further information, visit our website at www.cornellpress.cornell.edu.

Cloth printing   10   9   8   7   6   5   4   3   2   1

For Susan and Madeleine Honor

Contents

Acknowledgments

This book exists because of the mentorship and kindnesses of Dan Usner and Mary Beth Norton. I am grateful as well to those who read and offered comments on all or parts of the manuscript including Evan Haefeli, Isaac Kramnick, Ann Little, Neal Salisbury, Patricia Simpson CND, Michael Steinberg, Kevin Sweeney, and several anonymous readers. The archivists at the Congrégation Notre-Dame de Montréal, the Hôtel-Dieu of Montreal, the Hôtel-Dieu of Quebec, the Maison d'Youville (Montreal), the Archives Nationales de Québec, the Archives Nationales de Québec—Montréal, the National Archives of Canada, the Historic Deerfied-Pocumtuck Valley Memorial Library, and Neilson Library at Smith College rendered especially invaluable assistance. I thank Sheri Englund, Ange Romeo-Hall, and John LeRoy for their editorial guidance. The faculties of the History Departments at Stanford and the University of Pennsylvania, as well as Laura Free and Arthur Woll, provided always warm hospitality.

The Mellon Foundation, the Ihlder Fellowship, the Cornell Department of History and the Cornell Graduate School funded much of the research for this work. Finally, the very generous support of the Master and Fellows of Selwyn College, Cambridge, in concert with the Keasbey Foundation, allowed me to complete the manuscript during my first year in Britain.

An earlier version of a portion of chapter 1 appeared in *Women and Religion in Old and New Worlds,* edited by Susan Dinan and Debra Meyers, copyright 2001. Reproduced by permission of Routledge Inc., part of the

Taylor and Francis Group. An earlier version of a portion of chapter 5 appeared in *French Colonial History*, vol. 1, No. 1, 2002, published by Michigan State University Press.

Selwyn Gardens, Cambridge
September 2002

The Captors' Narrative

Narratives of Captor and Captive

*I*t is early October 1696, and in Montreal's compact market square, a block
away from the still unfrozen Saint Lawrence River, the onset of the wheat harvest lends a special urgency to the bustling activity of soldiers, shopkeepers,
farmers, merchants, nuns, priests, Indians, and English captives. In one corner of
the square, sisters of a Catholic women's missionary community and nurses from a
local hospital are discussing which of two captive Puritan men, exposed for sale there
by their Indian captors, they wish to purchase. They decide—and as a result one
man is led away to spend his captivity as a farmhand and general domestic for the
missionary sisters, the other is placed as a hospital orderly. . . . Sixty years later, a
similar event occurs. In the same market square the sisters of a new Montreal hospital buy captive British soldiers and sell others for profit. Twenty-one captives end
up on a community farm working for a single sister charged with their care during
the long years of war. Secular women participate as well. In the wake of the Deerfield
raid of 1704, which puts dozens of New Englanders on the market, one Montreal
businesswoman picks out men trained as weavers and sets them to work in the household textile factory she runs with her young daughter. . . . In the countryside of New
France, along the Saint John River, two Acadian sisters buy and sell captives taken
on the high seas. . . . In the town of Quebec, a fifteen-year-old girl dies of a fever she
has contracted from the prisoners she is caring for in the local military jail. . . .

From the seventeenth century to the present, Americans have imagined
the frontier captive as female. Her captor, by contrast, was normally a
male.[1] But when this foundational metaphor, based on the Puritan need
to portray a colony under siege as a woman in distress, is challenged by the

historical record of the early Canadian frontier, a different reality intrudes.
Men and boys made up over 80 percent of the approximately 2,600 Anglo-
American captives brought to Canada by the French or their Indian allies
between 1675 and 1763.[2] And the captors who determined their fate were
often women: Catholic French Canadians, young female captives-turned-
converts from New England, and Abenaki and Iroquoian women.

Gender roles, manifested in unexpected ways, defined the relationships
between captor and captive. Scholars have investigated the possible motivations that would lead their captive Puritan—almost always a woman—to
accept or reject Catholicism and Canadian life, but no one has yet asked
what these captive subjects meant to the Frenchwomen who sponsored the
captive trade, utilized captive labor, and sometimes successfully converted
their captives. In short, what was the *captors' narrative?*

In contrast to many of their literate New England captives, these women
lived their life stories rather than wrote them down. Their actions defined
their social roles. These roles included sponsoring and effecting the religious and cultural conversions of young female captives—who themselves
could and did quickly join the ranks of the captors holding their erstwhile
countrymen. The "captors' narrative" is unrelated to the written narratives
produced by their returned captives. The captors' narrative does not appear in the captors' own writing but emerges from the collected recorded
shards of the lives they led. This lived narrative provides our first insight
into the meaning and importance of the captivities to those women who
orchestrated them.

Ironically, the sites of female conversion—the religious communities,
households, wigwams, and communal fields—were also the places where
captive men resisted cultural and religious conversions. Men rejecting conversion were nevertheless retained as subordinates in the service of
women's religious and economic pursuits. The control of male subjects defined a great part of the captors' narrative.

In New France, the interests of French-Canadian women complemented
the mobile life of their husbands, fathers, sons, and brothers with their
long-distance trading and military service. By the outbreak of King William's War in 1689, reliance on indentured male domestic labor had created a condition in which the relationship between a mistress and her male
servant assumed real social importance. (Indenturing, or capturing, one's
labor force was a necessity in a colony in which free French men could have
land for the asking.) The onset of the war stopped the supply of indentured
servants. That same period produced numerous captive English-speaking
settlers, who would arrive in the public markets of Canada between 1689

and 1712. There they could be purchased by French-Canadian individuals—many of them women.

Though official documents occasionally expressed unease with the women's somewhat unorthodox roles and activities, free Canadian men did not generally oppose women's authority in the colony. Rather, they *depended* on the results of this exercise. Even the ruling officers and officials of colonial Canada relied on the services of independent medical workers, missionaries, and teachers from the women's religious communities, as well as on their wives and daughters in maintaining their fortunes at home.

While women's use of male subjects expanded their contributions to their families and colony, it also reveals hidden aspects of early modern masculinity. For an early modern male captive employed by a women's religious community, by a female merchant, or by groups of Native women agriculturalists, the world lost many of its familiar arrangements of authority. Even if employed doing traditionally male work—by no means an assured prospect—male captives would often be directed by a female mind and controlled by a female hand. Captivity at the hands of Catholic Frenchwomen in particular profoundly upset the patriarchal assumptions of male captives, especially those born free, English, and Puritan. The degree to which male captives chose to accept female authority depended on how legitimate they thought it was. In the case of the early Canadian frontier, the exercise of authority by French and Indian women often led to acts of physical resistance and to calls for a restored masculine version of freedom.

When read against other historical records, it becomes clear that many written accounts by or about male captives contain gaping holes or erasures concerning female authority. The consistent omission of women's authority reveals volumes about the Anglo-American male captivity narrative as a gendered document. This narrative sought nothing less than to rewrite the captivity experience itself, especially its subtext of reversals in the gender of authority. For returned captives, the act of putting pen to paper was the first step in claiming control of the intercultural encounter. Most often, captives wrote only about their "masters." When the presence of French or Indian women was admitted, these women were placed in the passive voice. In the author's hands, the captivity experience could be transformed from one orchestrated by flesh-and-blood women to one controlled, linguistically and ultimately historically, by the former captive himself. And to what purpose? Often to promote cultural superiority—as has been established by the scholarship of the Puritan captivity narrative. But even more fundamentally, at the level of the individual mind and heart, the act of writing was nothing less than an urgent act of restoring masculinity.

Seventeenth- and eighteenth-century observers as well as current scholars have been extremely reluctant to grant mastery to women engaged in the management of servants and slaves. But as this book demonstrates, the problem is not so much one of finding evidence of free women's involvement in systems of unfree labor as one of attributing significance to their actions. As it existed in colonial French Canada, female mastery—defined here as the *direct* control of captive laborers regardless of higher familial or societal structures of authority that may have been simultaneously in force—existed in response to tangible needs. Practices that evolved to meet those needs were imposed on captive cultural outsiders, male and female, with a clear purpose backed by unambiguous force. In constructing their version of intercultural captivity, women captors neither sought nor required external authorization of their mastery.

Ultimately, the extraordinary circumstances of captivity allow us to glimpse the routine yet hidden complications of gender relations in the early modern world. Reassembling captors' narratives permits us to see— in a time and place that has left no extant diaries—how women defined a significant part of their lives. Too often, the lives of women during this era are viewed through documents written by captive Anglo-American men who returned to the English-speaking colonies. The sources of evidence I examine, most previously overlooked or considered in isolation, offer a different picture of Canadian women's lives—one that allows us to see through the distortions perpetrated by the returnees. Sparse though the written records of French Canada may be in contrast to those of New England, when adequately contextualized they allow us to read, for the first time and with more faithfulness, the captors' narrative.

❧

This book is primarily concerned with the relationships between French-Canadian women captors and their Anglo-American captives. But Native inhabitants from the Iroquoian and Algonquian linguistic groups often held these same English captives while en route to Canada. The captivities among Indians therefore provide a crucial context for the chapters to follow. The experience of Iroquoian and Algonquian women yields an entire captors' narrative separate from that of *Canadiennes*. Moreover, it was among the Indians that captive New Englanders often first experienced gender power inversion, a foretaste of what was to follow.

On a summer's day in 1677, three individuals entered a secluded,

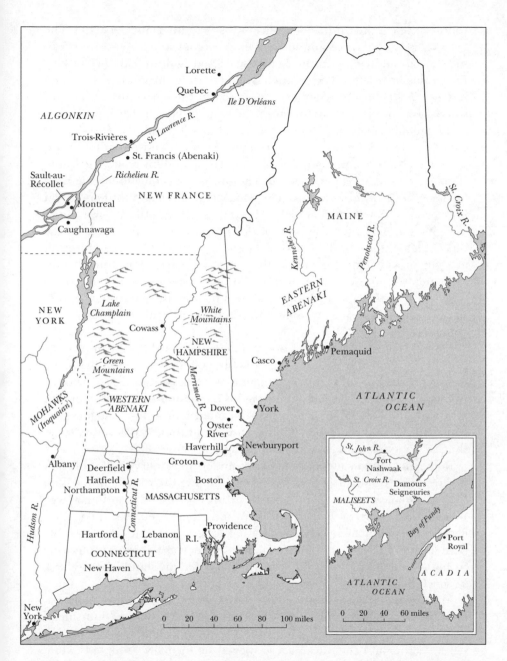

New England, New France, and adjoining Native areas, circa 1700. Adapted from Alden T. Vaughan and Edward W. Clark, *Puritans among the Indians: Accounts of Captivity and Redemption, 1676–1724* (Cambridge: Harvard University Press, 1981).

forested area of the Connecticut River valley to gather huckleberries. The
group consisted of two Algonquian Abenaki women and a twenty-four-year-
old Puritan militiaman in their custody named Benoni Stebbins, of Hatfield, Massachusetts. The women stopped in a promising spot and
instructed Stebbins to begin assisting them in their berrying. After they
worked for awhile, the attention of the women lapsed. Seizing the moment, Stebbins managed to jump on the women's packhorse and ride off
into the forest. Stebbins soon returned to Hatfield and recorded his ex-
ploit, tersely but triumphantly, in writing. He spared his readers the non-
heroic details of his experience, such as how he had come to be originally
in the custody of these two women, what his relationship to them might
have been, and how familiar he had become to their authority over time.[3]

Eighty-six years later, the narrative of John Rutherfurd, written in the
wake of his capture by the followers of Pontiac during the siege of Detroit
in 1763, provided more details on the role of women captors. Immediately
following his capture, Rutherfurd's new Indian "master" bound the young
man with a trinket-adorned rope and then handed the controlling end to
his wife standing nearby, who held Rutherfurd fast while the Indian man
"plundered the boat."[4]

From this point, Rutherfurd, about nineteen years old at the time, is deliberately excluded from the social roles inhabited by young Indian men.
Before proceeding on to the settlement that was to be Rutherfurd's home,
his master loosened the cords binding his hands and burdened him with
a heavy load of sticks, an action that relegated him to the female world.
Rutherfurd writes that whatever his master told him, "I was always to do
that, or whatever work his wife desired me."[5]

Rutherfurd then catalogues his work under the supervision of his new
mistress. He "broiled two hours every day, boiling their kettle with a little
fish or Indian corn in it" and "assist[ed] my Mistress in planting a large
field of Indian corn or maize, pumpkins, and other vegetables." Like other
captives, he complained bitterly of his nakedness, suffering "inexpressible
pain from not having any clothes on, not so much as a shirt to protect me
from the scorching rays of the sun, which burned my shoulders and back
so much that I was one continued blister."[6]

Enslavement was not, however, the only fate of young captives in his settlement, a fact that both encouraged and frustrated the young man.
Rutherfurd was highly conscious of the distinction between his own apparent status and the advantages enjoyed by formally "adopted" white
men. In Rutherfurd's account, the adoption of a man is defined as being
freed from the obligation to do women's work, which he refers to as
"drudgery."

Rutherfurd tells the story of an Ensign Pauli who had recently undergone such an adoption. "This gentleman made a very good Indian, being of a dark complexion, and he was much liked by his Master, who soon adopted him into his family, which exempted him from all drudgery."[7] It is unclear whether Rutherfurd is envious of Ensign Pauli or regards drudgery as the necessary price of fidelity to his home culture. Soon, though, perhaps desiring the safety of an adoption and seeing no other practical alternative, Rutherfurd accepts the Indian couple's offer to become their son.

Almost immediately, he is astonished to discover the contingent nature of being adopted:

> By this time our corn was grown up about a foot high, so that it became necessary to have it hoed and weeded, which was a severe task upon my mother and me for six days. I flattered myself that my being adopted into the family would have exempted me from this type of drudgery, as was the case with most of the other prisoners, but [Rutherfurd's "father"], having a particular regard for his wife, chose that I should assist her on many occasions, and she being fond of the ease laid most of it on my shoulders. She frequently made me pound or bruise corn in a large mortar till there was scarcely any skin on my hands, and when I showed them to her she only laughed and told me I would soon be better used to it, and that my hands would become hard like hers, which indeed were neither soft nor fine.[8]

Rutherfurd's "mother," then, demonstrated her desire—and her authority—to continue his enslavement indefinitely even while adopting him. Like Stebbins and so many other male captives caught within a woman's sphere of work, he found his lot intolerable and escaped back to British lines.

The enslavement of cultural outsiders was only one of a variety of culturally important strategies Indian women captor assumed within a so-called "mourning war" complex. In this set of interrelated customs associated with the Iroquois, a group pursued war with the objective of ritually replacing its deceased members. An individual—Indian or white—captured and held among the northeastern Native settlements according to the conventions of a mourning war might face ritual torture followed by execution, which satisfied the captors' desire for revenge and social reconstitution, or alternatively experience adoption along a continuum of treatment from true incorporation into the captor society to outright enslavement. While the more mobile Algonquian Abenaki did not often engage in the torture of captives, among the Iroquois the ritual assumed extreme importance as the part of the mourning war complex.[9]

Enslavement, whether or not intermixed with some elements of true adoption, remained a possible fate for Indian and white captives alike. Free male travelers into Indian country during the wars, who had no captive's pride to protect, confirm not only the ubiquity of slavery in northeastern Native communities but also the primary role of women in managing the practice. In the mid-1750s, during the height of the Seven Years' War, a French-Canadian trader and soldier who signed himself "J. C. B." wrote of precisely these circumstances in an almost casual and offhand manner. Concerning the disposition of British and Indian prisoners held in the local Iroquoian and Algonquian communities in the Saint Lawrence Valley, he wrote in his journal that "the prisoners taken are adopted, enslaved, or condemned to death. Slaves have to do the most menial work, such as cutting firewood, cultivating the fields, harvesting, pounding Indian corn or maize to make *sagamité,* cooking, mending the hunter's shoes, carrying their game, in short, anything that the women do. *The women are in charge of the slaves* [italics added], and deny them food if they were lazy."[10]

Similarly, a free Jesuit named Jacques Frémin recorded the lamentation of a mother whose Iroquoian daughter had recently died. The mother claimed her deceased child had been "Mistress here and commanded many slaves, who are still with me; she knew not what it was to go to the forest to get wood, or to the River to draw water."[11]

Neither "J. C. B." nor Frémin specify in their respective accounts that the female-controlled slaves were male. But the outline of the slave's duties, such as those performed by Stebbins and Rutherfurd and others—including even Jesuit priests such as Jogues and Bressani—make it certain that male slaves predominated among these subordinates.[12] The Quebec anthropologist Roland Viau interprets the function of male slaves forced into the economic role of females as not only providing increased labor capacity but also expressing a specific cultural aspect of Iroquoian warfare, one that sought to derive a sense of superiority by deliberately and publicly shaming defeated and captured men: "In 1676, the [Iroquoian] Onondagas traveled 200 leagues from their homes to raid, taking 50 [male] captives to whom they gave a new life—that of working their fields . . . they humiliated their male slaves by restricting them to generally female tasks."[13]

The Algonquian Abenaki, less settled than the Iroquois, also placed male captives in conditions of temporary or permanent enslavement.[14] Alice Nash has argued for a Western Abenaki version of what both Viau and the ethnohistorians William Starna and Ralph Watkins find among the Iroquois: true slavery coexisting with adoption. Her case studies reflect the larger reality of such captivities: the Abenaki succeeded in turning children of both sexes into fully acculturated adoptees, if they were young enough to incorporate fully. Interestingly, the cases she selects as examples of slavery all involve captured young adult men. The Abenaki, like the Iroquois, harbored no illusions that such captives could be transculturated. Implicit in Nash's analysis is the notion that the Abenaki had more than merely material motives for taking captives, be it for adoption, slavery, or something in between. "Masters and mistresses experienced complete power over their English slaves," she writes, "who provided tangible, visible proof of English vulnerability." One Abenaki woman, for example, enslaved the twenty-four-year-old captive Nicholas Woodbury of Wells, Maine. The woman kept Woodbury no fewer than eight full years after peace between New England and New France was declared in 1713, using him for "slave labor" and also hiring him out to others "despite his slight lameness due to an injury he received in captivity."[15]

Woodbury's lameness also raises a central problem of physical control. Historians have sometimes rejected the idea of female mastery simply on the grounds that women would have been physically incapable of dominating captured men.[16] Even those who have admitted the possibility of female authority over male captives among Native Americans emphasize that male captives would first have to be disabled in some way. One writer has suggested that among Iroquoians, part of a male captive's foot might be removed in order to prevent flight—a measure that could have eased burdens on female agriculturalists to control captive men.[17] But mutilation of this kind seems to have been practiced rarely, if at all, on European male prisoners. Most northeastern Native societies apparently found other ways to control Europeans. To maintain an orderly work environment, Iroquois women controlled their *esclaves masculins* by organizing them into work teams that could be closely watched by an even greater number of women agriculturalists.[18] Generally less sedentary than the Iroquoians, Abenakis practiced this same principle on a smaller scale—as the two women custodians who assigned themselves to Benoni Stebbins demonstrate.

Outnumbering a captive, however, seems not to have been deemed strictly necessary in the management of prisoners. A Mohawk woman simultaneously held two young adult male militiamen—Joseph Bartlett and Martin Kellogg Jr.—in her wigwam and did not seem to harbor reservations about her ability to maintain authority.[19] Nor did the unnamed young Iroquois woman who "commanded more than twenty slaves." But the authority of these women came not from physicality but from the hearth. As "J. C. B." points out, those slaves who did not succeed in convincing their mistresses they had worked hard enough during the day went hungry. The preoccupation with food in the Anglo-American captivity narratives suggests that withholding it was an effective punishment—especially for white prisoners unable to live off their surroundings as effectively as their Native counterparts. Control over food, as we shall see, would also be a tactic adopted by French-Canadian women in managing Anglo-American captives.

For the Indian women themselves, the enslavement of captives was just as important as adoption and torture rituals in providing gender-specific cultural power.[20] The enthusiasm and proprietary attitude taken by women in their direct, face-to-face control of captives is clear. Ritual torture and reconstitution of the community through adoption clearly informed women's social identities, but so did the enslavement of defeated enemies. The enslavement of captives allowed Iroquois women to play their part in the customs of war by reenacting a daily humiliation that dramatized the captives' loss of honor.

Indeed, tribal women used men's disdain of women's work against them as a potent weapon of war. For an enslaved male Huron captive, for example, simply being set to tasks he had traditionally consigned to his wife or daughters accomplished the intended humiliation readily enough. But for enslaved white Anglo-Americans, farming was familiar men's work and not at all humiliating. For the English, the real degradation of working in the fields, gathering wild foods, and general domestic service was that they *were directed in these activities by women*. Indian women, then, successfully manipulated common male attitudes to advance their own material and cultural interests.

Iroquoian and Algonquian women recognized that their authority rested in part on rituals of unmanning directed at captured enemies. In Iroquoia, women often began this process through the practice of finger amputation—a mutilation usually inflicted on men captives. The removal of the digits essential to drawing a bow or firing a gun permanently excised a man's ability to perform a male economic role while leaving him perfectly able to undertake the tasks of women. Finger amputation thus initiated social emasculation.

Algonquian Abenaki women engaged in an analogous practice. A schooner captain named William Pote, for example, reported this encounter with Eastern Abenaki women on his long march between the Annapolis Basin and the Saint Lawrence River:

> Some Days before us, at this place ye Squaws Came down to the edge of the [Saint John] River . . . Dancing Round us and Striking of us in ye face with English Scalps, yt Caused ye Blood to Issue from our mouths and Noses, In a Verey Great and plentifull manner, and Tangled their hands in our hair, and knocked our heads Togather with all their Strength and Vehemence,

and when they was Tired of this Exercise, they would take us by [the] hair and Some by ye Ears, and Standing behind us, ablige us to keep our Necks Strong so as to bear their weight, then Raise themselves, their feet off ye Ground and their weight hanging by our hairs and Ears, In this manner, they thumped us in ye Back and Sides, with their knees and feet, and Twichd our hair and ears to such a Degree, that I am Incapable to Express it, and ye others that was Dancing Round if they Saw any man falter, and did not hold up his Neck, they Dached ye Scalps In our faces with Such Violence, yt Every man Endeavoured to bear them hanging by their hair in this manner, Rather then have a Double Punishment, after they had finished their frolick, that Lasted about two hours and a half, we was Carried to one of their Camps.[21]

Such harassment was only the beginning of the unmanning process. The Eastern Abenaki had long showed a specific interest in retaining male captives in servitude. As early as the 1670s, they were recorded to have been enslaving groups of white males to employ them in the "women's work" of threshing corn.[22]

The physical control exerted by women is further illustrated by the experiences of Thomas Brown, a captive soldier during the Seven Years' War. Following a brief stay with the French at Fort Ticonderoga, Brown was reclaimed by his original Native captors and tethered to a heavily laden sledge. The mixed-sex group of Indians then bade him perform the exhausting task of drawing the sledge through the snow to their destination of Montreal. Wanting to be relieved of his burden, Brown, in his telling, suddenly invited three of the women accompanying him to sit on the sledge and then cheerfully joked, "I wished I was able to draw 'em [on the sledge]."[23] This attempt at jocularity apparently achieved the desired effect. The Indians thereupon dressed him in Native garb in preparation for a possible adoption. Some other British captives, no doubt to their consternation, were then tethered to the sledge in Brown's place. The escorting women, Brown then reports with no apparent discomfort, took it upon themselves to physically discipline those prisoners who were slow in obeying commands.

But what could never be conveyed to a New England audience was the scene painted by "J. C. B.": subordinate men living in the passive voice in a given Indian village. Absent in first-person form is any record of the perfect congruence between the needs of Algonquian and Iroquoian women as beleaguered agriculturalists and the suddenly available male farmers from the English-speaking colonies. The scene of groups of these men working at the behest of Native women is never described explicitly, but the experiences of the enslaved Indians and whites working in Iroquois fields sharpen our understanding of how this female-dominated space of the communal fields operated.[24] Free men might help clear the fields, but captive men were employed throughout the season as *gatsennen* or *ako-zene*—meaning domestic animals—in the service of the women's collective. Women decided under what conditions they would share their space with men.

The way these women ordered their world, however, is reported to us only in distorted vestiges. In Nicholas Woodbury's case, his father's long correspondence in pursuit of his redemption obliged Nicholas and his chroniclers to acknowledge his lengthy enslavement to a single woman. Their decision to emphasize his lameness can be interpreted as rationalizing such servitude. Also common was the "Pocahontas defense," in which the Indian woman was cast as a merciful deliverer from worse fates. Samuel Butterfield, a captive from Chelmsford, Massachusetts, was delivered by his Indian captors to the widow of an Indian he had killed. The "squaw-widow" protests that "if . . . by killing [Butterfield] you think you can bring my husband to life again, put him to what death you will. Otherwise let him alone and suffer him to be my servant."[25]

This Indian-woman-as-savior tale is unusual only in the explicit mention of the condition of servitude. Occasionally, similar echoes are recorded by family historians. During the mid-eighteenth century Winthrop Hoyt was said, with no supporting narrative or other evidence, to have been "held many years by a squaw of Caughnawaga."[26] Hudson River lore holds that one young captive of the "old French war" was saved on the verge of execution by a "squaw" who cried, "You shan't kill him! He's no fighter! He's *my dog*."[27] Such a tale would be indistinguishable from dozens of others and of little meaning but for the specific use of the word "dog." Starna and Watkins note that two separate Northern Iroquoian words both mean "dog" and "slave" interchangeably.[28] The chronicler of the story, from the Civil War era, does not seem aware of the double meaning of the term he relates. But we hear a distinct echo of the eighteenth century.

Age may have been a crucial factor in explaining and justifying the subjection of male captives. For example, in the wake of the American Revolution (the last era of captivities to be examined here) a returned captive named Jonathan Alder confidently assured his readers that among the Shawnees of the Ohio country "the boys are classed as squaws or work hands until the age of twelve." When a boy reaches this age, he is placed with the family of his adoptive "sister," presumably so her husband can begin training him in the ways of Shawnee men. Like John Rutherfurd's captor, however, Alder's teen-age mistress (whom he calls Sally) feels empowered to turn her captive adoptee into a slave. She calls Alder a "mean, low, sassy prisoner" and a "dirty, lazy dog," reimposing the alien status

Alder thought he had left behind. Sally feels within her rights to keep the boy within the female economic realm in spite of his approach to manhood. She proceeds to employ Alder as, in his words, "a kind of nurse to care of her children, which she seemed to produce as fast as I cared for. . . . This nursing business was a new thing to me and was by no means agreeable. I had to do all the washing of the children's clothes, which was neither a clean nor pleasant work."[29]

In Alder's telling, it is only because of the excessive beatings he suffers at the hands of Sally that his plight is noticed by a young Indian friend and ultimately by his adoptive parents, who remove Alder from Sally's custody. The captive leaves the reader with a portrait of Sally as an unnaturally lazy and vicious young woman who is able to get away with inflicting this treatment on Alder—at least for a while—because of his youth. But in the context of female authority in Native northeastern cultures, she appears to be an industrious, focused, and by no means unusual woman. That it took at least two years for anyone to intervene in Alder's situation suggests that his treatment was largely sanctioned by local custom. Sally's husband could certainly have intervened to put the boy back on the path to manhood had he wished—but he clearly felt Sally's utilization of him to be preferable. Sally acted within her rights, just as John Rutherfurd's mistress had when she enslaved her "adopted" nineteen-year-old.

Former captives portrayed female authority among the Algonquians and Iroquoians as a testing ground that would allow a male captive in his teenage years to prove himself and enter the male realm of hunting and warring. Amos Eastman of Rumney, New Hampshire, for example, "seized a club [while running a gauntlet of tormentors at Saint Francis] and knocked down the Indians right and left, escaping himself with barely a blow. Because of this the Indians liked him. Again, when ordered to hoe corn he, knowing that they considered such work fit for only squaws and slaves, cut up the corn, saved the weeds and finally threw his hoe into the river saying: 'It's the business not of warriors but of squaws to hoe corn.' They then called him young chief."[30]

Eastman may or may not have escaped from his condition in the manner he describes, but he does seem to have encountered "squaws and slaves" hoeing corn. For every captive like Eastman who escaped slave status, or for every Stebbins who escaped captivity altogether, many were either unable or unwilling to change their condition. Former captives continued to live as field slaves in Iroquoia or as corn threshers in Eastern Abenakia.

The Indian women who scripted their captives' lives regarded themselves not as *sauvagesses* but as land cultivators, mothers, daughters, and full participants in a war-making culture. Distortions introduced by Anglo-American captivity narratives cannot hide the fact that, ultimately, captives were just as much part of these women's stories as the reverse.

❦

Anglo-American captives who passed from Indian hands into those of the French found themselves in yet another new world. Canadian captivity consisted mostly of unwelcome and unpredictable experiences. John Demos has summarized the situation well when he wrote that "the circumstances of captivity were as varied as the numbers of people involved—on both sides."[31]

Temporary slavery was only one of the possible fates for captives among the French Canadians, as it was among the Iroquois and Abenaki. But since the Canadians could require involuntary servitude for those unconverted prisoners awaiting ransom, either short- or long-term enslavement—referred to as such by the authorities of New France—became the defining aspect of intercultural contact between individual Canadians and Anglo-Americans between 1670 and 1760. The captive Peter Labaree, appealing to a French-Canadian authority he called the "General Secretary" around 1754, wondered in dismay "if it was according to Christian law that a white man should be taken in peaceable times and sold as a slave." As Labaree related, the response was "the law of that country was what Mr. General said."[32]

What precisely was this phenomenon of captivity in New France? Though it often seems that in French- and English-language accounts of the time "captive / *captif(ve)*," "slave / *esclave*," and "prisoner / *prisonnier(ière)*" are used interchangeably, certain nuances can be discerned. In particular, the interchangeability of "captive" and "slave" is not necessarily a sign of the carelessness. Both words described an aspect of the experience.

When one entered "captivity" in New France, one became caught up in a netherworld of law where even the customs of the captors might or might not be applied in any given situation. But for French private individuals who dealt directly with the Indian captors or the Canadian governors to purchase captives, the action of ransoming an individual from their Indian allies invoked a general set of expectations. For these individual Canadian purchasers, the "captive" in question would be eligible for freedom when a profitable monetary redemption was received. This redemption might come from the captive's relatives, his home government, or another interested party on either side of the frontier. But as communication was rarely accomplished during wartime, custom demanded that the captive in question begin to repay the "debt" resulting from the prospective ran-soming by working for the purchaser.

Here the aspect of slavery appears. The bondservant status of captives was open-ended and might last indefinitely. No official, independent stan-dard informed a master or mistress when they had received sufficient rec-ompense in money or labor for the captive's release. That was left to the owner's discretion. The de facto and de jure status of Protestant Anglo-Americans was, in the words of one Canadian governor, that of "slaves fairly sold."[33] They could be bought, sold, leased, and disciplined at the sole dis-cretion of their masters and mistresses—who also determined the captive's employment and living conditions. The only evident restriction on private ownership of captives occurred in the cases of mandatory and universal re-lease of all those held involuntarily in New France, according to inter-colonial peace treaties such as those promulgated in 1698 and 1713. In the case of captives in private hands who had been leased by the govern-ment, those agreements simply ended. It is still mysterious, however, how or even if the government compensated individual owners after com-pelling them to set their Anglo-Americans free. (As we will see, some French families and communities simply ignored this order and retained their captives.) In the absence of documentation of compensatory trans-actions, we can only assume that peace was a hazard of the captive trade— *une fortune de la guerre.*

An important exception to this general outline was the case of military captivities between 1744 and 1760. As before, men designated as *prison-niers de la guerre* were often leased or sold to individuals and traders. After 1744, with the labor shortage no longer a pervasive problem, the French-Canadian authorities maintained military prisons for the confinement of excess prisoners (and a few civilian captives, women as well as men). All military prisoners were now more susceptible to official decisions regard-ing the condition and duration of their captivity. Before 1713, the rela-tively low numbers of captives and the acute labor shortage meant that almost all available Anglo-Americans would be seized upon in the market-place by individuals or institutions.

But it was never the intention of the French government or individual Catholic Canadian citizens to possess Protestant Anglo-Americans as chat-tels from one generation to the next. No such cases exist. Indeed, for Cana-dians, the treatment of the Anglo-Americans in their midst assumed a paradoxical character. French Canadians did not hesitate to subject newly arrived English captives to the full array of cruelties otherwise reserved for the truly enslaved Africans and Great Lakes and Prairie Indians: expo-sure for sale at markets, breaking up of families, extended deprivation of adequate food and clothing, and physical brutalization. At the same time, however, Anglo-Americans who showed a willingness of convert religiously and marry into French-Canadian society could be treated as the most welcome of guests. Thus the dehumanized captive servant in a household could eventually marry into that same captor family. As the case studies below indicate, factors of conversion included the social class of the captors (contrary to myth, English captives almost never married into the leading families of New France) as well as the age, sex, and martial status of the captive.

What importance did all these nebulous and ever changing customs assume on a society-wide basis in New England and New France? First, the total number of Anglo-American captives in New France is not known. Emma Lewis Coleman's still unsurpassed 1925 listing of 1,641 captives taken to Canada between 1677 and 1760 takes into account only those of New England origin. These results remain a fairly comprehensive guide to the captivities taken before 1713—when most were civilian frontier dwellers from Massachusetts, New Hampshire, and Maine. But in all likelihood as many as two thousand prisoners from non–New England colonies remain unnamed and uncounted.[34]

Even given this statistical gap, a few demographic patterns in the captivities are worth noting. Alden T. Vaughan and Daniel K. Richter have evaluated and interpreted raw data compiled mainly by Coleman and published the results as part of a larger study of transculturation among Indians and New Englanders in the colonial era.[35] Of the more than 1,600 captives they considered, at least 229 transculturated, that is, remained voluntarily with a captor society. Of these, all but the twenty-four known definitively to have remained with the Indians elected to settle among the French in Canada. As these authors succinctly put it: "French Canada, not Indian Canada, caught the New England captives' fancy."[36]

A more detailed breakdown of these basic numbers reveals that French Canada captured the fancy specifically of female New Englanders. As Vaughan and Richter put it, "the prime candidate for transculturation was a girl aged seven through fifteen." Regardless of age, almost one out of every ten men decided to remain among their captors, while about one out of every 4.5 female captives remained. Broken down by age, seven- to fifteen-year-old captives proved most willing to undertake transculturation. Captives of this age did not possess their own property to which to return, but they were old enough to successfully resist entreaties as well as various efforts at direct control made by surviving New England family members. An astounding 53.7 percent of girls aged seven to fifteen remained with the French Canadians. Of men classified as "adults" (all males older than fifteen regardless of marital status) only 1.8 percent elected to become Catholic Canadians.[37] The remaining men made up the demographic group the French Canadians were most likely to consign to involuntary servitude.

And how did New Englanders at home respond? On a societal level, the fight to restore the original religious culture of New England—after the decline evident at the end of the eighteenth century—started with words. Literate Puritan leaders found it necessary to turn the cultural civil war in New England into a united front against external threats. The Reverend Increase Mather had produced the narrative of Quentin Stockwell as early as 1684, but the height of this effort occurred in the wake of the Deerfield massacre in early 1704. The newly captured minister of Deerfield, John Williams, would relate in his manuscript written after his return to "Zion" (New England) that he had engaged in debate with his French Jesuit captor-hosts on the meaning of Providential signs. Was a French victory such as that which had brought the clergyman to Montreal a message to the earthbound that divine favor shone upon Canada? Or was it, as Williams maintained, a test of God's cherished Puritans?[38] An identical event could be made into a victory for New France or New England.

But New Englanders turned defeat into victory in very different ways according to their station in life and, ultimately, their sex. Men of the highest ranks of the besieged Massachusetts Puritan leadership, in particular Increase and Cotton Mather, closely monitored and packaged stories of civilian captivities for popular consumption. The prominent captivity narratives of this era—those of Williams, Hannah Swarton, Mary Rowlandson, Quentin Stockwell, and Hannah Dustan—were not entirely authentic voices of frontier folk. These narratives would never have been published, or even written at all, without enthusiastic editorial and promotional help.

The possible influence that these propaganda efforts might have had on frontier dwellers is impossible to judge. But the cases presented in this book demonstrate again and again that the New Englanders actually displaced by captivity led their wartime lives in ways that were based principally on contingency, material and familial interests, and in some cases the pull of the captors' religion. If Puritan elites were privately dismayed over the seeming attraction of French-Canadian society to ransomed raid victims, especially young unmarried women, then the Canadians themselves must have been at least equally dismayed when some converted captives chose to return to New England many years after settling in Canada. Almost always they returned because the settler or convert heard of an available inheritance back home across the frontier. Religious reconversion in the long period of almost unbroken intercolonial peace between 1713 and

1744 was little more than a formality.[39] Among the ordinary folk, people conducted their interests according to more immediate concerns than were attributed to them by their cultural and religious leaders.

And what of the Canadian motivations for captive taking? While Canadians certainly seemed to enjoy the display of captives as a sign of their cultural and religious superiority, especially before 1713, Anglo-Americans captives represented a significant supply of workers in the chronically labor-starved colony.[40] French colonial officials had long been horrified at the fact that over half of all their indentured men found a way to return to France—despite a number of preventative and even punitive measures taken to stop freedmen from leaving Canada.[41] The geographical expansion of New France trading routes into the *pays d'en haut* (Great Lakes region) and down the Mississippi River valley combined with the threats of their more populous English and Iroquois foes made the need for manpower especially acute.[42]

The entrance, then, of a few hundred New England civilian captives into the Canadian colony before 1713, many of them children and unmarried young adults, begins to seem more significant than the small numbers might at first suggest. During 1705, for example, perhaps 250 New Englanders, converted and not, lived and worked in Canada. In a colony of fifteen thousand, this was a small but not insignificant number. Captives were a larger presence in the towns of Montreal and Quebec—the combined population of which was only about nine thousand that year. Considering that French immigration had slowed almost to a halt after 1689, New Englander captives and converts actually became the principal coerced laborers and new permanent settlers in French Canada until about 1710. They would also be a significant labor supply after 1744—again novel only insofar as they represented a unique challenge of acculturation.[43]

Beyond brute labor, Anglo-Americans offered a unique benefit as potential settlers. The mostly Puritan villagers who arrived in the Saint Lawrence Valley were often skilled individuals—young weavers, artisans, and farmers accustomed to the regional climate. These skills must have proven attractive to Canadian authorities seeking settlers. The memory of the recent drop in skill level, social background, and moral character of the last generation of indentured servants from France probably made English-women and men seem like prime candidates for attempted transculturation.[44]

Regardless of the arrangements that private individuals made with their captives and their potential redeemers, it was unfortunate that the skills Canada's governors prized most were mainly characteristics of the adult

male captives, whom Canadians found to be the most difficult to accul-
turate. Men's labor usually had to be coerced—an activity the women of
New France did not hesitate to take on. But converted women and children of hard-working English frontier stock made more than adequate
consolation prizes: children could fully adapt to a new culture in a way that
adults of either sex never could, and a married *habitante anglaise* tied one
more Canadian settler to the land and to the colony.

❧

   This book is a history of the role that monastic and lay French-Canadian
women played in Puritan captivities. It is also necessarily the history of the
specific relationship between a woman captor and her male captive that so
often defined these encounters. The woman captor, a ubiquitous presence
along the Canadian frontier, has been largely lost to us because of an extreme difference in opinion concerning the legitimacy of women's authority in colonial North America. The Anglo-American men brought
across that frontier—many of them Puritan, most of them heads or future
heads of farming families, many of them having recently survived a period
of captivity among Indian women—responded with a silence that obliterated the memory of women's lives. For their part, these *Canadiennes*—often professionally oriented, often living communally with other women,
always Catholic–exercised the power authorized by their religious and cultural backgrounds and catalyzed by the fluidity of the New France–New
England frontier. The actions of these women suggest real surprise at the
frequent rebellion of their male captives—rebellions inextricable from the
fact that these women represented the foreign country and faith that held
these men.

CHAPTER ONE

The Farm: Lives of the
Congrégation Notre-Dame

J. G. worked as a servant to the nuns at their farm, and N. B. worked
for the Holy Sisters.

—STEPHEN WILLIAMS, *A Biographical Memoir*
of the Reverend John Williams

T he boundary of the Longley family farm, at the edge of the corn-
fields, was the edge of the English-speaking world.[1] The farm lay almost two miles northwest of the town of Groton, Massachusetts,
itself thirty-one miles northwest of Boston.[2] In response to the outbreak of
what the English colonists called "King William's War" with France, her
Canadian colony, and her nearby Indian allies, Groton had become one of
four designated garrison towns guarding the northernmost Massachusetts
and New Hampshire settlements. But the independent-minded Longleys,
whom some might have characterized as stubborn, lived a forty-five-minute
walk from that garrison. Correspondence exchanged between the appointed militia officers of the town and the Massachusetts authorities reveal that the threat of a French and Indian attack was foremost on the
minds of the families of Groton as early as 1689.[3] By 1692 William Longley, the family patriarch and a second-generation colonist, had been living
with the risk of raids for three harvest seasons.

A sense of community might have lessened William Longley's concern
about his large family's vulnerability. The eldest son of Will Longley—an
original Groton settler from Lincolnshire, a farmer, and a sometime town
clerk and constable—William Longley Jr. was one of the men who handled

town affairs, both the mundane and the extraordinary. These men had been tested by the brutal combat of King Philip's War in the 1670s and had continued to govern the community with an eye to maximizing their success in agriculture while providing for the common defense. William Longley's farm was physically isolated, but the feeling of remoteness was tempered by almost half a century of mutual reliance.[4]

But the large family nonetheless faced an unprotected frontier. William's first wife, Lydia Pease, had borne a daughter before her early death. His second wife, Deliverance Crisp, bore five more children, bringing the inhabitants of the house to eight. The eldest daughter, named Lydia after her mother, had recently turned twenty.

The family house was primitive even by the standards of the Massachusetts frontier in the 1690s, which meant that the family shared cramped quarters.[5] Village men did not choose it as one of the "garrison houses"— the homes, usually private, in which militiamen were quartered and that served as strongholds against armed raiders. A successful defense of the isolated Longley establishment would be of little tactical value to the village. But in times of alarm, a plan did exist for the protection of the family. The town militia assigned William Longley to the garrison house of James Parker in the very center of the village of Groton along with ten other adult men.[6] In theory at least, the Longley family could take refuge at the Parkers' place, but it was two miles away—a daunting distance during an attack, especially during the winter.

While William Longley maintained a prosperous enough farm, owned sufficient lands, and held a durable enough reputation to carry on his father's status as a mainstay of village government and defense, the remote homestead put extra pressure and responsibility on his wife, Deliverance, and his daughter Lydia.[7] At twenty, Lydia Longley stood on the threshold of marriage. With years of caring for her siblings behind her, she was probably well qualified to raise her own family and run a household with her husband. She would have been skilled in gardening; needlework and sewing; the crafts of brewing, cooking, and maintaining the hearth; the heavier responsibilities of drawing water, tending animals, and helping with planting and harvesting; and caring for infants and young children in countless ways. Although she was still unwed, perhaps because of her essential role at home, it was virtually certain that Lydia would marry within a few years. Her religious background is known—the Longleys attended the Congregationalist church of Groton, presided over by the Reverend Gersholm Hobart—but the degree of her fervor is not recorded.

When the almost twenty-year respite from frontier combat ended in Groton during the high summer of 1694, William Longley's plans for the defense of his family proved useless—there was no advance warning and no time to withdraw to the town. Oral tradition in the still close-knit town of Groton tells that the daylight attack on the Longley farm began with the gathering of a party of Penobscot Abenaki that had broken off from a larger band of raiders. Assembling at the edge of the far cornfield, the Abenaki first drove some cows into a yard where they would be seen from the farmhouse. The attackers then killed the unarmed William Longley as he rounded up the strays.[8] That left Deliverance and the six children defenseless in the house. But some form of physical resistance by the surviving women and children is a plausible explanation of events that followed. The Abenaki ended the lives of Deliverance and three of the children in the minutes following William's murder. An Abenaki tomahawk is not so much a hatchet as a three-foot-long club with a blade, capable of inflicting blunt as well as lacerating trauma. To bludgeon to death most of the eminently ransomable family members makes no sense, especially since French chroniclers report that booty was the principal motivation for the expedition that included the Groton attacks.[9]

Whatever happened next in and around the Longley cabin, when it was over three surviving children were in the custody of the Abenaki: Betty, aged four; John, aged twelve; and Lydia. As the day wore on the Indians added other captives to this group as other households at the northern edge of Groton suffered much the same fate as the Longleys. Among those taken with the Longley children were sixteen-year-old John Shepley and three other children of approximately ten years of age: Gershom Hobart Jr., the Groton minister's son; Phineas Parker; and Thomasin Rouse, the young daughter of the Longleys' nearest neighbor.

As the oldest survivor of the raid, Lydia presumably immediately assumed immediately a familiar role, caring for the surviving children—all well known to her. Soon after, though, she proved unable to protect her half-sister. Betty died or was killed soon after capture. (Abenaki raiders sometimes killed children unable to keep up with a rapidly withdrawing party. In the case of the Groton attack, such recourse might have proved advantageous since they were pursued by militia once the surviving Groton men had regrouped.) A clue to Betty's fate might be contained in a report by Thomasin Rouse upon the latter's return to New England, that an Abenaki chieftain had come close to killing her when she cried in response to being ordered to carry something.[10]

At some point on the journey north the party divided the children. John Longley ended up as servant to Madokawando, an eastern Abenaki chief notorious in New England for leading frontier raids. A group of captors led Lydia Longley north and west, 150 miles on foot through the summer heat to the market square of Montreal, where she was sold to a Jacques Le Ber, the richest trader on the upper Saint Lawrence.

The keeping of the children captured in the 1694 Groton raid suggests that at least temporarily they were, in Abenaki eyes, young enough to undergo true assimilation. This assumption was justified in the case of John Longley, who at twelve started training as an Indian warrior. At sixteen, however, John Shepley was more likely to have been enslaved. Lydia might have been deemed too old for transculturation—but the Indians must have known that she would bring a good price in Canada among the French, who had already discovered that young Puritan women found a certain attractiveness in things French and Catholic.

In the crowded Montreal's market square, Lydia Longley would have had ample time to take stock of her surroundings. Mid-August was not the busiest time on Saint Paul Street, but the bustle must have seemed considerable to a woman who had lived her twenty years in a forest clearing. If she had ever visited Boston, she would have found Montreal altogether different. Montreal was smaller and laid out on a slightly irregular rectangular grid parallel to the river, gently sloping up toward Mont Réal, a steep oblong hill a mile and a half behind the settlement. Behind the town's wooden palisade stood about two hundred wooden houses and some larger buildings of gray stone. The gray structures looked like a fortress, especially when contrasted to the whitewashed and rough-hewn buildings in Groton.

To a newly arrived woman from Massachusetts, the people would have presented a novelty greater than the architecture. Both men and women in Canada favored relatively ostentatious dress that called rather more attention to social rank and occupation than did the subtle distinctions in the dress of puritanical New Englanders. Prominent Frenchmen sported brightly colored and ornate ensembles imported from Europe, as did their wives. Women of all ranks made color an obsession, another contrast to the Groton frontier. But Canadian men and women did not sacrifice practicality to fashion—they integrated the two. The deerskin garments of voyageurs and habitants, contrasting with the colorful garments of town dwellers, reminded the viewer of the raisons d'être that had by 1694 come to replace the Société Notre-Dame's missionary idealism: the fur trade and war. Gray-coated *troupes de marine* and black-robed priests would have passed frequently in the square, emphasizing to the newly arrived New Englander that she would have real differences to reckon with. Austerely dressed religious sisters, ordered and lay, further delineated difference.

But perhaps the most striking visual difference was the tendency for women of all but the highest rank to wear skirts *à la sauvagesse*—roughly reaching mid-thigh—for ease of work and comfort during the humid summers. The lack of modesty drove visiting European men to distraction and provoked enraged sermons from local priests—much to the apparent amusement of the wearers of the novel garments, sported probably nowhere else in Christendom in 1694.[11] This sense of surprise was probably shared by Lydia Longley. Clearly, more than religion separated the young Puritan woman from the *Canadiennes* surrounding her.

Before long, a fatherly man entered the market and paid the requested ransom for her. This gentleman's appearance combined several aspects of Canada. Jacques Le Ber, though dressed as a gentleman, was a trader, businessman, and soldier. Sixty-one years old in mid-1694, he had come to personify the self-made *Canadien*. Arriving in Ville-Marie in 1657 from Rouen, where he had been born into a landowning family, he quickly made his mark and a fortune in the fur trade along with his business partner and brother-in-law Charles Le Moyne. His extensive landholdings and position in the western fur trade gave him wealth unprecedented in Montreal—two years later he would purchase outright a letter of nobility from Louis XIV. And he remained, in genuine Canadian fashion, active in military life until the end, personally fighting Mohawks on an expedition mounted the year before, at the age of sixty.[12]

After being conducted a short distance down Saint Paul Street to Le Ber's spacious house, Lydia Longley would have learned more about this man and his family. Le Ber had become a widower in 1682 and had not remarried. In 1691 his third son, Jean-Vincent, had been killed fighting the English at Laprairie, and the next year word reached Canada that the family's eldest son, Louis, had died in La Rochelle, France, where he had worked as his father's agent. The second son, Le Ber's namesake Jacques, was living in France as an officer in the French army.[13]

When Lydia arrived at the Le Ber house, one of her patron's adult children still lived under that roof; the other lived nearby. If Le Ber's deceased and absent children reflected his interests in business and military affairs, his two children in town reflected his piety and aesthetic interests. The unmarried youngest son, Pierre, two years older than Lydia, avidly pursued a highly unusual career for a Canadian man, that of an artist. He worked as a painter of religious subjects. Pierre also spent considerable time and energy endowing, improving, and, of course, decorating the various religious communities of the town. The year of Lydia's arrival, Pierre had begun living at the settlement of the Charon religious brotherhood to which Le Ber *fils* had directed his share of his father's fortune. This money underwrote the founding of Montreal's first *hôpital général,* which would serve, it was hoped, as a refuge for destitute and infirm men and as a school for boys to be run by the Charon lay brotherhood.[14]

But it was Jacques Le Ber's only daughter, Jeanne, his only child living at home, who might have exerted the greatest influence on Lydia Longley. Thirty-two years old in 1694, Jeanne Le Ber was one of the most talked-about women in Montreal, principally because no one ever saw her. Nine years before, the "pensive, withdrawn, and introverted" woman had taken a "simple vow of perpetual seclusion, chastity, and poverty."[15] Ensconced in her room in her father's house, she continued to a limited extent to manage the extensive property she held in her own name, although she evidently refused to replace her mother fully in the management of the household on Saint Paul Street.[16] The circumstances of the seclusion of the wealthiest young woman in the colony aroused much curiosity in Montreal, and any possible appearance by her was a marked occasion.

Upon arrival at the Le Ber house, her patron installed Lydia as a guest and potential *Canadienne* rather than a servant. That she was never listed as "in service" to the Le Bers is significant because the house already had a white captive who Le Ber designated specifically as *dans la service:* an Irish-born New Yorker named John Lahey.[17]

Lahey had arrived at Saint Paul Street by a circuitous route. Born a Catholic in County Tipperary, he had immigrated to the English-controlled Hudson River valley, settling eventually in Corlear (present-day Schenectady) in what had previously been New Netherland. He had embraced Protestantism at Corlear, presumably to fit in with his adopted society. Taken captive in a major raid on Corlear in 1690, he was brought to Montreal and bought by Jacques Le Ber.[18] At the time of Lydia's arrival, Lahey had been working for Le Ber as a domestic for over four years. This *hibernois* had not converted back to the religion of his birth but instead remained, perhaps defiantly, Protestant in the face of the ardently expressed Catholicism surrounding him.

The contrast between the household positions of Lydia Longley and John Lahey must have struck both of them from the beginning. We cannot know whether Lahey actively resented the somewhat more privileged status of this new female arrival. For her part, Longley could not have failed to suspect that the determining factor separating her from Lahey was her sex—and she may even have begun to link her status as a young, unmarried woman with her potential cultural and religious value as a convert. But she would also have recognized the complexities of birthplace and religion that determined status in New France. Also serving the Le Bers within the household was a slave of African origin, known in the records only as

Jacques. Jacques may have also been a familiar presence to Lydia Longley, as he had been taken from New England, where he had been a slave, and purchased from the Indians by Le Ber. Certainly, like Lahey, he spoke English as well as French. English speakers may have been crucial to the adjustment of the newly arrived Longley, who presumably spoke no French. Jacques had just that year accepted baptism and become a Catholic, although because of his race he was destined to remain a slave.[19]

Freedom in New France rested on a combination of factors. For an unmarried female like Lydia Longley, religious conversion and the desire to settle permanently in Canada as a married woman or a religious sister was all that would be required. Though she was not obligated to work as a servant in the Le Ber house, the barrier of Lydia's redemption price remained—her status continued to depend on the wishes of Jacques Le Ber. For John Lahey, a somewhat less desirable settler, freedom in New France depended on conversion, citizenship, and actually working off his monetary debt to Le Ber. Evidently there was no one back in Corlear able or willing to pay his ransom. And for the slave Jacques, neither sex nor religion but race alone sealed his permanent status. He could never be free, nor could he marry without his master's permission.

Between mid-August 1694 and March 1696 Lydia Longley lived at the Le Ber house. When she arrived she had been a young woman who had just witnessed the violent death of her father, stepmother, and five of her six siblings. She was then in the hands of one of the most prominent citizens of the society that had sponsored that raid. The next record we have of her is from March 1696, when she moved into Marguerite Bourgeoys's community of lay sisters known as the Congrégation Notre-Dame de Montréal, having decided to "abjure her heresy" and adopt the Catholic faith. Her decision to join the Congrégation implies that she had progressed far beyond simple religious conversion. She had resolved, at the age of twenty-two, to join Bourgeoys's community as a religious sister and a professional teacher. What had happened in the intervening nineteen months?

The first question is why she had not entered the Congrégation as a student right away but had remained instead in a state of social limbo with the Le Bers. Her age at the time of arrival would perhaps have made it awkward to begin schooling with younger girls with less experience but greater knowledge of catechism. And the language barrier would have been a problem. Given these factors, the Le Ber household was probably the ideal vehicle of conversion. Her good treatment in a home of what must have seemed, to a former frontier dweller, unimaginable opulence no doubt speeded her recovery from the long, uncomfortable, and terrifying journey from New England. Even the presence of the servant John Lahey and the now Catholic slave Jacques must have eased her immersion in French language and culture: they gave her a link to her past during her exposure to, and eventual apparent acceptance of, a new faith, culture, and understanding.

Furthermore, Marguerite Bourgeoys and her sisters of the Congrégation lived right around the corner from the Le Bers'. Walking from Jacques Le Ber's front door to the Congrégation would have taken no more than six or seven minutes. Her decision to live there in March 1696 suggests she was already intimately acquainted with the community, perhaps visiting in the company of other women—including the young noblewoman Marie Madeleine Dupont de Neuville, who would serve as Lydia's godmother, or perhaps even Pierre Le Ber, who was a frequent visitor to the Congrégation.[20] She discovered at the Congrégation Notre-Dame a world she could not have known: an existence under the exclusive authority of women leading communal, celibate lives in the practical service of God. There was no Puritan equivalent.

Marguerite Bourgeoys, who had retired from the leadership of the Congrégation in 1692, doubtlessly impressed her young visitor. Lydia would have also met other former New Englanders, specifically the two Sayward sisters—one of whom, Mary Sayward, then a student, already possessed the spiritual power and proselytizing zeal that would soon mark her career. A final key individual at this time was Marguerite Le Moyne, already in 1694 a redoubtable thirty-year-old mistress of novices and, not incidentally, Jacques Le Ber's niece.[21]

Within the institutional memory of the Congrégation is the belief that the self-styled recluse Jeanne Le Ber had a primary religious influence on Lydia Longley.[22] No evidence casts doubt on this assumption—but it is one based solely on the physical proximity of the two women. Whereas efforts to bring Canadian, Indian, and New England women into the Catholic faith and community is a recurrent theme in the recorded lives of Marguerite Bourgeoys, Mary Sayward, and Marguerite Le Moyne, the figure of Jeanne Le Ber remains ambiguous.

Jeanne Le Ber demonstrated acts of faith that were extreme even in her time: social isolation, self-flagellation, nightlong prostration before the altar. Yet she retained the essential prerogatives of her social position at the pinnacle of New France society: acting as a benefactress, attending to some affairs of business, and retaining a personal servant in her comfortable "isolation."[23] Jeanne Le Ber never resolved the central paradox of her own life: her evident desire to be humble before God but not before God's people. Her contrariness might explain why she never actually joined a women's religious community. She disappointed the Ursulines in Quebec,

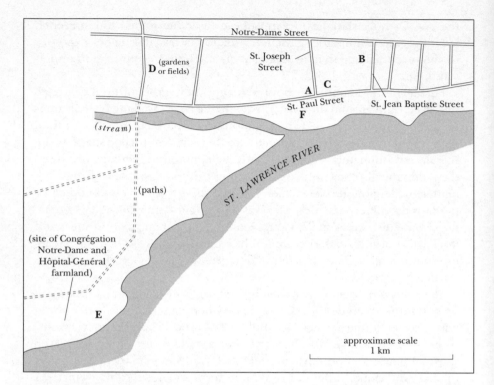

Montreal, mid-eighteenth century. *A*, the Le Ber household; *B*, the Congrégation Notre-Dame mother house and gardens; *C*, Hôtel-Dieu; *D*, Marguerite d'Youville's Hôpital-Général; *E*, Pointe Saint Charles; *F*, the market square off Saint Paul Street. Based on a drawing attributed to P. L. Morin, date unknown.

from whom she had received her early education, by not joining that community despite her obvious piety and suitability for the religious life. She also never became a sister of the Congrégation despite a long and intimate association. To do so would have meant long apprenticeships subject to the authority, not only of her social peers like Marguerite Le Moyne, but of her distinct inferiors—such as Bourgeoys's immediate and hand-chosen successor, the carpenter's daughter Marie Barbier.

This tendency to remain aloof from the missionary efforts of the Congrégation to attend to the needs of her soul found expression in her relocation in June 1695, halfway through Lydia Longley's tenure at the Le Bers', in the Congrégation's newly constructed church. Jeanne had partly financed the new church—intended to replace Bourgeoys's modest chapel—on the condition that a three-level apartment in which she could live be built behind the altar. Jeanne's actual move took the form of a public procession that led down Saint Paul Street, back up Jean-Baptiste Street, and ended with a mass in front of Jeanne's new apartment, during which she made the vows of a recluse devoted to God. She now looked on Montreal and the Congrégation as if through a one-way mirror—seeing all who came to the church but never herself being seen. She also was able to enjoy fresh air without being viewed by a curious public—her apartment featured a door that opened onto the Congrégation sisters' private walled garden.[24]

It is impossible to know what Lydia, or anyone in the motley crowd of onlookers, made of the singular, even bizarre spectacle of the procession. Lydia Longley might have indeed been influenced by this powerfully spiritual individual. But it seems more likely, especially given the practical turn her life made once within the Congrégation, that Lydia's main influences were Bourgeoys, Le Moyne, and her fellow New England students.

And what of Jacques Le Ber's motives? He must have found great satisfaction in providing his old friend Marguerite Bourgeoys with her first formerly Puritan woman to take the vows of postulant and lay sister.[25] But was he reluctant to let her go? Would marriage to Lydia have been a realistic possibility? The age gap would have been unusual, but not unprecedented for men of Le Ber's status. Perhaps the most visible marriage in the colony in 1696, that between Montreal's governor Philippe de Rigaud, sieur de Vaudreuil, and his wife Louise-Élisabeth Joybert, would have been similar to this hypothetical union. In 1696 Governor Vaudreuil was fifty-three years old and Louise-Élisabeth was thirty years his junior. But Louise-Élisabeth, unlike Lydia, came from a socially prominent family.[26]

Jacques Le Ber was, in fact, a mainstay of the circle of elite Montrealers, mostly women, routinely in the business of redeeming Anglo-American captives and then sponsoring those who converted for marriage and settlement.[27] The majority of sponsored captives married into a social class comparable to their own in the English-speaking colonies. Seigneurs with extensive landholdings, then, married off their captives—those who were willing—to their own *habitants* and *habitantes* and not, with only a very few exceptions, to their own sons and daughters from the landholder/merchant caste.

But by the 1690s Le Ber occupied a social position distinctly superior even to that of his fellow seigneurial merchants. His spectacular wealth would lead to his securing a letter of nobility in 1696, which put marrying Lydia into a different light. The French and French-Canadian noblesse generally did not marry outside their caste without the perception of scandal. (Nor did the presence of the frontier seem to matter much. Agathe Saint-Père, from Montreal, a friend and distant relative by marriage of

Jacques Le Ber, warned her own younger half-brother and voyageur Nicholas Le Moyne that a contemplated marriage to a common *Canadienne* would lead to his expulsion from the family.)[28] It seems quite unlikely that a marriage between Jacques and Lydia would have been accepted by his circle—the most illustrious in New France.

And as for the son, Pierre Le Ber would not in all probability have entered anyone's mind as a suitable partner for Lydia. The problems of social standing would have been the same as for the father. And his residence among the Charon lay brothers made the question moot—Pierre Le Ber never demonstrated any desire to marry.

Marriage between two captives who wished to become Canadian settlers, however, could be and often was encouraged by their elite sponsors. John Lahey's eventual conversion and marriage to another former captive, Mary Swarton, originally of Casco Bay, Maine, raises the question of why Lahey and Longley failed to make a match.[29] The two would certainly have been legally and socially acceptable once both of them had accepted Catholicism and Lahey had satisfied his debt of service to Le Ber. But Longley's increasing attraction to the Congrégation also made these plans, if they ever existed, as moot as the hypothetical joining of herself to Pierre Le Ber.

Interestingly, however, almost to the day that Lydia Longley left the Le Ber household in March 1696 to enter the Congrégation, John Lahey made the decision to return to the Catholic faith of his birth, indicating his intention to remain permanently in Canada. His baptism record lists him as still in the service of Le Ber, but his obligation to his master must have soon ended. In September 1697, Lahey married Swarton and became one of the first Irish-born permanent immigrants to the Saint Lawrence Valley. He and his new wife settled in Montreal, and in time thirteen children were born to them, four of whom survived to marriageable age.[30]

While both Lahey and Longley converted to Catholicism and remained in New France, their paths separated when Lydia separated from the network of Anglo-American captives and settlers in New France. John Lahey and Mary Swarton were fully integrated into this network, as demonstrated by the participation of several other former captives as godparents to their later children. Lydia Longley's name does not appear on the long list of baptism witnesses, even though she lived in Montreal through most of Mary Swarton's childbearing years.[31] (That she was a religious sister would not exclude her from such activities, as the record of her later life would show.) Perhaps the divergence was Lahey's doing—if, for example, he harbored resentment of Lydia's relatively privileged life in the Le Ber household. Most likely, though, the separation was Lydia's doing. Her failure to join her New England and New York counterparts in observing their significant life passages was an early sign of her total immersion in the Congrégation, which would define her existence for the next sixty-two years.

In March 1696 Lydia Longley took up permanent residence at the Congrégation Notre-Dame and a month later accepted baptism. Before the broader conversion of her new life among women took hold, she had had to adopt the Catholic faith as presented to her. The appeal of Catholicism probably owed much to its specific feminine manifestation in Bourgeoys's community. Bourgeoys's vision was hardly Calvinist—yet certain parallels helped Puritan women like Lydia find common ground with their new teachers.

The first parallel was the simplicity with which Bourgeoys's faith and mission were carried out. A central theme in early modern anti-Catholic thought was derision of the supposed tendency among Catholics to show "ostentatious humility." Bourgeoys and her followers demonstrated to their students that their humility was genuine and manifest in myriad ways: "If we remind ourselves of the life of Our Lord and that of Our Lady," Bourgeoys wrote, "we will let holy poverty appear everywhere: simplicity in our food, our clothing, our rooms, our furniture, and even in the infirmary among the sick and the infirm. For it is in these things that we discover the marvels of God. A careless, lax, easy life is a dense cloud which hides from our eyes the boundless treasure of his goodness."[32]

Certainly their sober and simple dress style—Bourgeoys mandated a long black dress with woolen belts and headdresses until 1698, when a more traditional habit was adopted—recalled Puritan admonitions on the evils of self-aggrandizement through conspicuous sartorial ornamentation.[33] But this superficiality was only the outermost layer of a whole way of thinking about the Marian apostolate. Inherent in the practice was the idea of social leveling—not as an articulated societal goal but as an essential characteristic of a women's religious mission. "All sisters must be equal," Bourgeoys had written, "each one should be employed at whatever she is fitted for. It must be so that the superior could be the cook and the cook, superior if they are capable of it."[34] And Bourgeoys required no *dot* (dowry) for her novices: they stood before God, all equally capable to continue the Virgin's apostolate, much as the freeholders of the Groton stood before the Almighty, all equally capable of advancing the errand into the wilderness.

An additional parallel would have been Bourgeoys's subtly subversive avoidance of the Catholic church hierarchy through her community's status as a lay sisterhood. Bourgeoys and her sisterhood emulated Mary without dependence on an intervening clergy. Neither Bourgeoys, her col-

leagues, nor her successors, of course, denied clerical authority or sought
to revolutionize the structure of the church. They simply sought a way to
hear Mary's voice without the competing cacophony of the often rusty
wheels of the mother church. As Puritans, Lydia Longley, Mary Sayward,
and Esther Sayward certainly understood the concept of listening to God
without the intervention of clerical hierarchy before they first arrived in
the house of the Congrégation sisters.

But along with parallels to Puritanism came a theological factor novel to
the New Englanders, which may well have proved decisive to the captives—
the idea of salvation attainable through good works. The rival Calvinist notion of a divine list of the elect remaining largely unknown to the earthbound proved often bedeviling to Puritan women—especially in times of
high infant mortality. One can only imagine the balm to the soul that the
belief in salvation through good works must have held for one as deeply
and profoundly affected by recent tragedy as Lydia Longley. Moreover, this
belief could be interpreted as a clarion call to an active life addressing the
afflictions of the world. Here, theology became firmly grounded in practical enterprises and in a professional life.

Conversion for Lydia Longley, now Lydia Madeleine, must have meant
more than the triumph of one theology over another. She lived for the
remainder of her life within a women's community whose structure and
activity were outside the boundaries of the Puritan life. Her cultural conversion and professional life had just begun. It was to find its full fruition
on a cultivated stretch of land along the Saint Lawrence at Pointe-Saint-
Charles—and was defined in significant part by the men who worked that
land.

❦

October 9, 1696, proved a busy day for Bourgeoys's successor, Congrégation *supérieure* Marie Barbier. The problem of labor on the farm at
Pointe-Saint-Charles could wait no longer. The ongoing war with the English had led to a sharp decrease in the indentured servant trade and to
increasing difficulty in securing free contracts for casual labor. When not
fighting, most men had to attend to their own property and affairs. There
remained precious little time in those days for anything else. And the farm
itself had its own problems.

First, there was now no farmhouse. The large structure built on the land
at Pointe-Saint-Charles in 1668 had burned down in 1693, taking with it a
good deal of Montreal's history. The original farmhouse had served not
only as the center of wheat production and animal husbandry supporting

the Congrégation but as a site of acculturation to Canadian life for the royally sponsored young female immigrants, the *filles de roi* (king's girls). Earlier incarnations of a school building in the town of Montreal itself could no longer handle the new arrivals. The farmhouse-school at Pointe-Saint-Charles, given the name "La Providence," and the surrounding lands had become the ideal site to instruct the young women on the demands of Canadian farm life for which most were destined.[35]

But by the time of the 1693 fire the *filles de roi* had stopped arriving at La Providence, and the farmhouse was now the exclusive domain of the *soeurs fermières,* their domestics, and students from the main house in Montreal who assisted in the work of the farm. The original manager, Catherine Crolo, was—the year of the fire—seventy-four years old but had retired from her strenuous post some years before. The historian Emilia Chicoine has speculated that Crolo could have been succeeded by Catherine Bony, one of Bourgeoys's recruits from France—but she would have been approaching fifty-six years of age in 1693.[36] A final difficulty with recruiting new farm managers was that most of the new entrants to the Congrégation in the 1680s were daughters of artisans such as bakers and shoemakers, and had not been raised on farms. Clearly a crisis in management had occurred by the time of Marie Barbier's accession to community leadership. To make matters worse, the formidable expense of building a new farmhouse had not been met as yet, and the strain of having sisters, students, and servants walk the mile and a half between the motherhouse and the fields made a demanding job even more so.

Barbier was well qualified to evaluate the situation and improve it. Unlike Bourgeoys, she knew firsthand the demands and responsibilities of working as a *soeur fermière.* One of the very few nonspiritual experiences she related to her spiritual director, Father Charles Glandelet, was the experience of driving cattle through the paths of Sainte-Famille on the Île d'Orléans near the Congrégation's outpost above Quebec.[37] Early in Barbier's tenure, no doubt through her experience at Île d'Orleans, she recruited a youthful corps of new, able-bodied *soeurs fermières* from the island and brought them to Montreal: Marie-Anne Guyon, aged thirty; Marie Gagnon, twenty-eight; and Marguerite Letourneau, twenty-one.[38] The Massachusetts farm girl Lydia Longley, now also called Sister Sainte-Madeleine, had joined them earlier that year.

But Barbier judged that even more help was needed to assist the new *soeurs fermières* in meeting the needs of the rapidly expanding Congrégation. The first opportunity she pursued on behalf of the community was the offer of a local farmer to become an indentured servant of the community and assist the sisters as the *contremaître* (foreman) at Pointe-Saint-

Charles. Born in Normandy in 1650, Pierre Picard had come to Canada as
a teenager and had worked as a servant to Paul Boucher.[39] In 1669 he had
married Jeanne Cederay and started a family as a habitant, probably in the
Boucherville region, where most of his children were born. Presumably he
did not prosper, because in 1696 at the age of forty-six he was willing to
sign away his freedom.

Picard, though, gained much in the contract he signed on October 9.
He gained a place to live (apparently a hut or small outbuilding surviving
on the Pointe-Saint-Charles property) and the assurance that his two sons
and three daughters still living with him would be sheltered, fed, and educated.[40] For Barbier, assuming the burden of five more dependents was
no doubt a serious matter, but it was important that the community acquire
someone with the years of experience that Picard brought.

With the supervisory personnel at Pointe-Saint-Charles thus substantially augmented, Barbier turned her attention that very same day to the
problem of farm labor. There is no extant list of servants of the Congrégation between the census of 1681 and the list 1699. Nevertheless, the situation must have been dire due to the general unavailability of indentured
labor. The *soeurs fermières* and their new *contremaître* would have had to rely
primarily on their own sisters, the remaining indentured servants, girl and
boy students, and whatever short-term help they could arrange.

The market for New England captives must have been intriguing to
Marie Barbier. The sudden availability of Anglo-American men could be a
financial and practical boon to the entire community. There were some financial risks: escape, uncompensated forcible reclaiming by the Indians,
or a government-mandated order of release could mean the loss of the entire investment. But in the event of a long war or the failure of the ransoming system, the community could hold their captives indefinitely. After
being purchased from the Indians, the English Protestants became legal
slaves of their purchasers.[41]

On that same October 9, Marie Barbier purchased a twenty-five-year-old
man from Deerfield, Massachusetts, named John Gillett. Perhaps she had
heard that he was being held nearby and made the trip out of Montreal to
make the transaction directly. Or perhaps the Indians knew of the labor
needs of the religious communities and peddled Gillett door-to-door.[42]
But the transaction could also have taken place in the small market square,
for this was the most common way to sell captives to the public. Offered
with Gillett was a slightly younger friend and fellow Deerfielder named
Nathaniel Belden. Each man was purchased by a different religious community. While Gillett went to the Congrégation, the *supérieure* Marie Morin,
acting on behalf of the Hospital Sisters of Saint Joseph, acquired Na-

thaniel.[43] The Sulpician brothers of Montreal bought Daniel Belden, Nathaniel's father, who had been taken in the same raid. The three purchases make eminent sense based on the needs of the respective communities. As the more experienced farmer of the two younger men, Gillett would have most closely fit the Congrégation's need for farm labor. The Hospital Sisters, who employed most of their captive men as orderlies, would foresee little difficulty in training the youthful Belden to his many daily tasks.[44]

Lydia Madeleine may have first encountered John Gillett at this sale. Since she seems to have been the only English-speaking sister that year (the Sayward sisters were as yet too young to have become novices), Barbier and Morin could have used her when questioning the captives about their backgrounds and capabilities.

Whether she was involved directly with the sale or not, the universe of difference between her own arrival in New France and that of Gillett and his companions could not have been lost on her. Before their capture these men had shared Lydia's experiences on the New England frontier to a remarkable degree. The Gillett family had paid a dear price to live on that frontier. John, at twenty-five, had been steeped in the world of frontier warfare and captivity from his earliest childhood.[45] John's father, Joseph, was born in Windsor, Connecticut, in 1641 into one of the original landowning families of what would then be considered the upper Connecticut Valley.[46] Joseph, his wife Elizabeth Hawkes, and their six young children became in 1673 some of the first settlers of the newly cleared four-year-old settlement called Pocumtuck—later referred to as Deerfield. Nearby lived Joseph's younger brother, Samuel, who with his wife had been raising his own family four miles away in Hatfield since about 1668.[47] The closeness of the two families is reflected in the fact that Joseph and Elizabeth Gillett named their first and only Deerfield-born child Hannah, after Samuel's wife.

But the brutal and widespread fighting of Metacom's rebellion, also known as "King Philip's War," fractured the promise of the newly established lands. Joseph Gillett was killed near his home in the fighting at Bloody Brook on September 18, 1675. His brother Samuel was fatally wounded eight months later at Turner's Falls.[48] Nor did the surviving family members remain unscathed. Samuel's widow, who had married a local man named Stephen Jennings in early 1677, had the distinction, along with two of her four children by Samuel Gillett, of being among the first group of New England captives taken to New France. On September 19 Hannah, her children, and fourteen others were taken from their houses by Housatonic Indians of the Hatfield-Deerfield area and sent on a long journey by foot to Sorel, on the south bank of the Saint Lawrence.[49] (These Housatonics, some of whom had long known their victims personally, have never received what is perhaps their due for ingeniously adapting their age-old hostage and captive-taking practices to the French-English inter-colonial rivalry. New Englanders were not fighting the French during Metacom's rebellion, but these Housatonics, by moving north and insert-ing themselves in a preexisting network of French-allied Indians, created a situation in which they could profit from ransoms paid by New England emissaries through the mediation of French authorities in Quebec. This raid would serve as a model for others that would plague English settle-ments for almost eighty years.)

Stephen Jennings and Benjamin Waite, who also had family members in captivity, took it upon themselves to follow immediately the trail of the cap-tives to the Saint Lawrence Valley and obtain their release in Quebec. At Sorel, Jennings first saw his new daughter, named Captivity Jennings, born to Hannah on the trek north. This Christian name suggests the religious context in which Hannah Jennings placed her captivity. Nouns or verbs used as female Puritan names could be addressed directly to God (e.g., "Submit," "Obedience"). "Captivity," a human reflection of God's will, was Hannah's one-word narrative, a word that recalls the spiritual wilderness preoccupations of her contemporary Mary Rowlandson. The indelibility of that name also reflects how the experience permeated the later life of the Jennings and their extended family.

John Gillett grew up, then, with the memory of his father's and close un-cle's violent frontier deaths as well as the living presence of his aunt Han-nah and young cousin Captivity Jennings, the redeemed captives. Other events of that time drew John closer to the Jennings household. After the battle at Bloody Brook the residents of Deerfield abandoned their embry-onic settlement. Elizabeth Hawkes Gillett was one of the former Deer-fielders who resettled in the comparative security of Hatfield, perhaps residing with the Jennings family until her own remarriage in 1680. What-ever their living arrangements, John Gillett at the age of six must have been an eyewitness to the Hatfield raid and the Jennings family's drama—and lucky to have eluded capture himself.

As a young man, Gillett sought to reestablish his father's settlement of Deerfield. His mother, Elizabeth, had died in 1682, his younger sister Hannah the next year, and his older brother Jonathan in 1686. Elizabeth's second husband, Nathaniel Dickinson, saw that the interests in Joseph Gil-lett's Deerfield land were divided fairly, with the eldest son receiving the use of the land until his brothers came of age.[50] When John did come of age he established himself at the resettled Deerfield. Having received his share of his father's land and whatever else of his inheritance remained, he was, in 1696 at the age of twenty-five, a reasonably prosperous and self-sufficient bachelor farmer and militiaman.

But the beginning of John Gillett's own pioneering in the upper Connecticut Valley was cut short as suddenly as his father's had been. The onset of King William's War placed the northernmost line of villages in constant peril, but since the abduction of his aunt and cousins nineteen years before, only one captive had been taken from the Deerfield-Hatfield area, Martin Smith, who disappeared alone in 1693.[51] On September 16, 1696, John Gillett and his militia companion John Smead were by their own account "tracking bees" when set upon by a small band of Mohawk. Smead managed to slip away but the Indians held Gillett fast. The Mohawks then proceeded further into Deerfield and raided the prominent Belden household.[52] The party returned to Gillett's location with three r.ew captives in tow: Daniel Belden, the family patriarch in his mid-forties; his son Nathaniel, a young man about Gillett's age; and his daughter Hester, a few years younger than Nathaniel.[53] The Beldens were doubtless much aggrieved, at that point having witnessed the death of Daniel Belden's wife and three of the Belden children. The four captives were then conducted up the Connecticut and White River valleys at a fast march, appearing in the Mohawk settlement of Caughnawaga (then at Sault-Saint-Louis on the Saint Louis rapids above Montreal) no more than three weeks later.[54]

At Caughnawaga, the Mohawk introduced John Gillett and the Beldens to the differential treatment of captives by sex. The three men were separated from Hester, stripped naked, and made to run a gauntlet of Mohawk women and children. Most blows were directed at Nathaniel and John— thus sparing the older Daniel. For some unknown reason the Mohawk elected to keep Daniel Belden and his daughter at their settlement for awhile. They conducted John Gillett and Nathaniel Belden to Montreal for sale to the French. The captives arrived there on October 9, 1696, only twenty-three days after their original capture.[55]

That past spring, Lydia Longley had experienced a kind of rebirth at her Catholic baptism and her subsequent entry into the Congrégation as a postulant. She took a new name, adopted new clothing, assumed a new social role and professional identity, and adopted a new faith. There was also an element of rebirth in John Gillett's entry into that same community. As Iroquoians, the Caughnawaga Mohawk had known for uncounted generations that the first step in enslaving a man is to infantalize him. Whether he was to receive a new adopted identity or be retained as a subservient member of the community, the removal of his previous identity and status was vital. These thoughts lay behind the Indian custom of requiring captive men to strip naked whenever they came to a French settlement.[56] A captive's nakedness while being sold to Canadians served the practical purpose of allowing for inspection of sound bodies. But the ritual symbols ran deep and crossed cultures. Gillett entered his new world as he had entered his previous one. And once conveyed from the marketplace to his new custodians at the farm—Marie-Anne Guyon, Marie Gagnon, and Marguerite Letourneau—he would call them "sister." He would be newly clothed as well as fed, cared for, instructed—and controlled—by these fictive elder kinswomen.

But this passive, infantile state was not enforced solely to communicate and enforce subjugation. It carried powerful elements of potential regeneration or, specifically in this case, conversion. When Guyon, Gagnon, and Letourneau set to their own task of counter-reformation in training the Protestant Gillett for his servant's role in a women's community devoted to the Catholic faith, the question arises, What were their intentions for him? In the market square, did Marie Barbier see in Gillett only a body for sale? Or, did she see as well a lost soul, as she had in the young woman guest residing with Jacques Le Ber? To answer this question we must first consider the inner nature of the Congrégation, and in particular its identity as a community for women.

❧

As it grew from its modest beginnings, Marie Barbier's community took on the challenge of converting an astoundingly diverse group of resident subjects: French immigrants, English captives, and local Indians. Bourgeoys enacted one version of the belief central to French-Canadian religion, culture, and imagination: that any individual could be made suitable to live and survive in the colony of New France. As Bourgeoys and the sisters gradually moved from the periphery to the center of the French colonial project, the men of the community, having initially played an important supporting role, were pushed toward the margins.

Marguerite Bourgeoys herself, a young woman rejected as a postulant by the contemplative Carmelites of Troyes, France, refocused her sense of mission to face the North American wilderness on her own terms.[57] Sidestepping the severe restrictions on women religious imposed by the Council of Trent, Bourgeoys sought to emulate those French lay sisters devoted to social service.[58] Her vision amounted to a specifically New World version of a Marian, wandering, and apostolic life for laywomen. This was the life she called the *vie voyagère*.[59] Bourgeoys intended this wandering to be nothing short of an explicitly female apostolate running parallel to the original male-centered apostolate of the disciples of Jesus:

> The apostles were sent in the name of Our Lord and they worked wonders. The sisters of the Congregation are sent under the protection of the Blessed Virgin to teach school and they instruct girls as though they were very learned. . . . The apostles were unfaithful in abandoning our Lord at the time of His passion. They needed the Holy Spirit to make them strong. The sisters of the Congregation are timid and slow to advance in perfection. They need the help of the Blessed Virgin to obtain the Spirit of God who will give them courage. The apostles went out to all parts of the world. The sisters of the Congregation are ready to go anywhere they are sent in this country.[60]

Bourgeoys created the means to this end through the office of *filles seculaires* (secular sisters) who took simple vows of poverty, chastity, and service. But most crucial to her community's internal structure and external relations were her views on male authority. Bourgeoys's reasoning was subtle. She posited first that the apostles of Jesus had also followed Mary, and that the Virgin had in turn acted as a "mistress of novices" to them. In this conception Mary began to regard the apostles as her superiors only after God gave them the power to "remit sins." Nevertheless, according to Bourgeoys, the apostles always continued to regard Mary as "their mother" and continued to take her advice. This rather obvious analogy to her own mission is indicative of her thinking. Although she did not deny the technical and public superiority of the clergy, she was fully resolved that the clergy ought not to interfere with her mission, which functioned outside it. Bourgeoys further believed that as followers of the Virgin, she and her sisters should be accorded due respect from non-clerical men as well as women.[61] Armed with this belief in an authority to do God's work through the mediation of a blessed feminine presence, Bourgeoys and her sisters-in-religion felt, not surprisingly, as little hesitation in gathering in and fashioning the lives of male subordinates as they did in resisting the concerns and admonitions of the clergy.

That her new sisterhood actually realized this ideal and established its independence continually rankled a series of Quebec bishops. But the *vie voyagère* was not in any sense a utopian vision. Bourgeoys harbored no illusions regarding the workings of human nature, in monastic garb or not, and its rather limited capacity for improvement.[62] This unadorned Gallic pragmatism created the conditions necessary to effect her New World innovations. And unlike the Beguines and other earlier groups of itinerant laywomen, who were never faced with the challenges of trans-racial or trans-gender inclusion, Bourgeoys held a nonrestrictive vision of the *vie voyagère*. "If you act as an advocate for the church," she wrote, "its own baptised members will be converted, and unbelievers as well."[63] Her actions reveal precisely how wide a net she cast.

Her original conception of service had included teaching and catechizing Indian girls, which placed Bourgeoys squarely within the larger missionary guidelines of Montreal's founders: Maisonneuve's Société de Notre-Dame. It also followed previous missionary forms widely known and admired in France: that of the long-suffering Jesuits and the cloistered Ursuline mission pioneered by Marie de L'Incarnation.[64] But when the local Iroquois proved hostile to the inhabitants of Montreal, Bourgeoys's mission by necessity turned inward to her own people. She began a school for Canadian girls in a converted stable on the farm, and in a nearby structure she housed and instructed the *filles de roi*.[65]

The policy of welcoming sisters from all social backgrounds set the Congrégation Notre-Dame apart from their socially elite Ursuline counterparts in Quebec—and proved congruent to the needs of the rough-and-tumble frontier settlement. By taking in students from merchant, artisan, and farming families, La Providence demonstrated its practical and vocational emphasis. In 1684 Bishop Saint-Vallier wrote that approximately twenty "*grande filles*" (teenage girls) resided at La Providence, alongside at least the same number of younger students.[66]

Bourgeoys's conception of a *vie voyagère* on the New World frontier required that her community be completely self-sufficient rather than dependent on potentially fickle and controlling patronage of wealthy individuals or on mercurial and preoccupied French colonial authorities.[67] Dependence could quickly turn fatal in that particularly harsh environment if the tide of benevolent favor suddenly receded. Self-reliance left Bourgeoys with a stark challenge: the colony needed women, but Marguerite Bourgeoys needed men—to physically sustain her community with their labor. And as for the male residents, the material needs of the community meant ultimately that men and boys could, at least for a time, be offered a chance to walk in the Virgin Mary's footsteps as well.

Before Marguerite Bourgeoys had even departed France for Canada in 1653, she had included a man among her tiny band of sister-travelers: "A young man, a student, also offered himself to serve this house, to give himself to the service of God for his whole life. He followed us on the voyage and took his quarters [on the ship] near ours. But while he was on board, he was attacked by dysentery from which he later died in our house two years after his arrival in Montreal."[68]

Three types of male residents lived among the sisters during the early days of the Congrégation Notre-Dame. Male servants, or *engagés*, were indentured to the sisters collectively for a specified period. These men worked alongside others referred to as *donnés*—men who had pledged their service in perpetuity to the community in exchange for a guarantee of food, shelter, and religious guidance. The sisters also instructed boys as student-domestics under a contract that their parents could break only with difficulty. In the first years of the colony Bourgeoys educated a few young boys in the absence of available priests in Montreal—but even after the educational opportunities had expanded in the city (and in Quebec) by the 1670s, parents or guardians of modest social standing continued to indenture their sons to the community with the understanding that they would be both servants and students there.

Just as Bourgeoys and her companions mapped their own path in dealing with male superiors, they did so as well with their male subordinates. They included their servants in the vital life of the community, and—unlike their French counterparts and the Sulpicians and Jesuits in Montreal—they even went so far as to blur the distinction between sister and servant.

Bourgeoys considered men to be an integral part of her novel New World mission.[69] She writes, for example, that the sisters and servants shared bread.[70] More than an incidental note, this detail reveals that the Congrégation excepted themselves from at least one symbol of the social hierarchy separating the classes. Bourgeoys thereby included male servants in certain aspects of community life, much as she had earlier when she broke with common practice of not fully integrating female students and wards of inferior status. Both actions deeply troubled some of her fellow sisters of the Congrégation and would define the battles fought by her successors.[71]

Bourgeoys also decided to include servants as co-worshippers with her lay sisters in the tiny stone chapel built into the palisade surrounding Montreal in 1675. The inclusion of servants in the back pews at mass would not have been so unusual in an isolated French monastery or seigneury, but having men accompany women religious to worship made a public statement about the nature of the mission—unmistakably contrarian in terms of expected class as well as gender distinctions.[72] At the founding of the community, Bourgeoys described her "brothers" in intimate terms. Beside the name of twenty-five-year-old Jacques Hordequin on the 1667 census appear the words *frère donné*.[73] Bourgeoys addressed her three fellow *congrégationalistes* as *soeurs,* or sisters. And here in Jacques Hordequin she claimed a *frère,* a brother. Thomas Mousnier, another *donné,* appears in Bourgeoys's own writings as *"frère* Thomas".[74] These were dependent brothers, fictive "little" brothers, but brothers within the sisterhood nonetheless.

Though her outreach was genuine, the frontier pragmatism of Bourgeoys and her companions never let the women lose sight of why the men had been brought in to the community in the first place—to carry out the physical work needed for survival. An element of coercion always underlay the ideals Bourgeoys held about the male presence at the Congrégation. The institution of indentured servitude unmistakably held most men to the community, and unceasingly shaped the actions as well as the perceptions of sisters, students, and servants.

As the community expanded, men in the Congrégation became more marginalized. The 1668 establishment of La Providence created the new role of chief *soeur fermière* for one of Bourgeoys's original companions, Catherine Crolo. From the beginning Crolo had seen her duty at the house as that of housekeeper, going so far as to refer to herself as the "donkey" of the community. After the community started its wheat crop and animal husbandry program, she became principally concerned with the direction of men. Crolo walked each day with the men servants from town to farm and back again. And when Bourgeoys finally purchased a large house adjacent to the first acreage capable of providing ample living space, Crolo took up year-round residence at Pointe-Saint-Charles. The servants slept wherever their work dictated.[75]

As the men of the Congrégation became increasingly identified with field work instead of household activities, the male *engagés* found themselves outnumbered. By 1681 the membership of the Congrégation had grown to twenty-four sisters, who taught and met the needs of perhaps forty or fifty girl students of all ages. The number of *filles de roi* during their peak arrival years in the 1670s easily exceeded that of the Canada-born students, although the immigrants had largely stopped arriving by the mid-1680s.[76] The census of 1666 and 1667 lists the names of four "*domestiques engagés*" employed by Bourgeoys who had served her and her original companions. By the next census in 1681, only twelve more servants had been added, aided marginally by a handful of indentured boys.[77]

While the character of the community became increasingly female, the age differential between sisters and servants widened. The median age of women in the community grew progressively younger while Bourgeoys acquired increasingly older male servants. In the fourteen years separating the 1667 and 1681 censuses, when the number of sisters had increased sixfold, an influx of young, Canadian-born sisters pushed the median age of the sisters down to only twenty-five. In addition, large numbers of students as well as a small group of associated free servants (known as the sisters of the grey robe) also took an active role in the management of the communal property—so that the median age of all females giving daily instructions to the *engagés* was certainly no more than twenty. As for the men, in 1667, the median age of servants had been twenty-two. By the 1681 census, the Congrégation, perhaps wanting more experienced help, had selected servants whose median age approached thirty-four.[78] The younger sisters were also increasingly originating from the same tradesman caste as their new female employers in Canada.

Men in the community—increasingly marginalized, outnumbered, and managed by younger women of their own class—saw that the bourgeois gentility and maturity of the maternal founders of the community had been undermined. A culture of rebellion began to take hold among menservants of the Congrégation.

Unlike the acculturated female immigrants, the men of the community left at a greater rate than servants in Canada generally, often risking draconian punishment by escaping. Despite the determined and imaginative efforts of Marguerite Bourgeoys, only two of all the indentured servants present at the Congrégation in 1667 or 1681 are known to have stayed permanently in Canada.[79] The 10 percent rate of success enjoyed by the sisters in settling their male dependents was a bare fraction of the 50 percent general rate of return for *engagés* before 1690.[80]

Though there is no census data for two decades after 1681, what we know of the escape attempts by later arrivals strongly suggests a continuation of physical resistance by male servants.[81] It doubtless surprised these sisters profoundly that the *donnés,* the men held closest to the center of community, outdid even their indentured counterparts in resistance. Certainly one of them, and possibly two, took the extreme measure of running away—a criminal act of breach of contract. Heavy penalties, including extended service, could be administered by civil authorities. A returned servant's master could supplement this sanction liberally by the administration of corporal punishment or the imposition of hard living conditions. But flight meant above all elimination of one's support and food-supply network. In the brutal Canadian environment—cold for eight months, hot and humid for four, and surrounded by hostile Iroquois year-round—these absences can only be considered genuine acts of desperation.

Jacques Hordequin, a *donné,* disappears from the records between 1667 and 1681, and the lack of a record of his death in the generally meticulous parish record suggests he fled—perhaps to France or to the Great Lakes fur-trading region. The case of another *donné,* Thomas Mousnier, is more complex and represents the subtleties of gender relations within the community. Though Bourgeoys had the right to retain a *donné* under any circumstances, she wrote in 1682 that Mousnier had been "dismissed" after less than three years of service, apparently after demonstrating some sort of recalcitrant behavior. Bourgeoys, who later encountered Mousnier by chance on a Montreal street, reported that he "regretted" his actions and that he "believ[ed] he could return" to the community.[82]

The confrontation with *frère donné* Thomas Mousnier presented Marguerite Bourgeoys with several options. She could have simply accepted him back into the community on the same terms as before. Even had the *donné*'s contrition proved fleeting, she would have been well within her rights to have him apprehended and delivered back to the community in Montreal by force. When the moment came, Bourgeoys chose neither to enforce her contract nor to accept the servant's contrition. Contracts aside, Bourgeoys did not want *frère* Thomas within her mission unless she could be convinced his heart and soul were engaged in the community's mission. For Bourgeoys, sincerity took precedence over the advantages of the potential labor power.

Donné rebellion would continue under the regime of Bourgeoys's successor, Marie Barbier. Her fugitive *donné* proved to be none other than *contremaître* Pierre Picard, who had signed his contract with Barbier on the day of John Gillett's purchase. Picard abandoned his obligations as well as his wife and children a short time later. The sisters did not pursue Picard, as was their right, but nevertheless honored their commitment to educate his offspring, perhaps because Madame Picard took on the role of farm *contremaîtresse*.[83]

Why, despite their concerted efforts, did the sisters fail to win new male settlers for Canada when their counterparts in the male religious communities proved to be relatively successful? The simple fact that the men lived under indentured servitude did not account for the extent of flight. Other masters obviously had far greater success than did Bourgeoys.

Did the sisters offer fewer prospects for success for freed servant men? Servants came to Canada seeking upward mobility, and an indenture contained an expectation of reciprocal advantage. The authority of the patron rested on being able to secure the allegiance of the servant. But the sisters were no less able to provide for their servants than other masters in the colony. Relative access to land was not an issue—property could be had by freedmen simply by signing a contract with a local seigneur. And though not seigneurs themselves, as were the Sulpicians and many servant-holding families, the sisters of the Congrégation Notre-Dame enjoyed the aid of benefactors such as Jacques Le Ber, who could provide at the sisters request a network of patrons equal to any in New France. In short, a servant leaving the sisters on good terms would have the same relative advantage as his counterparts. The only real difference was the gender of those in authority.

When some French servants rejected an unconventional women's religious mission, they also rejected by extension female authority in the monastic setting. The idea that *women's* authority was rejected cannot be proven but should be considered. Bourgeoys's insistence on a loyal heart as well as an obedient mind may well have alienated the servant men. As all servants discovered, the uncloistered nature of the Congrégation did not mean a laxity in monastic discipline. Bourgeoys's effort to make her sisterhood legitimate in the eyes of the skeptics, especially clerical skeptics—combined with the educational mission of the community—perhaps hardened her resolve to live by the strictest internal standards. The residents at La Providence, for example, ordered their lives according to the ringing of bells.[84] Bourgeoys advised aspirant sisters that they must "obey promptly in everything and obey everyone who has any jurisdiction over her without murmur or complaint."[85] Less could hardly have been expected of the servant men. Perhaps the weight of Bourgeoys's insistence on a complete immersion of servants into the life of the community fell most intensely on the pledged-for-life *frère donnés*. The magnification of an adult male servant's fictive childhood status—a status continually reinforced in the households and fields of the Congrégation—might have proved cloying. Circumstances could lead the ascription of child status to offset the pious resolve to give oneself to a religious community.[86]

The difficulties encountered in Bourgeoys's cross-gender experiment indicate the magnitude of the gender barriers present in the early modern world. Within the Congrégation community, women and men failed to find a common language. But the failure was not exclusively that of rebellious male servants. Bourgeoys's complex mission did not survive her leadership. The foundress stepped down from the position of *superieure* in 1692, eight years before her death. In her increasingly bitter writings Bourgeoys noted that in the 1690s the humbler-born sisters became more cognizant of their vastly improved social status as sisters of the Congrégation. The sisters sought to reestablish the distinction between themselves and those servants who shared their social backgrounds. Under the new *supérieure*, for example, servant's bread was now of an inferior quality.[87] "I notice," she writes, "that there are sisters who show more esteem for a girl who has social rank than for one who might be more virtuous. Some are also harsh with the poor, both in giving them pleasure or in lending to them even when this can be done without inconveniencing themselves."[88] By claiming the social privileges of monastics, Bourgeoys's daughters-in religion could now feel unrestrained in treating servants in a stricter, more traditional manner.

There is also evidence, however, that the conditional inclusiveness offered to servants had always been a fiction. The Congrégation took some pride in accepting boy students, but they were sometimes seriously marginalized. In 1687 a shoemaker named Vivien Magdelaine and his wife Marie Godin contracted the labor of at least three of their sons aged six, twelve, and fifteen to work for the Congrégation for a period of nine years.[89] In exchange, the Magdelaine family were relieved of the support of their children, and the indenture included the provision that the sisters would educate them. The Magdelaine brothers were listed with other boys not as students but as "taken on as domestics" *(engagés en qualité de domestiques)*—and they apparently lived ambiguous lives as both students and a servants.[90] Along with disproving the frequent assumption among historians that Canada's women's religious communities educated only preadolescent boys, the lengthy terms of indenture served by the Magdelaine boys meant that they would have left the community, at the earliest, when they were fifteen, twenty-one, and twenty-four.

The experience of Vivien Magdelaine's oldest son, Joseph, raises the question of the inherent limitations of male inclusion in the community. He was indentured to the Congrégation at the age of fifteen for a term of nine years, but the nature of the "education" he actually received or expected to receive is far from clear. At the beginning of his term, Joseph had already reached the age at which most of his male peers had completed their educations and had gone on to apprenticeships, joined the military, or undertaken trading voyages to the West. By the time he completed his term at the age of twenty-four, he was already older than almost half of his teachers and the substantial majority of the sisters and female students supervising his work. That he was a student in any but the most rudimentary and occasional sense, then, strains credulity. To the sisters, his nine-year presence was defined not by pedagogy or even faith but rather by what could simply be defined as a relationship of the hearth—a common struggle against the literal and metaphorical cold of the frontier. His prospects could hardly have been much better after his release than at the time of his arrival.

Race became another yet another dividing factor between the sexes at the Congrégation. In 1676, twenty-three years after her arrival in Montreal, Marguerite Bourgeoys finally succeeded in opening a tiny wilderness mission at the Jesuit outpost known as the Mountain Mission on Montreal Island. Three years later, the Congrégation welcomed the first two Iroquoian sisters, Marie-Barbe Attoncion d'Onotais, twenty-three years old, and Marie-Thérèse Gannensagouas, fourteen.[91]

Marie-Thérèse Gannensagouas remained at the Mountain Mission to teach and catechize Indian girls alongside her fellow sisters.[92] Marie Barbe d'Onotais accompanied her new sisters back to lead the life of a teacher and farmer. In the transcultural sense, d'Onotais's transformation proved more radical than that of her younger counterpart. But in another sense, d'Onotais's life as a teaching and farming sister featured a powerful continuation of the female elements of Iroquoian life. For both Iroquoian women and French-Canadian monastic women, agricultural knowledge possessed a spiritual as well as a practical dimension when shared among adult women, between mother and daughter, or between student and teacher. Whether instructing students or assisting Catherine Crolo, d'Onotais would have been in regular supervisory contact with the French indentured servants.

The cultural viewpoint of the Iroquois as personified by d'Onotais represented a middle ground. For d'Onotais, that monastic sisters did much of their own field work and directed the men assisting them possessed a certain familiarity. The feminine exclusivity of farming in Iroquois settlements was breached only by those male captives who had been spared execution in favor of liminal adoption. The Iroquois, then, regarded men working for women in the fields as a gender power inversion—but a deliberate and, above all, *legitimate* one. Somewhat ironically, d'Onotais may well have shared with her servants the perception that the service of the men possessed a quality of shame. Yet, if she shared Bourgeoys's vision for the men, her activities supported the purpose of cultural integration for men and boys.

As in the Le Ber household, gender, rather than race or social origin, joined religion as a principal determinant of authority within the community. The French servants probably understood this, although they may not have conceived it in abstract terms. Who in Canada, after all, had never heard the stories in the *Relations* about Jesuit fathers like Isaac Jogues, priests whose forced subjection to Iroquois women had been made an integral part of their martyrdom? By putting an Iroquois woman in authority over them, Bourgeoys went well beyond stretching legitimate gender boundaries that determined the ways of the lay sisterhood. In the French male view the presence of d'Onotais might also be said to have appropriated and perverted the church for which the martyr Jogues gave his life: the Congrégation had dressed up feminine "savages"—and by extension savagery itself—in pious clothing. And, once again, men failed to be promoted fully for acculturation.

The efforts of Marguerite Bourgeoys to create a center for a women's voyage along the periphery of the French-speaking world proved, like all intercultural middle grounds, ephemeral and transitory. Like Marie de L'Incarnation, the Quebec Ursuline who became influential through her paradoxical cloistered missionary work, Marguerite Bourgeoys established a local center of religious activity and transculturation.[93] Her troubled efforts to include all of her residents in the Marian *vie voyagère* tells us not only about the nature of the small community made by women but also of their unhesitating efforts to define her mission. Of more importance to the community than struggles with male clerical authority were the entrenched views of male servants—men who perceived themselves, not as creating their own centers from margins, but rather as being pushed ever closer to the sharp edge of earth. The life of the Congrégation in the five decades after its beginning forces us to consider the implications of men living at the margins of smaller worlds made by women. No matter the destination, men often refused to proceed along a path not just cleared by women but *defined* by them, even if these women were followers of Mary herself.

❧

Whenever it was that Lydia Madeleine and John Gillett first met—in the market square on the day of his purchase or on the next harvest day as one of his custodians—the two of them soon inhabited different worlds within the same small community. Both had departed from the prevailing customs governing the early modern European world and had entered a zone in which women made the rules and formed the religious and secular values. Lydia took her place in a twenty-year tradition of successful female secular acculturation and mission building. John, however, found a history of male resistance to the ever more circumscribed role of men within the Congrégation. When he first arrived, the Congrégation was beginning its experiment with mid-level authority wielded by a man, Pierre Picard, who himself had worked under the three *soeurs fermières*. But in a very short time even the role of *contremaître* would fall back into female hands. In all the tasks he was given, Gillett found his relationship with women radically and continually redefined.

Gillett was not necessarily the only English male captive present at the Congrégation (an eighteen-year gap in the record of servants at the Congrégation leaves this unresolved). We know of the locations for the Gillett and Belden captivities only because of an offhand notation by their Deerfield friend Stephen Williams. This suggests at least that others held there may not have been forthcoming about the identity of their captors. Considering the desperate need for labor in Canadian monastic communities, the availability of captive men during the 1690s and 1700s, and the large numbers of such men employed by the women's hospital communities, it might seem unlikely that Barbier and her expansion-minded successor Marguerite Le Moyne would keep only one English captive. The Hôtels-Dieu of Montreal and Quebec, as we will see, continued to purchase male Anglo-Americans in significant numbers during every war until the British conquest in 1760. At least John Gillett did not lack for a relatively sympathetic ear. Nathaniel Belden worked just on the other side of the hedge that separated Montreal's Hôtel-Dieu from the Congrégation. Under the watchful eyes of the sisters, the two men perhaps were able to converse from time to time.

Shortly after Gillett's arrival, the frenetic activity of the wheat harvest ended and most servants, including Gillett, would have spent much of their time in town, in or around the Congrégation's main house and gardens. In the winter the day began with the obligatory shoveling of snow and removal of ice. Several servants would spend a significant part of the day drawing water from one of the small streams flowing through town into the Saint Lawrence, or, if these were frozen, from the great river itself. This was heavy work—two wooden buckets had to be balanced on a heavy five-foot-wide wooden yoke.[94] (The blunt symbolism of the yoke, a ubiquitous biblical metaphor for slavery, would not have been lost on anyone.) Another constant task was the cutting and hauling of firewood for cooking and the occasional warming fires. During the few warm months, male servants were also employed keeping the gardens and grounds surrounding the main house. Unlike the private houses surrounding them, the lay sisters maintained a certain quality of modesty. Cooking, serving meals, and attention to the women's quarters were the province of the small number of hired free girls.[95] These sisters of the gray robe represent yet another layer of female authority to which the menservants and, later, captive men of the Congrégation were made subject. As keepers of the kitchens and fires, the young women would have directed the gatherers of water and wood as well as the laundrymen and maintenance workers.

The care and herding of the cattle and assorted beasts of burden required that sometimes servants sleep outdoors or in the stable to ensure the animals' survival in the bitter cold. In warmer weather, those servants designated for work on a given day assisted the *soeurs fermières* tending to the wheat crop. Keeping that crop required a fair bit of judgment and short bursts of intensive, ordered work to maximize the possibility of success.[96]

John Gillett had worked hard throughout his life; overwork was not what planted the seeds of rebellion in his mind. What kind of life had Lydia Madeleine adopted? he must have wondered. A resisting captive could see in her the perversion of Puritan womanhood. For a Puritan, to adopt the Catholic faith was to forswear one's salvation and to accept instead a grov-

eling allegiance to what was seen to be a corrupt clergy and a devotion to
the muddled idolatry of the saints. Of more immediate and visible concern
to a captive would be the commitment of the sisters to a communal and
celibate lifestyle. Communal life for women meant a disavowal of a home
and husband, and a commitment to celibacy meant a sacrifice of children—a repudiation of the divine directive of multiplication.

Different meanings of celibacy were manifest. The sisters obliged their
men to live as they did—communally as well as in celibacy. For an early
modern Euro-American man, celibacy denied identity—the roles of husband, father, and household master in which the act of procreation signified the genesis of one's "little empire."[97] Celibacy for women meant
freedom from this same domestic empire. The release from the two-year
cycle of pregnancy and childbirth meant that other categories of activities
could be pursued. While celibacy would not have necessarily connoted
"freedom" to early modern Frenchwomen in this family-oriented epoch,
many women found the celibate life attractive, while most men found it
profoundly debilitating.

The communal life of the mission gave it strength. The dynamic sisters
made an errand into the wilderness a woman's own business. Thus the
Congrégation completely reversed the New England stereotypes of the active man and the passive, homebound woman. The sisters were the ones
leading an active public life; the passive domestic life was that of the servants.

Such was the authority that directed John Gillett's daily activities. The
same three sisters who had conducted Gillett's initial training—Marie-
Anne Guyon, Marie Gagnon, and Marguerite Letourneau—were later responsible for his ongoing care and discipline. The conflict that Marguerite
Bourgeoys had unintentionally provoked in her original French servants
was visited anew on Gillett. If, as seems most likely, the sisters coupled the
overseeing of Gillett's labor with an attempted conversion of his mind and
soul, the perpetuation of the conflict was assured. The sisters may have
thought that the combination of coercive labor with spiritual guidance was
helpful and merciful. But in Gillett's mind, it is likely that these two factors
were negatively reinforcing. Gillett's alienation would have been worse had
its agents been Lydia Madeleine or the fifteen-year-old New Englander
Mary Sayward, who would have been even less acceptable to him as authority figures. Sayward, for example, was doubtless active in the conversion of nonbelievers at an early age. Only three years later she was
appointed to lead the Congrégation's mission at Sault-au-Récollet, where
she would be guaranteed contact with incoming New England captives.
Presumably, Marguerite Le Moyne, who made this decision, had some ba-

sis for recognizing Sayward's qualities—the appointment was made soon after her profession to the community.

So it is perhaps not so surprising, then, that like some of his French predecessors, Gillett rebelled against the women's community that held him. In the end, he worked on the farm and in the house of the Congrégation for only eleven months. When, during a lull in hostilities, a joint English-Dutch mission made a second visit to Canada in April 1698 to negotiate with Governor Frontenac for the release of captives, the English emissary, Peter Schuyler, was in for two surprises. First, although the French citizens and "convents" holding captives were instructed to bring out their captives, almost all the New Englanders—presumably converts like John Lahey, Mary Swarton, Lydia Longley, and the Sayward sisters—refused to come home. Only four New Englanders, including the three Beldens, returned with Schuyler to Deerfield, which they reached in June 1698. The second surprise that greeted the delegation was that John Gillett was nowhere to be found in New France.[98]

Seven months before, in September 1697, Marie Barbier had dispensed with the services of John Gillett. The manner of this severance almost cost Gillett his life, for he was sent on a ship to the prison in La Rochelle, France, where he suffered confinement for some months.[99] Why had this happened? Why would Barbier have disposed of Gillett just before the harvest?

Barbier could not have known of the impending peace (although the Treaty of Ryswick was signed that same month, word did not reach New France until the ice cleared the entrance to the Saint Lawrence the following spring), so a fear of losing the community's investment through a declaration of peace would not have played a part. The later shipment of other captives to La Rochelle, and Gillett's eventual redemption by the "Charitie of some English marchants," suggest the existence of a network whereby Canadian captive holders could profit by trading through middlemen in France.[100] That Barbier took this opportunity implies that two factors were in play. First, she could not send her captive directly back to New England without losing her financial investment entirely, with continuing intercolonial hostilities preventing ransom talks. Second, Gillett had become a rebellious or uncontrollable servant who was no longer an asset to the community. Dispossessing the community of Gillett at that time under any other circumstances would have been nonsensical, and certainly not the act of a supremely competent *supérieure* like Barbier. The advantages of having a farmhand at harvest time and through the long winter to come would have far outweighed any monetary gain Barbier could have realized through the ransoming deal she negotiated with the agents in La Rochelle.

John Gillett had clearly rejected not only the possibility of conversion but also a willingness to continue working within a women's mission. If Bourgeoys had not won the hearts and minds of the French *engagés,* and had not even been able to prevent her three local *donnés* from illegally escaping, perhaps it was inevitable that a Puritan militiaman would not have remained for long in Barbier's more emphatically female-oriented mission, which excluded men from the central life of the community. Journeying in a disease-ridden ship sailing from New France to La Rochelle and spending several months in a filthy French prison were life-threatening undertakings—an ordeal that Gillett could have avoided had he chosen to remain where he was.[101] But it appears that the physical hardships he was to experience on his seven-month intercontinental odyssey back to Deerfield were an acceptable risk to ensure his release from the Marian mission.

❧

And what of the captors' narrative emerging from this encounter? Legitimacy of authority is in the eye of the beholder. Servants and the sustaining of the community played relatively small parts in the mental universe of the sisters. There is only a single mention of servants in Marie Barbier's recorded communications with her spiritual director, Charles Glandelet.[102] Indeed it seems as if there were two Marie Barbiers: the *mystique canadienne* that she presented to her fellows in religion and the practical agent of the Congrégation's expansion that she presented to those she charged with carrying out her instructions.

This double identity also characterized to some extent the rest of the sisters, regardless of their background and offices. But some members of the community tended toward the emulation of the career of Catherine Crolo and felt themselves suited best to the biblical work of Martha. Lydia Madeleine was so inclined. The religious conversion that had begun under the roof of Jacques Le Ber and in visits to the Congrégation sisters proved only the first stage of a larger conversion

For Lydia Madeleine, the fields of Pointe-Saint-Charles were a blank slate on which she could rewrite her life. Although she would not become the chief *soeur fermière* of Pointe-Saint-Charles until 1736, her previous lengthy tenure as the superior of the Congrégation school and farming community at Sainte-Famille on the Île d'Orléans allowed her to best express her new profession.[103]

For Lydia Madeleine, that the Congrégation was Catholic, communal, celibate, physically active, and professional had almost the opposite meaning it had for Gillett. The appeal of Catholicism to Puritan women bears emphasizing. The community's special devotion to a Marian itinerant life cast the divine presence in a distinctly feminine light. The articulation of the Virgin as a guiding mother gave the community its model for the familial relations of mother, sister, or daughter. Clearly the familial element had a strong appeal for those whose original families had been lost or fractured beyond repair.

The familial aspect of communal existence informed Lydia Madeleine's whole life. When the community walked beyond the palisade to gather the harvest, Lydia did not see an unnatural or disorderly concentration of female authority but a united family of women working together—*serving* together—in a common purpose.

Here was the root of the conflict between sister and servant. Male servants rejected the reality of women's rule, but from the women's viewpoint, this rule was actually service—even though it entailed acting with authority. This service-through-power paradox is a constant theme in the captor's narrative of Canadian women. Lydia Madeleine's life expressed it well.

The sisters of the Congrégation, however, were not unaware of the social and cultural impact of their lives. We see, especially in Lydia Madeleine's life, the importance they assigned to celibacy and professional service. For some of them, celibacy meant far more than being bound in marriage to Christ. Marie Barbier and Catherine Crolo had apparently both been victims of sexual assault early in their lives, and Lydia Madeleine's mother had in all probability died giving birth to her.[104] They saw that life in the sisterhood could yield earthly advantages and freedoms.

And in the realm of professional service, the shift of identity accompanying the transformation from a frontier farm girl to, in Lydia's case, a professional manager of large landholdings carried with it an increase in public social standing. Lydia Longley had emerged willfully from the circumstance in which the only way to share a domicile with John Gillett would have been to live as partners in marriage.

The Canadian members of the Congrégation also could not have failed to notice their new status. Marie Barbier rose from a sexually compromised carpenter's daughter to one of Montreal's most prominent, visible, and influential citizens—fully capable of hard dealing with secular and clerical elites. When interacting with subordinates she redefined her personal power. Barbier's sense of powerlessness during two episodes in her life—the assault against her and later the death of her brother when fighting the English—was certainly nowhere evident when, exercising her authority, she purchased an English man in Montreal.[105]

In the end, the presence of John Gillett at the Congrégation Notre-

Dame signifies the true close to Marguerite Bourgeoys's original experiment—the inclusion of male subjects as willing partners in the Marian apostolate. Men from outside the French Catholic tradition could be expected to participate in this singular purpose envisioned by the sisters of the Congrégation to an even lesser extent than had been the case with the restless French servants.

Marie Barbier and Marguerite Le Moyne, the formidable and aristocratic woman who succeeded her as *supérieure* in 1698, together set the tone and provided the example for the impersonality and increasing strictness with which the community's servants had to be treated. Other events overtaking the Congrégation would bring to an end more than the experiment with men. The acceptance of a formal rule in 1698 (by which the lay sisters became women religious under the authority of the bishop in Quebec) as the price for further expansion of the Congrégation and the death of Marguerite Bourgeoys during the first days of the eighteenth century eliminated the entire context of the world known by the *frères donnés*.

Lydia Madeleine's life, though, did not end with the scattering of the New Englanders present at the Congrégation in the last years of the seventeenth century. Thirteen years after her first arrival in Montreal, the French-English frontier war still raged, producing in its wake an odd repetition of the past. In 1707 Lydia Madeleine's first cousin, Sarah Tarbell—whose birth thirteen years earlier Lydia had in all probability attended—arrived as a captive in Canada.[106]

The raid that had left most of the Longleys dead and two of the children captured certainly became an integral, perhaps defining, story in the minds of Sarah and her brothers. If the resonance of the story faded at all in the first years, it was rekindled when Lydia's younger brother John Longley returned to Groton—involuntarily—after four years as an Abenaki warrior in training. As Sarah grew to understand what had happened to the Longleys, it was already known in Groton, courtesy of the returned John, that Lydia lived among the "nuns" as a converted Catholic. Did Sarah follow the professed wish of her fellow Groton residents and wish for Lydia's return from her deceived or forced conversion? Catholic nuns could hardly be seen as independent agents of their fate from the vantage point of this New England village. But John Longley nevertheless remained an ambiguous and slightly unsettling figure. After returning to Groton in 1698 at the age of sixteen, he successfully reintegrated into the life of the Puritan town. But there remained the four happy years among the Indians—and the involuntary return. Did Sarah feel some exoticism emanating from her cousin, and did she perhaps imagine Lydia's life as one of adventure, novelty, and escape?

The elements of these musings unfolded before her eyes with arresting suddenness. Captured by Indians outside her house on July 1, 1707, she was forcibly parted from her brothers and conducted many days through the forest to Montreal. No armed house raid this: Sarah then aged thirteen, and her brothers John and Zechariah, aged eleven and six, were by themselves when picked from a cherry tree by a small roving group of Caughnawaga Mohawk. Like the Longleys before them, the Tarbells were separated by sex. The Mohawks reserved the older girl for monetary ransoming while deeming the boys of suitably young age for adoption as future warriors, which they in due course became.[107]

One Jacques-Urbain Rocbert, sieur de LaMorandière, purchased Sarah Tarbell. So, like Lydia, she was relieved of the Indians by a benevolent and wealthy bachelor redeemer. Unlike most such redeemers, LaMorandière had no immediate family. His intentions for acquiring a thirteen-year old captive girl must be considered honorable, however, as LaMorandière's extended family, the Rocberts, were active in captive redemption, and in any case the redeemed Tarbell did not reside in Montreal after her redemption, but rather among the Congrégation sisters in the Indian mission at La Chine, to the west of the town.[108] LaMorandière in all likelihood simply did his patriotic and religious duty in bankrolling Tarbell's redemption and placement among the sisters.

So Tarbell's life played out much as she imagined Lydia's—the sudden capture, the weeks in the summer woods, the separation from her brothers, the redemption by a wealthy man of Montreal, the arrival in a community of French Catholic sisters. But upon arrival she did not immediately stand face to face with Lydia Longley, now the established Soeur Sainte-Madeleine, but remained among the sisters in the Indian mission upriver at La Chine. Lydia may certainly have visited Sarah or vice versa, but they remained physically separate. The intriguing prospect of a reunion of the cousins probably never materialized, partially because of Sarah's location at La Chine and also because she disappeared from the Canadian records after 1710. She did not return home, marry in Canada, or remain among the sisters.[109] In all likelihood she died at La Chine while still a student—and possibly a novice, of the Congrégation sisters there.[110] Despite her death, she followed her cousin in faith.

Sarah Tarbell's tale indicates that Lydia Madeleine felt some reticence toward New England captives, for she makes no appearance in the accounts of fellow captives who appeared periodically in New France throughout the remainder of her long life. Lydia did not make the succor of captives her business; instead she immersed herself in the business of a *soeur fermière* at Saint-Famille and at Pointe-Saint-Charles. Her name appears in documents only in the rarest of occasions—as when she agreed to act as the witness to the baptism of a local girl named Marie-Madeleine Prémont of Sainte-Famille, a niece of a colleague at the Congrégation, Sister Marie Prémont.[111]

Her immersion remained complete. Generations of descendants of converted captives were baptized without her blessing or participation, and generations of captives endured physical and mental suffering without her comfort—those taken after 1744 were routinely imprisoned instead of being placed in private homes. The Congrégation gave Lydia a way not only to transform herself professionally but to withdraw from the concerns and dislocations of the kind that had so radically altered her life.

And what of the New England village she had left behind? Especially during the long peace that lasted from 1714 to 1744, interrupted only briefly in the early 1720s, Lydia Madeleine had the opportunity to communicate with her relatives at Groton and visit her birthplace. Here the local memory of the town of Groton may grant insight or alternately obscure what actually occurred. In 1890, the local historian Francis Marion Boutwell recounted that a friend of hers named Miss Farnsworth had actually seen an old pincushion in the possession of her grandmother, Lydia Longley Farnsworth—the niece of Lydia Madeleine. Lydia Longley Farnsworth told her granddaughter that the pincushion had been sent to her by her aunt from the Congrégation Notre-Dame in Montreal. Though aunt and niece never met, Lydia Longley Farnsworth reported that from time to time her aunt had sent little gifts to her.[112]

There is no real reason to doubt this story. Although it might seem that this picture of a kindly aunt sending pincushions to her namesake fits a little too closely into a sentimental nineteenth-century vision of a nun's passive and sequestered life (Lydia is universally described by Groton writers of this era as "having been placed" in a convent), fine needlework had been a tradition at the Congrégation as a money-making activity since the days of Marguerite Bourgeoys.

Of more importance is the report by the meticulous and preeminent historian of colonial Groton, Samuel A. Green, that John Longley received a letter from his sister in Canada urging him for the sake of his soul to abjure Protestantism, as she had done. Uncharacteristically, Green does not cite the source for this information.[113] Further inquiries as to its existence and the present whereabouts of the letter have turned up nothing. Perhaps the story of the letter is simply a bit of family lore—but the supposed content of the letter certainly rings true. Lydia Madeleine would have known of the eventual return of her brother to Groton and would be understandably concerned with the state of John's soul—especially if she had also learned he had become a deacon of the Congregational church. The missing Longley letter also recalls the existing letter written by the Quebec Ursuline Esther Wheelwright to her mother in Maine in 1747, stating how happy Esther would be if her mother could see the light of the true faith.[114] But the Wheelwright letter also conveyed the genuine affection she felt for her family despite their differences in religion. If the pincushion and letter stories are true, and possibly even if they are not, Lydia did not forget the home from which her new faith and new profession had inalterably separated her.

Lydia Madeleine survived almost long enough to live again under an English flag. The record of her death read: "July 21, 1758, was buried in the chapel of the infant Jesus in the parish church the body of lidie longlé de Ste. Magdelene, English woman, Sister of the Congrégation de Notre-Dame, deceased yesterday, aged eighty-four years. There were present M. Vallières and poncin priests."[115] Lydia Madeleine might have immersed herself in her new faith, new society, and new profession for sixty-two years—but it is telling that Father Poncin had written, "lydie longlé . . . English woman." Her complex identity accompanied her in death as it had in life.

And what had the conversion of Lydia Madeleine meant to the community that had accepted her? Again, the choice of names is important. Perhaps with guidance or suggestion, Lydia Longley chose "Madeleine" as her baptismal name and later, with the acceptance of the rule in 1698, selected "Soeur Sainte-Madeleine" as her name in religion. "Madeleine" in this context recalled the repentant sinner Mary Magdelen. Did Lydia and her sponsors link her conversion from the Protestant "heresy" with Mary Magdelen's conversion to renounce her ways to walk with and tend to Jesus? If so, we can best understand Lydia's meaning to the community and perhaps the meaning of the community to Lydia by reading the words of Marguerite Bourgeoys on the subject of Mary Magdelen:

> Our Lord granted St. Mary Magdelen the grace of responding to the love He bore her. The gracious savior had a love of complacency for her, seeing her detest her sins; a love of benevolence, seeing her at His feet and washing them with her tears; a love of beneficence, letting everyone know that many sins were forgiven her because she had loved much. This dear lover carried her gratitude as far as a creature could. She had a love of complacency for all that she could understand of His divine perfections; a love of benevolence, drawing everyone to follow Him, a love of beneficence, proclaiming His resurrection wherever she could. She entered upon the love of union by purging her soul by perfect contrition.[116]

John Gillett arrived back in Deerfield in the late spring of 1698, reclaimed his property, and through Samuel Partridge requested that he be granted monetary relief in consideration of the fact that he was "Destetute of Money or Cloathes." On June 17 of that year the Massachusetts House granted him six pounds.[117] He told Partridge and the House nothing of the Congrégation Notre-Dame, at least in the official correspondence.

Shortly after Gillett's return to Massachusetts, he decided to end the frontier experiment begun by his late father. He had had enough of the edge of the world. Somehow he heard of a new location, called Lebanon, then being cleared and laid out in the Connecticut colony east of Hartford.[118] This would give him the experience of starting a new life in a new settlement without the inherent dangers of the northern and western frontiers. Still a single man, John Gillett became one of the original fifty-one purchasers of deeds in Lebanon. Another was Josiah Dewey of Northampton, Massachusetts, perhaps an acquaintance of Gillett before the latter's capture. In any event, Gillett married Josiah's daughter, Experience Dewey, and with his wife raised four children while working as an independent farmer.[119] In the end, Gillett achieved the life he had wanted: to be the first white settler to work a certain parcel of land, and to become the master of a small world.

Daniel and Nathaniel Belden returned to Deerfield to stay, and subsequent events inflicted even more pain on this long-suffering family. His first wife having been killed in the raid in which he and his son and daughter had been made captive, Daniel decided in 1699 to marry a woman named Hepzibah Buel Wells. Wells had already suffered the loss of two daughters in an Indian attack in 1693, an episode in which she herself was apparently "scalped" by the attackers. Although both Daniel and Nathaniel were spared in the subsequent and devastating 1704 Deerfield massacre, Hepzibah was captured and killed before her party reached Canada.[120]

And there would be yet more. Although Daniel's daughter Hester had been captured in 1696, another daughter, Sarah, had escaped on that occasion, only to be captured in 1704. Interestingly, she and her husband, Christopher Burt, were, according to family tradition, "employed in convent and Jesuit [probably Sulpician] academy."[121] Was it possible that Daniel Belden's daughter knew enough of his captivity to seek out her father's former captors? The couple eventually returned safely to Deerfield—the family's price for their place on the frontier finally paid.[122]

Lydia Madeleine Longley certainly found a new faith—but did she exult in the new roles this faith delivered to her? Did she reflect on her long journey as she regarded the men in the fields whose bodies were an extension of her will? The gift of Marguerite Bourgeoys, perhaps, was not so much what she gave to Montreal but what she imparted to the individual women who followed her.

From the perspective of the Congrégation, the men of the Congrégation Notre-Dame had been given a gift of remarkable generosity—the opportunity to become Canadians, and Catholics, under the direction of supremely dedicated female teachers, farmers, and missionaries. But the Congrégation sisters must be forgiven for perhaps not realizing what they were asking of their subjects. Their French servants had rejected the colony—finding it uncomfortably embodied in the feminine nature of the authority that held them. And a later captive and newly liminal freeman from Deerfield would have under almost any circumstances of captivity gravitated toward home. But the life of a servant to women, the submergence of a man's free-born will, would never be an acceptable outcome of a Puritan man's errand into the wilderness. To John Gillett, the price of Lydia Madeleine's freedom was his own servitude, and eventual salvation lay not in transforming his identity but in reclaiming it.

CHAPTER TWO

The Frontier: Girls' Own Errand

into the Wilderness

An English woman, who belonged to one of the French nuns, came
in [to the wigwam], and told me I need not fear, for I was given to
this squaw in lieu of one of her sons, whom the English had slain;
and that I was to be master of the wigwam; but she being a papist,
I placed little reliance upon her assertions.

—JOSEPH BARTLETT, "Narrative"

In the late summer of 1708, the writer of these words, militiaman Joseph
Bartlett, had not yet celebrated his twenty-second birthday. The Newburyport, Massachusetts, native had been pressed into militia service
and quartered along with four other soldiers with a frontier captain named
Simon Wainwright and his family at Haverhill.[1] Wainwright had earlier
married the widow Mary Silver, who brought her young daughter, also
named Mary Silver, into Wainwright's house. In 1708 the fourteen-year-old
Mary Silver had lived under the same roof as Bartlett for several months.

Earlier that summer at Montreal, Governor Vaudreuil had decided to re-
cruit "mission Indians" mostly from the Saint Lawrence settlements of
Caughnawaga for a season of harassing the New England frontier under
the command of French officers. Originally the objective was ambitious:
Portsmouth, New Hampshire. But attrition on the trail south combined
with the failure of a large group of mission Iroquois to join the Caughnawaga Mohawk led the commanders to revert to a less demanding raid
on a frontier Massachusetts village.

Nevertheless, the party would meet stiff resistance from the frontier outpost. On the morning of the August 29, the French-Mohawk party set upon

the modest but fortified houses of Haverhill. The attackers focused particularly on the centrally located Wainwright house. Bartlett recorded the spirited but confused combat that followed. When the captain's wife, Mary Wainwright, felt the house should surrender lest they be burned out, Bartlett replied to her that they should keep on firing—as he believed he had already killed six of the aggressors. But before he could load, lock, and fire again, others in the house had already surrendered it. Then Mary Wainwright took the initiative. Greeting the French and Indians cordially at her door, she negotiated with the aggressors and agreed to go to another room to get them money. On this pretense she slipped out of the house with all her children but her daughter Mary, who had at that instant somehow become separated from the rest. That moment's separation would stretch into a lifetime. The French and Indians, discovering the ruse and none too happy, rounded up the remaining survivors and in revenge for the defense and deception killed Simon Wainwright on the spot. They then departed for the Saint Lawrence with all the valuables they could carry and three captives—including Joseph Bartlett and the younger Mary Silver.[2]

The attackers separated into French and Mohawk bands, dividing the captives between them. Bartlett traveled north and then west with the Mohawks. He later recalled in detail the specific hardships of his journey, during which he was physically bound and in fear for his life. He nevertheless credited his captors with sharing food generously when they themselves could obtain it. Eventually they reached the Saint Lawrence region, where he underwent the cutting of his hair on one side of his head. He then was taken to Montreal, where Governor Vaudreuil personally interviewed him on the future military intentions of the English.

After the interview, the Mohawks took Bartlett north around the base of Mont Réal to the Catholic Indian settlement at Sault-au-Récollet (which Bartlett remembered as being called "Sadrohelly") on the north shore of Montreal Island. Before the captives entered the fort, they received the same gendered treatment that previous male prisoners experienced. The party entered Sault-au-Récollet and presented the scalps and captives to the women. One Indian woman beat Bartlett with a pole, a second amputated one of his fingers, and yet a third woman assumed custody of the captive and installed him in her wigwam.[3]

At this point a strange event occurred. Bartlett met the young white female who assured him that he was to be the "master of the wigwam."[4] She was, in fact, Lydia Longley's fellow sister Mary Sayward of the Congrégation Notre-Dame.[5] Here for the first time a written male captivity narrative recorded the lived captor's narrative of an English apostate woman.

In the 1690s the Puritan captivity narrative had not yet developed into
the style of personal memoir it would assume among New Englanders in
the mid-eighteenth century. Early narratives such as those of ordinary citizens like Mary Rowlandson, Hannah Swarton, and Quentin Stockwell
were heavily edited, if not actually ghostwritten, by elite figures like the
Mathers in order that the reader might experience the appropriate form
of religious enlightenment. Probably the only substantial early narrative
actually written by its purported author was that of a returned captive representative of the theocracy, the Reverend John Williams. Accounts of pre-
1713 captivities are brief, matter-of-fact statements composed either upon
a captive's return when petitioning for relief or years later for the benefit
of local chronicles.[6]

Not until 1807, by which time the American captivity narrative had become a popular literary genre, was the narrative of Joseph Bartlett published in pamphlet form, although Bartlett had been captured a century
earlier. It had been given to the publisher by a Bartlett descendent and had
evidently been written for the benefit of his family by Bartlett himself sometime before his death in 1754. The authenticity of the account is certain;
his highly specific details of the locations he visited and people he encountered correspond well with other accounts and known events.[7]

How was it, then, that the position and social role, the lived narrative, of
Mary Sayward at the Mountain Mission proved beyond the grasp of the captive Joseph Bartlett? He had identified her as "an English woman, who belonged to one of the French nuns." If he was not referring to Sayward,
could this instead have been Sarah Hoyt, the only other English female at
Sault-au-Récollet old enough to be reasonably described as a woman? But
Hoyt belonged to an Indian family, not to a "French nun," and there is no
record of her, or her husband, becoming a "papist."[8]

How could Bartlett, confined for six months in the claustrophobic mission, have failed to understand that the "English woman" did not "belong
to" the French nuns but rather directed her French associates, held a substantial degree of religious authority among the Indians (including the
woman who "adopted" him), and actively taught the girls of the settlement? That the mists of age had obscured his memory on this point seems
unlikely given his accurate recall of other events in his captivity.

It is virtually certain, then, that Bartlett very deliberately distorted his account. The specific purpose and effect of this distortion was to denigrate
the authority of Mary Sayward within the mission. By making the sister "belong" to one of nuns, he placed her in the customary passive position that
women most often assumed in the Puritan captivity narrative. Her being a
"papist" was apparently offered as evidence that she was a deluded female.

But identifying her as a religious sister—let alone a religious sister in authority over others and as an active agent of the enemy faith—was evidently beyond the pale.

Strange as well is the extremely upbeat tone of the succor and assurances Bartlett ascribed to Sayward. That he was soon to be "master of the wigwam" as a result of his "adoption" not only seemed unlikely: adult Protestant men never transculturated to this degree and the Indians at Sault-au-Récollet already had long experience with captives, and the amputation of Bartlett's finger suggests the Indians themselves did not expect the English woman's prediction to be realized.[9] Perhaps the encouragement was embellished to fit Sayward into a more conventional narrative role—that of a source of mercy—even if he immediately dismissed her advice on the grounds of her religious conversion.

Bartlett's slighting of Mary Sayward's status proved congruent with his narrative treatment of his "adoptive mother" and his systematic omission of demonstrably present female authority. The Congrégation Notre-Dame's record of Sayward's activities provide external evidence of Bartlett's distortions, but in the case of the Mohawk woman his own version of events betrays him. Whatever his female Indian captor had in mind for Bartlett, "adoption" was certainly not among them.

Only two weeks after Bartlett arrived at Sault-au-Récollet, for reasons he does not explain, he was moved to "another fort about eighteen miles distant" where he spent two more weeks before being returned to Sault-au-Récollet.[10] To be shunted about in this way is reminiscent of the sort of captivity experienced by Nicholas Woodbury, alternatively utilized and leased out by his Indian mistress.[11] Although Bartlett at first praises the Mohawk woman for her kindness, upon returning to Sault-au-Récollet he complains of being "poorly clad" and "destitute of proper food."[12] Further confirmation of the fact that he was anything but in line to become "master" of this wigwam was the arrival of a second captive, Martin Kellogg Jr. Also obscured by Bartlett—deliberately—is the treatment and employment of Bartlett and Kellogg, with the exception of a single hint of reality. The only Indian economic activity Bartlett describes is the women's work of soaking and boiling corn. Hunting is not mentioned. As the slaves of the same evidently enterprising Mohawk woman, Bartlett and Kellogg became quite familiar with the tasks of processing corn. Kellogg's subsequent dramatic escape, in which he accomplished the extremely difficult feat of walking from Montreal Island to Northampton, Massachusetts, strongly suggests that no love was lost between Kellogg and his Indian captors.[13] That Bartlett himself was sold to the Delude family in Montreal six months after his arrival confirms the purely fictional nature of the captive's "adoption."

The words of comfort and adoption from the mouth of Mary Sayward were, then, far more likely to have been Bartlett's own words of comfort to his readers about the "Englishwoman." He maintains this fiction even to the point of hinting at his own subjection to surviving Mohawk unmanning rituals and practices. He leaves open the question of why he never became "master" of his mistress's wigwam—only familiarity with Iroquoian customs would make this clear. As for the New England missionary sister, the mission with which Mary Sayward transformed herself into the professional intercultural teacher called Soeur Marie-des-Anges, or Sister Mary of the Angels, remained alive in the collective memory of her adopted community, but it was never conveyed back to her land of origin.

And what of Joseph Bartlett's young fellow captive, Mary Silver? Like the sister he would meet at Sault-au-Récollet, Silver would also come into the sphere of the Congrégation Notre-Dame. Unlike Lydia and the Saywards, however, Mary chose to make her profession not with the teachers and missionaries of the Congrégation but with the Hospital Sisters of Saint Joseph. Her decision represented the purely professional element in individual women converts' conceptions of their new lives in Canada.

Whether Mary Silver also resided at Sault-au-Récollet alongside Bartlett in some capacity is uncertain. With unsure authority, the renowned nineteenth-century Quebec historian F.-X. Garneau believed that Silver was placed in the care of a "M. Dupuy of Quebec," who safeguarded her and helped Silver negotiate the long march to Canada. Coleman speculates that this Dupuy, perhaps Louis Depuis, *dit* le Parisien, may have directly placed Silver as a student at the Congrégation, presumably with no interlude among the Indians.[14] Such a scenario seems unlikely. If Dupuy indeed was "the Parisian," he may well have physically conducted Silver to Montreal, but he certainly lacked the monetary means to sponsor a captive by placing her as a student among the Congrégation.

A far more likely candidate for Silver's sponsor was in fact listed on Silver's record of Catholic baptism as her original captor: Antoine Pécaudy, sieur de Contrecoeur. The illustrious list of those who attended as witnesses at Silver's Catholic baptism in 1710, including Governor Vaudreuil, who signed as her godfather, suggests she had been sponsored by the high society to which Contrecoeur belonged. The connection here was strengthened by the fact that Marie-Charlotte Denis (Madame Ramezay) signed as Silver's godmother. Marie-Charlotte Denis was the niece of Barbe Denis, Contrecoeur's wife.[15]

But Contrecoeur's status would not necessarily have been enough to convey Mary Silver directly to Montreal if the Indians had an original claim on her, as they did on Joseph Bartlett. Mohawks, as evidenced by the captivity of Eunice Williams and others, could demonstrate reluctance to part with their impressionable, and soon marriageable, teenage female captives.[16] Silver could have easily lived at Sault-au-Récollet under the tutelage of Mary Sayward, who had been *supérieure* there for close to nine years by the summer of 1708. Being placed with the Congrégation Notre-Dame may have been Silver's own wish—made in the mission among the frontier Catholic women's network. Sponsorship (in the form of redemption from the Indians by the elite Canadian clique who eventually saw to her baptism) may have come later and at the behest of Sayward and Catherine Charly, Marguerite Le Moyne's temporary replacement as *supérieure* of the Congrégation Notre-Dame in 1708.[17]

Finally, Bartlett's failure to mention Mary Silver's presence at Sault-au Récollet in his narrative does not mean she was not there—especially in light of his omission of Sayward's name and position at the mission. He would have been likely to omit the tale of the girl he had defended with his musket from Catholic and Indian attackers because he had certainly failed later to protect her from the seduction of Catholicism. Describing Mary Silver's conversion would have required disrupting the foundational assumptions of the Puritan captivity narrative. Confined to his washing, grinding, and threshing, he was helpless to prevent the girl from becoming increasingly "savage" and Catholic. And as always there would have been the unspeakable issue of inverted authority. Bartlett was captive in Sault-au-Récollet through a harvest and a planting season. If the Mohawk women there held to age-old practices, they would have on each occasion assembled all subordinated men for team labor in the fields. Directly or indirectly, Silver's relationship to Bartlett would have then transformed unimaginably as that of an overseer to a slave.

For her part, Mary Sayward had by 1708 taken a far longer path to Sault-au-Récollet than Bartlett. The journey had begun with a simple calculus of power politics among warring colonies. During the winter of 1691–92 the outlying settlements of Maine stood even more exposed to tension among empires than the peripheral farms of Groton. French and Canadian leaders regarded the tiny English settlements hugging the craggy coast as a growing menace, potentially a shortcut to a flatland assault by the English on Quebec City via the Saint John River. Such a threat was a rational fear at that time. Even the start of such an invasion might suggest French vulnerability and lead the Eastern Abenaki into an alliance with the New Englanders.

So it was that a party of 150 Eastern Abenaki under the command of Madokawando (later John Longley's master) spent the night of January 24, 1692, in a heavy snowstorm under Mount Agamenticus readying for a

French-authorized sabbath-day attack on the coastal village of York. The objective was not general harassment, as would be the case at Groton four years later, but annihilating the inhabitants in hopes of stemming the tide of Maine settlement, abating the Saint John River threat, and most importantly, solidifying the Abenaki alliance. The alliance as well as the promise of profit motivated Madokawando and his lieutenants. The Indians' attack proved astoundingly successful, coming as it did on a religious feast-day (January 25 was the Puritan Candlemas). The raid produced the third-largest single-day civilian losses New Englanders suffered during nine decades of fighting the French and their allies. Survivors buried forty-eight victims in the end, ranging in age from infants to the elderly. The number of profit-bringing captives, mostly women and their young children, was about eighty. This total would be surpassed only by the 1684 Oyster River and 1704 Deerfield raids.[18]

The captives, along with the gunpowder and window leads (for making ammunition), proved almost immediately profitable. After conducting the numerous prisoners seven miles northwest along the coast to the village of Wells, the Abenaki approached some local Maine townsmen to say that those who wished to ransom relatives or friends would have a chance to do so at a specified location ten days hence. Here, thirty-six captives were ransomed thanks to a generous and immediate response from colonists along the coast. Historian Charles E. Banks has inferred that the ransomed captives tended generally to have "friends" who were financially able to pay for their release. This inference seems confirmed by the fact that unredeemed captives, who made the long wintertime march to Canada, tended to be socially and economically marginal.[19] Among those marginal York residents left friendless in those woods was thirty-two-year-old Mary Plaisted as well as eleven-year-old Mary Sayward and her seven-year-old sister Esther, both daughters of Mary Plaisted by a previous marriage.[20]

At the time of her capture, Mary Plaisted lived with her daughters and her fourth husband, James Plaisted, outside York in an area called Cider Hill, three miles in from the coast. James Plaisted probably worked as a hardscrabble farmer, as had Mary's three former husbands. The small estate left by at least one previous husband suggests that these were people of extremely modest means. Where James was during the raid, why he was not captured, or why he failed to secure the release of his wife and two stepdaughters has never been explained.

Who may have sponsored the entry of the Sayward girls as students at the Congrégation Notre-Dame is also uncertain. One likely candidate is Catherine Gauchet, the wealthy French-Canadian widow who ransomed Mary Plaisted and trained the New England woman as a household domestic servant.[21] Gauchet would have certainly had the means to ransom all three and place the young girls with Bourgeoys in the pious and patriotic fashion of Jacques Le Ber and his female acquaintances dedicated to captive sponsorship, most prominently Marguerite Bouat Pacaud.[22] The separation of impressionable daughters from their mothers would be the most logical course for the French-Canadian mind intent on conversion. The Sayward girls were entering an age susceptible to religious conversion and social acculturation. Gauchet perhaps regarded their mother as perhaps too old to be acculturated and thus consigned her to service. But Gauchet did not spare her new *domestique* exposure to the Catholic faith.

The simultaneous Catholic baptism of Mary Plaisted, Mary Sayward, and Esther Sayward is an enduring puzzle. On December 8, 1693, Father Jean Prémont baptized Plaisted in Montreal. On the baptism record is an annotation stating that the two girls were baptized on the same day—but in a separate location—presumably the nearby chapel of the Congrégation Notre-Dame.[23] Do the three baptisms indicate a shared bond of devotion or a common experience of coercion? The future actions of the converts suggest a more complex reality. The mother's baptism cut many ties, for it apparently invalidated, at least in Puritan eyes, her marriage to James Plaisted—who Mary must have known or strongly suspected was still alive.[24] The sincerity of her conversion must also be questioned because Mary Plaisted chose to return to Maine (and her husband and modest property) in the truce and prisoner exchange of 1695. What had she gained in the interim? Had her conversion been wrenched from her involuntarily, making the decision to seize freedom an easy one? Mary Plaisted left no extant record of her thoughts on the subject. But Hannah Swarton, herself a married woman captive in service to a French-Canadian matron, has written:

> For the Lady, my mistress [Marie-Madeleine Chaspoux, wife of the intendant of New France Jean Bochart, sieur de Champigny], the nuns, the priests, the friars, and the rest set upon me with all the strength of argument they could from scriptures, as they interpreted it, to persuade me to turn papist, which they pressed with very much zeal, love, entreaties, and promises if I would turn to them, and with many threatening and sometimes hard usages because I did not turn to their religion.[25]

The explicit mention of "threatenings" and "hard usages" may well be due to the intervention of the propagandistic pen of Cotton Mather, who heavily edited the Swarton narrative in order to instruct a lapsing Puritan audience in the hazards of heresy. Though the editing in this passage is suspect, the underlying facts are not. Louise Dechêne and other observers of French-Canadian society point out that although servants of that society tended to be well treated by early modern standards, the routine and ordinary "light corporal punishments" meted out to all servants—captive or not—could well have been conveniently interpreted by Swarton, Mather, or Plaisted as special persecution directed at Puritan holdouts.[26] Conversion alone would not have meant release (as we witnessed in the case of John Lahey) and would therefore not have lessened the burdens of "hard usage"—unless conversion was a first step to true transculturation. Plaisted's actions indicate this was never her intention.

Becoming Catholic, though, even while still confined as a servant, would have gained for Mary Plaisted increased access to her daughters. The fervor continually demonstrated by Mary Sayward later in her teenage years indicate that in December 1693, near her thirteenth birthday, the two-year-long exposure to the magic of the sisters of the Congrégation had taken hold—no doubt pulling Esther Sayward along as well. The conversion of the mother would have preserved what could be left of a familial bond. By 1695, though, Mary Plaisted must have known that the fight for her daughters had been lost—and decided to salvage what she could and return to her previous life. The agency of the Sayward daughters is undeniable here. Although on occasion New England emissaries successfully prevailed upon the Canadian authorities to force their masters, sponsors, or communities to give them up, such an effort, if made at all, was not successful because the former captive girls refused to go with their mother.[27]

After her return to Maine, Mary Plaisted actively protected the complex financial interests of her daughters at the cost of a legal dispute with her son, John. She obviously held out hope for their return. But she had had enough of religion. The year after her return, town authorities fined Plaisted for not attending sabbath services in York.[28] It has been suggested that this minor rebellion reflected the vestiges of her former Catholicism.[29] However, it could just as easily have represented bitterness at the destructive effects of any brand of faith.

As students at the Congrégation, the Sayward girls received an education that served them well in their respective ambitious lives. Mary, renamed Marie-Geneviève after her baptism, and Esther, now called Marie-Josèph, achieved a good level of literacy and competence in basic mathematics in addition to receiving an extensive course in religion. They also as a matter of routine learned the domestic and agricultural skills practiced by the Congrégation sisters—students, as we have seen, helped on the farm at planting and harvest time—and they may have learned animal tending from their fellow students. Needlework and other domestic skills rounded out the curriculum.

The precise dates of Mary Sayward's baptism and formal entry into the Congrégation are unknown, but by 1701, at the age of nineteen, she had been placed by the *supérieure* Marguerite Le Moyne in charge of the Congrégation's small mission at Sault-au-Récollet, the second location of the Indian settlement popularly called the Mountain Mission.[30]

The selection of Mary Sayward for that position reveals several characteristics of this convert from Maine. First, she was spiritually zealous. The mission of the sisters at the settlement was teaching with a specific eye to the conversion of the Indians, especially young girls. Second, the placement of an English speaker as the director of the mission was a canny move on the part of Marguerite Le Moyne, who must have known that the Sault-au-Récollet mission served as a frequent transit point and even place of residence for New England captives. Placing Sayward there was part of an explicit strategy to win New England converts.

Indeed, Mary Sayward presided over the conversion of several young captives in 1704 and 1705 in the aftermath of the Deerfield raid, when the traffic in captives at Sault-au-Récollet reached its height. Here children were separated by sex, the boys receiving catechism from the Sulpicians at the Mountain Mission and the girls from Sayward and her two or three companions.[31]

Complicating the work of the sisters was the ownership or adoption of these children by various Indian families of the settlement. Because it was the mission of the male and female missionaries at Sault-au-Récollet to bring the civilizing force of religion to the Indians, it must have been a frustrating, continuing paradox for the brothers and sisters to see the New England captives advancing from Protestantism to Catholicism while simultaneously regressing from European civilization into "savagery."

Nevertheless, at least temporarily these New Englanders became Catholic. The frontier mission of Mary Sayward proved successful from a religious point of view, although perhaps less so from a cultural standpoint. But the boys and girls from Deerfield could not have failed to notice the presence of a female analogue to the priests. The Sulpicians of Sault-au-Récollet held no authority over the sisters of the Congrégation. Priests and sisters worked as complementary male and female elements in the mission of conversion and transculturation. Further, the director of the female element was a young English woman from Maine, living a life well outside the boundaries of anything possible in the land of her birth.

Meanwhile, on February 2, 1710, the Sulpician priest Henri-Antoine de Meriel baptized Mary Silver in front of a group of socially formidable Montrealers. Silver's own signature appears at the end of the document, written in a somewhat unsteady hand, suggesting she may have found at least a minimal literacy along with her Catholic faith among the sisters of the Congrégation. However long her stay there, Silver, like Lydia Longley before her, found English-speaking women among the sisters. Silver's network in fact was even more extensive than had been Longley's. Sister Lydia Madeleine lived and worked in Montreal that year, and Mary Silver certainly met her there.

Montreal in 1708 still featured many lingering New England-born survivors from the earlier raids of Queen Anne's war, many of them Deerfielders. Some were still captive *domestiques* working off ransom payments, and others lived there already as free citizens, having converted to the captor's faith and married either French Canadians or one another. A third, smaller group, mostly teenaged females, lived on the narrow cusp between the two fates. Such was the status of Mary Silver upon her arrival at the Congrégation Notre-Dame. In addition to Soeur Sainte-Madeleine (Lydia Longley) and Esther Sayward, then twenty-one years old but still living there as a student boarder, Silver found two thirteen-year-old New England girls who were being educated by the sisters in outlying missions: Sarah Tarbell and Martha French.[32]

That Mary Silver did not choose the life of a *religieuse*—a professed sister—in the community in which she had been educated is perhaps comprehensible, for the network of New Englanders within the Congrégation Notre-Dame at that time was a loose assemblage of individuals, not a tight group dedicated to the Congrégation's mission.[33] Their freely chosen and very distinct career paths indicate that New England-born women, instead of associating with one another, sought out those French-Canadian sisters and secular women with whom they felt a kinship by virtue of their chosen profession. Among those choosing the religious path, Mary Sayward chose life among her fellow missionary sisters, Lydia Longley remained dedicated to securing the community's sustenance, and Mary Silver sought to become a *hospitalière*, a hospital sister. Those who chose to leave the religious life married into varying social strata. Esther Sayward married brilliantly into the French-Canadian nobility, while Martha French, at the age of sixteen, married an illiterate farmer. Elizabeth Price, who left the Congrégation before the arrival of Mary Silver, married a master shoemaker.[34] And friendships seem to have been selective as well. Although Esther Sayward signed as a witness at the marriage of Elizabeth Price, Lydia Madeleine Longley, maintaining her characteristic absence from the affairs of her former countrywomen, did not.

Mary Silver's decision to become a *hospitalière* is especially understandable in view of the close physical connections between the two communities of women. Except when they were forced to live under the same roof because of a fire in 1695, the congregants of Notre-Dame and the Hôtel-Dieu of Montreal were separated by only a short hedge that one could easily see over and talk across.[35] The sisters of the two communities visited each other frequently. But for all their mutual contacts, the two communities were separate and distinct. The Congrégation focused increasingly on wilderness missionary work under Barbier, Charly, and Le Moyne, but the Hospital Sisters of Saint Joseph, who embodied the mission of their Hôtel-Dieu, found their purpose within their hedged confines. The rules of each community defined and responded to the realities of its service. The Sisters of Saint Joseph had made vows of *clausura,* imposing on themselves the physical restraint of the cloister. But in a frontier hospital, cloistering only kept the sisters within—it did not keep the world out.

Mary Silver adopted this life of a hospital sister. After her conversion in 1710, the sixteen-year-old Mary left the tutelage of the Congrégation Notre-Dame and entered the service of the Hôtel-Dieu. Apart from the sisters' living quarters and chapel, which provided a refuge for at least part of each day, the environment of the walled hospital was a varied world very much reflective of the larger town of Montreal itself. Rich and poor, male and female, French and Indian, African and English, young and old, prisoners, slaves and freemen mixed among the sisters who cared for them.

Fires have consumed a great portion of the Hôtel-Dieu's records of Mary Silver's first years there. The two principal surviving sources of information are the annals of the sometime *supérieure* Marie Morin and a map of the physical layout of the community. This layout is even more helpful than the annals in piecing together everyday life in the community—not a subject deemed worthy of ink in most religious community chronicles of the day.

On a typical autumn day in 1711 or 1712, for example, Silver might have visited and cared for sick or injured patients in the infirmary set aside for well-off citizens as well as attended to the poorer patients and prisoners in a larger ward in another wing of the main building.[36] Because of the time she spent learning farm work as a student at the Congrégation Notre-Dame, it is even possible that Mary Silver may have helped her fellow sisters oversee the French-Canadian workmen, impoverished patients, and captive New Englanders set to work in the extensive gardens within the walled grounds of the Hôtel-Dieu. These "gardens" in fact were more properly described as small agricultural fields, providing as they did most of the vegetables, wheat, and corn vital to the food supply of the community.[37]

The presence of captives at the hospital is certain because of those who are known to have died in Montreal following an illness or wound. But that other New England captives worked there after their recovery, or alternatively were purchased especially by the Sisters of Saint Joseph during the early tenure of Mary Silver, can only be inferred. The certain presence of Nathaniel Belden as a captive *domestique* at the Hôtel-Dieu of Montreal between 1696 and 1698 indicates that *supérieure* Marie Morin was well aware of the possibility of procuring needed labor from the captives of the Indians and was quite prepared to exercise this option. Further, the records of the Hôtel-Dieu in Quebec during the last years of Queen Anne's war do survive, indicating that recovered captives, all men, sometimes were appropriated to serve as community *domestiques,* as they would be again in the 1740s and 1750s by Marguerite d'Youville's Grey Sisters (see the next chapter). To suppose that the Hôtel-Dieu of Montreal would not have engaged in this practice is unrealistic, especially given the greater number of available captives in Montreal as compared to Quebec.[38]

Even though Mary Silver chose to leave the teaching community and place herself in the hospital, she is best remembered in New England (courtesy of antiquarian Charlotte Alice Baker) as the successor to Montreal's ubiquitous (and English-speaking) catechist-priest, Henri-Antoine Meriel, who died in 1713.[39] Despite the durability of this tale it is probably a flight of fancy, if only because all New Englanders remaining in the Saint Lawrence Valley had been given leave to return home in late 1712. Silver cannot properly, then, be said to have succeeded Meriel as the catechist to "captives." Second, it is not clear how the restlessly itinerant Meriel could be adequately replaced by a cloistered nun who under ordinary circumstances would not have ventured beyond the property boundary of the Hôtel-Dieu. Unless granted special dispensation, Silver certainly would have been able to access only those captives brought there as patients or purchased as bondservants in the manner of Nathaniel Belden. Furthermore, the strong linkage Baker draws between Meriel and Silver seems to be based on the assumption that Meriel, as the baptizing priest, would have been the principal spiritual influence on her. But as we have seen, the sisters of the Congrégation Notre-Dame required little help in providing the inspiration for the conversion of New England girls.

Nevertheless, the final section of Joseph Bartlett's narrative, devoted to religious and even theological sparring with Meriel, leads back to the question of Bartlett's failure to mention Silver again in his narrative. Regardless of whether they had been together at Sault-au-Récollet, Silver's fate would certainly have been of more than passing interest to the Newburyport militiaman who had been captured alongside her in the Wainwright house in Haverhill.

Bartlett came to Montreal in February 1709 and remained there until the general return of captives in November 1712. During the first fifteen months of his Montreal sojourn, Bartlett, by his own account, worked as an attendant to his master, a rich "captain" named Delude who had been afflicted with gout. He also was permitted to work at his shoemaking trade during his "times of leisure."[40] During most or all of the time he was with Delude, Silver would have not yet become a *hospitalière* but was still a student of the Congrégation. If the root of Silver's legendary status as the successor to Meriel is her acting as the priest's earnest catechist *protégé* before becoming cloistered or even officially Catholic, then Bartlett is likely to have omitted Silver's authoritative religious role in precisely the same way as he slighted Mary Sayward's authority at Sault-au Récollet.

Bartlett seems to have held a specific aversion to acknowledging the authority of New England women whom he regarded as apostates from Puritanism. He had no trouble, for example, in portraying the Catholic proselytizing of Captain Delude's wife. Bartlett, in fact, describes her religious exhortations to him in some detail. But there remains the mystery of his last two-and-a-half years in captivity. Where was he between the time he left the Delude household in May 1710 and his release in November 1712? And why did he keep those circumstances hidden?

Bartlett's status as a shoemaker might provide the reason. He could not have "wrought at shoe-making," at leisure or otherwise, without working for an established master at that trade.[41] Presumably Monsieur Delude had entered into a lease agreement with such an established master. This shoemaker, whoever he was, may have eventually wished to stop sharing the profits of Bartlett's work with Delude and purchased the captive outright from the elderly Frenchman. One candidate for the purchaser is Jean Fourneau, master shoemaker, who had married Elizabeth Price, a Deerfielder, four years before in 1706.[42] The possible Fourneau-Bartlett connection is strengthened by the fact that Jean's shoemaking establishment possessed a decidedly English character, given the presence of Elizabeth as well as her converted Catholic brother, Samuel Price, who also apparently worked in the shop.[43] Moreover, Joseph Bartlett's signature as a witness at the October 1712 marriage of two New England Catholic converts, Elizabeth Hurst and Thomas Buraff, establish Bartlett's presence in a network of New Englanders, some converted and free, others still Protestant and captive, under the sponsorship of the aforementioned Montreal noblewoman Marguerite Bouat Pacaud. Elizabeth and Samuel Price, Esther Sayward, and Martha French with her sister Freedom French (both of them Deerfield captives turned Congrégation students) consistently appear as witnesses to baptisms and marriages of former New Englanders sponsored in some way by Bouat Pacaud.[44] When Bartlett witnessed the marriage of Hurst and Buraff, he too became part of this network, but a perhaps unwilling one. Bartlett's presence at masses as an admitted unbeliever had shown that one did not have to be a Catholic to be permitted to attend sacramental ceremonies. The additional presence of the unconverted captive Jacob Gilman at the Hurst-Buraff marriage suggests that Bartlett's presence was not an indication that he had become a last-minute, unrecorded Catholic.[45] But, as he remained a *potential* convert, someone had pressed him to attend and sign the witness document. From the tenor of his self-reported resistance to Catholic ritual, he would seem to have been loath to do this, even had he been close friends with the betrothed.[46] Unless he was then a captive of Marguerite Bouat Pacaud herself, the Fourneau-Price family are the only candidates with the interest and ability to forcibly incorporate Bartlett within this tiny network.

There is the possibility, then, that not only did Bartlett serve Jean Fourneau and Samuel Price at his craft for two and a half years, but Elizabeth Price became his mistress in the household. The presence of Elizabeth Price would explain the complete omission of that time period from Bartlett's account. His narrative treatment of Mary Sayward, his omission of not only Mary Silver but any other converted Puritan female, and his distorted but relatively straightforward relation of Indian, French, and male authority suggest the presence of a hidden New England woman in the two-and-a-half-year gap. Elizabeth Price could well have been an even more unacceptable as a figure of power than Mary Sayward or Mary Silver, who at least associated themselves with the respectability and legitimacy of a religious community. Elizabeth Price, as the illiterate former wife of a local Deerfield Indian, would have still carried the stigma of social marginality across the border into New France. Her subsequent conversion and upward mobility into the master artisan class, which Bartlett probably considered himself a part of as well, would have only amplified harsh feeling against her in his still Puritan eyes. And, at twenty-six years of age in mid-1710, she was only three years older than he. And for Price, Bartlett's arrival in the role of a captive servant would have been a constant signifier of the satisfaction and pride inherent in her new status as a master artisan's wife and household mistress—a status that had eluded her as a white woman in western Massachusetts.

Joseph Bartlett carried the memory of his life in captivity back to New England, where he raised a large family as a prosperous New Hampshire deacon. Here he reflected on his experiences and eventually put them in writing. Consciously or not, he created a narrative in which he had been subject to the authority of Indian, French, and New England women. The account he produced assumed the more familiar and comfortable form of a man in motion, resolutely struggling with other faiths, other societies, other men. But several women who had encountered him had also incorporated him into their stories—as a finger amputee, as a slave in a cornfield, as a witness at a mass or a wedding, and as a shoemaker. These stories remained hidden in New England and to English-speaking posterity, but nonetheless entered the lived captors' narrative.

The life of Mary Silver was misrepresented by persons other than Joseph Bartlett. Her mother Mary Silver Wainwright, resolute and now twice widowed, whose level-headed actions in combat saved all her children but the eldest daughter, had not given up on seeing again her missing child, presumed converted. In a heart-rending petition in her own hand addressed to Joseph Dudley, governor of Massachusetts, dated April 29, 1710, she wrote:

> Now Lett the petition of Widow Mary Wainwright humbly showeth that Whereas my Daughter hath for a long time in Captivity with ye French in Canada and I have late reason to fear that her soul is in great Dainger if not all redy captivated and she brought to their ways theirefore I would humbly Intreat your Exelency that some care be taken for her Redemption before Canada be so Endeared to her that I shall never have my Daughter any more; Some are ready to say that there are so few captives in Canada that it is not worth while to poot ye Country to ye charges to send for them but I hoope your Excelency no[r] No other Judichous men will thinck so for St. James hath Instructed us as you may see Chap. 5 v 20 Let him know that he which converteth the sinner from the errour of his way, shall save a soul from Death and shall hide a multitude of sins this is all can do at present but I desire to Begg of God that he would Direct the hearts of our Rulers to do that which may be most for his Glory and for the good of his poor Distressed Creatures an so I take leave to subscribe myself your most Humble petitioner Mary Wainwright Widow.[47]

Casting her daughter in the passive role to the men of the Massachusetts Assembly ended up being a futile exercise. The legislature read the petition, but it was not acted upon. Two years later, when the issue of publicly funded ransom was made moot by the freedom granted to New Englanders remaining in Canada, Wainwright's fears were realized. We do not know if mother and daughter directly corresponded with one another. But a contemporary of Silver recorded the response she sent to her godfather, Governor Vaudreuil of New France, when that governor had been contacted by Mary Wainwright regarding the return of her daughter: "Monsieur, I tenderly love my dear mother, but before everything I am bound to obey God, and I declare to you that I am resolved to live in the holy religion which I have embraced, and to die a Sister of Saint Joseph. My dearest wish is, before my death, I may see my mother embrace the holy Catholic faith, with the light of which it has pleased God to enlighten me."[48]

Mary Silver's mother had quoted scripture in her entreaty to Governor Dudley, and Silver herself had explained herself to Governor Vaudreuil in terms of the hold of her new faith. Clearly, Mary Silver had been raised a Puritan—but the female version of Catholicism presented by her Congrégation sisters, and reinforced among the Sisters of Saint Joseph, had captured her mind beyond redemption. The letters reveal how Silver cast the meaning of her life in terms of faith, valuing it above a reunion with her family. Redemption to her was not a physical return home but the spiritual journey it would be necessary for her mother to take in order to join her in salvation.

Further, Mary Silver was using her knowledge of scripture not to beg favors from male elites, as her mother did, but to steer the souls of subjects, mostly men, in her charge. Such was the change the Canada frontier wrought on the lives of women.

Silver spent most her days until her death in 1740 neither in quiet religious contemplation nor as a catechist of the faith. She lived instead primarily as a nurse in a tumultuous hospital, supervising subordinates who physically sustained the community. Hers was a life of enacted *professional* skills. Further, Silver specifically chose one form of professional service—nursing—over another—teaching. To understand Mary Silver, one must understand the profound radicalism of being in a position to make such a decision. A frontier Puritan girl's life proceeded within defined frameworks of farm and town. Variations within these frameworks as the girl advanced into womanhood consisted of the social roles portrayed so aptly by Laurel Ulrich: wife, mother, mistress, captive.[49] For a sixteen-year-old girl to combine the mothering skills needed for professional nursing and the mistressing skills required for supervising laborers—and to usurp the Puritan male roles of religious minister and ultimate household authority—implies she has undergone a major shift in mental orientation. The ability to *choose* among these evolved professions within the context of a celibate, communal, female-controlled institution was far more than an expansion of social roles—it was, from the perspective of the world in which Silver had been born, a step out of time.

Mary Silver died young at forty-six, but Mary Sayward's life proved even shorter. Sayward eventually left her post in the frontier mission and served with evident and characteristic distinction in the Congrégation's new school in Quebec city. In 1717 an unknown sickness swept though the sisters' residence. Two sisters were treated at the Hôtel-Dieu at Quebec and recovered.[50] Mary of the Angels died on March 28. Her brief life, long journey, and fulfilled mission would be remembered by the women—if not the men—who had known her.

❋

In 1707, the most renowned narrative of the Puritan trials in the wilderness, *The Redeemed Captive Returning to Zion,* electrified New England from Boston to the Connecticut River valley. John Williams's tale of how he, a minister from Deerfield, forged spiritual victory on the anvil of military defeat has for many observers defined the wilderness and intercultural experiences of second-generation Puritans. The narrative continues to be a main focus of New England captivity studies.[51]

A passage of the narrative, sometimes overlooked, touched directly on the captors' narrative of Catholic women:

> One day [at the Abenaki settlement of Saint Francis on the Lake in April 1704] a certain savagess taken prisoner in King Philip's War, who had lived at Mr. Buckley's at Wethersfield, called Ruth, who could speak English very well, who had often been at my house but was now proselyted to the Romish faith, came into the wigwam. And with her came an English maid who was taken in the last war, who was dressed up in Indian apparel, could not speak one word of English, who said she could neither tell her own name or the name of the place from whence she was taken. These two talked in the Indian dialect with my master a long time after which my master bade me to cross myself. I told him I would not; he commanded me several times, and I as often refused. Ruth said, "Mr. Williams, you know the Scripture and therefore act against your own light, for you know the Scripture saith, 'Servants, obey your masters.' He is your master and you his servant." I told her she was ignorant and knew not the meaning of the Scripture, telling her [that] I was not to disobey the great God to obey any master, and that I was ready to suffer for God if called thereto. On which she talked to my master; I suppose she interpreted what I said.[52]

The Deerfield minister did not identify the "English maid" later in the narrative, and editors of reprinted editions have not offered a possible name.[53] While absolute certainty is impossible without Williams's own statement, a review of those known present at Saint Francis in April 1704 makes it likely that the "maid" was Mary Anne Davis of Oyster River (now Durham), New Hampshire.

Other New England-born unmarried females who lived at Saint Francis could have been called maids. Davis, however, was the only one of these "taken in the last war" (King William's War, 1689–98). Moreover, Indians captured Davis in 1693 when she was five. Nine years later, she might have lost, at least in the eyes of Williams, much if not all of her facility with English. Less certain was why Williams would have reported that she could not disclose her name, when her confessor and catechist at Saint Francis, Père Bigot, clearly knew her as Mary Anne Davis. Possibilities include that Williams committed an intentional obfuscation. Alternatively, Williams's account could have been based on a deliberate deception on the part of both Ruth and the "maid"—in order that the latter might remain unknown to potentially meddlesome redeemers in New England.

A final possibility is that in fact Williams had it right—that the "maid" did not know her name. In this case, "Marie-Anne" could have been bestowed by her Catholic sponsors and added to a generic "Davis" when she went to live among the French five years later. This final theory is supported by the fact that the names of her parents and her birthplace are not identified in the French documents—highly unusual for a convert—suggesting that in fact she did not remember them. "Marie-Anne" as a baptismal name and "Davis" as a generic surname might have been derived from, or given in honor or emulation of, the previously arrived Quebec Ursuline of New England birth, also named Mary Anne Davis, Soeur Saint-Benoit.[54]

The final evidence pointing to the meeting between John Williams and Mary Anne Davis in 1704 is her role as a proselytizer. Aged about sixteen in 1704, Mary Anne had already been under the tutelage of the Jesuit Père Bigot at Saint Francis for close to ten years and had become an ardent Catholic convert.[55] The mission to Williams in the wigwam of his captivity would have been natural for her to undertake as a further expression of her fervor.

Her lack of facility with the English language would have limited her effectiveness as a proselytizer of New Englanders, except through the conduit of Ruth. Nevertheless, she watched with Ruth as the scene concluded in the wigwam. According to Williams:

> My master took hold of my hand to force me to cross myself, but I struggled with him and would not suffer him to guide my hand; upon this he pulled off a crucifix from his own neck and bade me kiss it, but I refused once again. He told me he would dash out my brains with his hatchet if I refused. I told him I should sooner choose death than to sin against God; then he ran and caught up his hatchet and acted as though he would have dashed out my brains. Seeing I was not moved, he threw down his hatchet, saying he would first bite off my nails if I still refused; I gave him my hand and told him I was ready to suffer. He set his teeth in my thumbnails and gave a grip with his teeth, and then said, "No good minister, no love God, as bad as the devil," so left off.[56]

Whether Mary Anne Davis or Ruth remained in the wigwam with Williams, we do not know. But the encounter suggests another clash of the narratives of captor and captive. The Indian Ruth clearly perceived the power inversion in their situation, and perhaps relished doing unto others as had been done to her while enslaved in New England during King Philip's war.[57] Mary Anne Davis's perception of the event remains hidden. But the meaning of the encounter is deepened by the fact that her involvement with unconverted New England men had begun many years before. The meeting with the Reverend John Williams might have been novel due to his preeminence and the fact he was a transient visitor to the settlement. But every indication was that by April 1704 facing intransigent Puritan men had become a familiar experience for her.

Davis herself was not a captive at Saint Francis. Father Bigot's reference to Davis's "bonds" among the Abenaki was a figurative contrast to the true freedom she finally found as a hospital sister in Quebec. Abbé Casgrain as well as Bigot's contemporary Mère Juchereau, the Hôtel-Dieu annalist who personally knew Mary Anne Davis, confirm that Davis passed her life among the Indians largely in religious contemplation. While these views may be idealized, they at least confirm that she was not a "slave" in the community.[58] Although Davis was "free," there were English slaves, all men and boys, already at Saint Francis by the time Williams arrived there.

The year before, 1703, two brothers from the Jordan family of Spurwink, Maine—Dominicus Jr., aged twenty, and Samuel, nineteen—were delivered to Saint Francis. They did not leave written narratives, but from other such arrivals it is possible to estimate in what manner they arrived. The Deerfield captive Joseph Clemmon, taken alongside John Williams, entered several Indian missions during his captivity and reported a procedure in which the prisoners approaching a French mission settlement had their faces painted red, were forced to strip naked, and ran a gauntlet. The Abenaki did not generally apply this practice to female captives. Amos Eastman, taken in the Seven Years' War, reported that upon arrival at Saint Francis he was put to women's work, hoeing corn, until his rebellion against the treatment raised his status in the eyes of the Abenaki. Alice Nash tells of the captive John Stark, who resented being put to women's work as a slave at Saint Francis.[59]

But whatever their exact form of initiation, both men suffered a long and debilitating captivity at that settlement. Unlike Mary Anne Davis, Samuel Jordan considered himself to have been enslaved outright at Saint Francis from age nineteen to twenty-five. He described the experience later in an unrelated petition as one of having been "kept in Miserable captivity for the Space of Eight Years." The Saint Francis Abenaki kept his elder brother even longer. Dominicus Jordan Jr. probably did not emerge from captivity at Saint Francis until 1713 and possibly as late as 1716—thirteen years after his capture. In fact he was never really released. Perhaps distraught at being left behind as a captive long after peace had been established between New England and New France, he finally escaped from his captors.[60] That the Jordan brothers resisted conversion and never married in all that time suggests that their promotion to warrior was not forthcoming, as it was for Amos Eastman.

As available Saint Francis narratives confirm, Dominicus and Samuel Jordan would have been most often under female supervision while planting and hoeing corn, beating kernels into flour, carrying burdens, drawing water, maintaining fires, and assisting with the hunt. The brothers eventually spent seven years working in the small settlement, in the close and uncomfortable company of the increasingly devout Mary Anne Davis.[61] And they were not the only New England slaves Davis met. A year after the Reverend John Williams's brief stay, his twelve-year-old son Stephen spent a full year in the Saint Francis area as the property of "Sagamore George," under the direction of George's wife.

The failure to mention years of association with Mary Anne Davis on the part of the Jordan brothers and especially by Stephen Williams, who produced a full-scale captivity narrative, adds a new dimension to the omissions seen in the accounts left by John Gillett, Nathaniel Belden, and Joseph Bartlett. (Significantly, perhaps, the extremely brief "narratives" of Gillett and Belden appeared in the Stephen Williams manuscript.) The omissions of the Saint Francis captives must be considered within the framework of the narrative archetypes of Indian women as put forth by Anglo-American men. Was Davis a benevolent mother, a smitten maiden of salvation, or a monstrous shrew of revenge?

Mary Anne Davis fitted none of these types. From Stephen Williams's point of view, perhaps, Davis's failure to try to alleviate his father's torment at the hands of his Abenaki master suggested she was not given to offer succor, as was expected of virtuous young women who after transculturation become maidens of salvation. Davis's behavior, even if she had not taken part in the physical torment of Stephen's father, was instead typical of those bullying and haggard old squaws typically described as furies.

The problem is that Mary Anne Davis acted as a fury while physically appearing as a maiden of salvation. In the case of Davis we have the rare benefit of an actual physical description by those who knew her. Upon her entrance to the Hôtel-Dieu six years later, the sisters described her as a striking figure with blond hair and pale skin and wearing a white winter robe.[62] But her appearance did not conform in Puritan eyes to her behavior. That Davis did not participate in the torment of John Williams was by no means certain, because by her age a typical young Indian woman would have already accrued experience in the gauntlet lines. Since the two acceptable images of Indian women—succoring maiden and fury—could not be combined, both were omitted.

The contextual evidence allows a rough reconstruction of the relative statuses and corresponding actions of the native New England residents in Saint Francis. One of the returning men, Samuel Jordan, could not resist the image of the smitten maid of salvation, though he would later characterize his captivity as eight years of misery. After being transferred to the French for the last year of his captivity, he reported that he and an English companion had been aided in an escape back to the Maine coast by a "friendly squaw" known, phonetically at least, as "Molly Mun." There is no way to verify or disprove this story smacking of romantic fiction. But whether Jordan expressed the literal truth, the partially truth, or concocted the story, his choice to emphasize the actions of "Molly Mun," the maiden of salvation, and to omit the actual seven years as a slave in close proximity to the very real Mary Anne Davis, reveals the representational priorities of the Puritan male captivity narrative in regard to free former countrywomen.

And for Samuel Jordan as well as the other captives, the appearance of the white "savagess" at Saint Francis underscored the savagery inherent in the inversion of gendered power. This issue of legitimate authority comes up in the Reverend John Williams's account of his encounter with Ruth and Davis. When Ruth proposed the Biblical admonition of "servants obey your masters" as an absolute principle, it perhaps came as no surprise to her when the Puritan minister rejected it as applying to him in his servile position. Because in Williams's eyes God's chosen people were Puritans, legitimate authority rested only within themselves.[63]

But the captives felt it necessary to spare New England readers any contrary lessons that could be derived from their years with Mary Anne Davis. The inversion of authority between John Williams and his male Indian "master" was about as far as a narrative could push the acceptable boundaries of the portrayal of illegitimate power. Davis's youth, gender, and Puritan origins underscored and intensified the inversion of power and the illegitimacy of her authority. But to accurately portray this circumstance in writing was not possible at this time. Puritan *manhood defeated* could not be presented as a prelude to an ultimate victory—the stigma of defeat would have been difficult to dispel.

And what of this captor's narrative? Davis left no direct evidence from her years at Saint Francis as to how she felt about her life and destiny. The opinion of Father Bigot, transmitted through an intervening source, that Davis was devout and preferred quiet solitude, does not seem so far-fetched since very soon she elected to become a Hospital Sister of Saint Augustine. But that does not reveal her thoughts about the Abenaki society in which she once lived. How she might have regarded her prospects for marriage among the Abenaki, her adoptive family, or her original home in New England all remain unknown. Practically the only real pathway to her mind and heart is through her later choice of professional career. Caring for and directing captives from her former home continued to be a focus of her activities and identity. We glimpse her life among the Abenaki only by considering the lives of these captives. The Williamses and the Jordans might have regarded Mary Anne Davis as an unfathomable perversion of womanhood, but there was at least a hint in Mary Anne's later life of what she had valued at Saint Francis. In regard to the English slaves there, she had learned that the appropriation of bodies could necessarily coexist with service to souls.

Not all the captives of New England origin in New France are presently known. The decades of research on the New England captivities culminating in the publication of Charlotte Alice Baker's *True Stories* in 1897 and Emma Lewis Coleman's *New England Captives* in 1925 continue to be the indispensable starting point on the subject today. Even in their 1980 statistical review, Alden T. Vaughan and Daniel K. Richter indicate their belief that there are most likely only a very few captives yet to be found beyond the nearly 1,700 named by Baker and Coleman.[64] But one vein of evidence that Baker, Coleman, Vaughan, and Richter left undisturbed is the list of patients in French Canada's hospitals. A few archivists of the religious hospital communities have noted the presence of captives in their records, but the phenomenon of recovered prisoner-of-war patients put to work as captive bondsmen remains unanalyzed.

One such relatively unknown individual was Matthew Pauling. In January 1690 "Mattieu Paulling" is listed in the patient register of the Hôtel-Dieu in Quebec: age thirty, a native of London, England, and a patient in the prisoners' ward. Three years later he is listed again, this time in the same volume in the expenses ledger with a note indicating his new status: English domestic servant.[65]

What sort of transformation had occurred for Pauling? The expense of three livres was paid directly to the actual owner of Pauling. Since the London native had come to the hospital as a patient, not due to ransom actually paid by the Sisters of Saint Augustine, the sisters would have had to arrange to lease him if they wished to keep him. In this case, the sisters did precisely that.

An actual owner for Pauling is not listed, but a leasing arrangement is confirmed by a similar entry for another New England captive who served the Sisters of Saint Augustine alongside Pauling. A Jean Andresse (probably John Andrews) is listed as having been a patient at the hospital for just three days in 1693, but he reappears in the record almost immediately as a community *domestique*. Doubtless the three livres was paid to the original monetary redeemer—a Monsieur Madous.[66] As for Pauling, his owner was not recorded. Pauling might have still been an Indian captive, and the scribe possibly found it too hard to identify his owner or owners.

The community's expenses ledger indicates that the owners of captives were paid a fair market rate for labor. The sisters scrambled to acquire a variety of types of laborers, signing most of them on a free-contract basis. Three presumably Canadian domestics, for example, were paid 100 livres over one year, aggregate, for their services.[67] The annual rate of about 33 livres per man roughly equaled the rate of 3 livres per month paid to the master of each English captive. To put the overall expense of labor into perspective, during the year 1694 the sisters paid for labor only about 5 percent of the annual expenditure for that year of about 11,000 livres—a fair bargain by any measure.[68]

But the English captives were not the only form of relatively inexpensive labor employed at the Hôtel-Dieu. Between the peace of 1713 and the resumption of intercolonial war in 1744, when there were no captives available, the Sisters of Saint Augustine supplemented free contracted labor with that of convicts transported from France. One such unfortunate named Pierre Monet began serving his indeterminate sentence under contract to the sisters in January 1742. His age that year, fifty, suggests, however, that there was an element of mercy in the sisters' action. There could not have been much demand for a untrained convict of modest origins whose capacity for hard labor was largely over. In New France, an unwanted convict could go cold and hungry in the streets as easily as anyone else.[69]

The investment in captive labor proved to be especially beneficial to the Sisters of Saint Augustine. The large influx of New England prisoners requiring care during both King William's war (1689–98) and Queen Anne's War (1702–13) demanded not only extra domestic help but the specific skill of English-speaking help in the prisoner's ward. The intake could be overwhelming at times. The *Registre journalier des malades* records over two hundred admissions of New England prisoners for treatment during these two wars. In one sample day in 1709, for example, the Saint John Indians held claim on nine English patients at the Hôtel-Dieu alone.[70] And, of course, the *hospitalières* were asked to care for the New Englanders alongside war causalities in the French army and Canadian militia. And in wartime the usual range of civilians afflicted with common illnesses and injuries continued unabated.

In 1709, on the eve of Mary Anne Davis's arrival at the Hôtel-Dieu, Pawling and Andrews no longer appear in the community records, presumably having returned home at the end of the previous war in 1698. But Queen Anne's War had brought a steady stream of new prisoners who were treated in the same manner. Two of the Saint John captives were listed that year as *engagés* (in this context not indentured servants but contract workers). Doubtless the Saint John Indians received payment for the work that "Jean" and "Louis" performed. One other captive *domestique* that year was known by name: a Captain Edward Barlow.[71]

For Barlow and his counterparts, captivity assumed a complexity unknown in most prisoner-of-war or enslavement situations in the early modern world. A New England militia captain working in the wards entered into a kind of partnership with skilled women in professional service. The work of such captives could be as varied as the activity of the community and certainly might include the menial work of gardening, kitchen work, water carrying, snow removal, and general cleaning, depending on the season and the needs of the community. Sometimes an English captive's usefulness as a communicator led to a linkage between him and the *infirmier* (male nurse) that appears in community documents.

The element of coercion in this situation was possibly complicated by the gratitude that patients feel toward those who care for them in life-threatening situations. But certainly even patients who were not the leased property of the Hospital Sisters could not have failed to perceive the bizarre hierarchy of authority around them. Here before them one of their militia captains did the bidding of Catholic sisters—some of them half Barlow's age.[72]

The importance of youth within this community cannot be overemphasized. When Mary Anne Davis entered the Hôtel-Dieu sisterhood in 1710 at the recorded age of twenty-two, she was already older than half of the professed sisters there. Of thirty-five active professional *hospitalières* in 1710, fully two-thirds were younger than thirty years old, and one-third of the community had not yet celebrated their twentieth birthday. The youngest was fourteen.[73] As with the previously discussed Congrégation Notre-Dame, this demographic situation imparted a physical dynamism that propelled the community through its daily hardships. Combined with the experience and resolve of their elders, the sisters' youthful strength enabled them to prevail over the environmental and human challenges of running a frontier hospital where many of the patients were captive soldiers of an enemy power. A hospital sister was therefore the very opposite of the silent and acquiescent contemplative—an image so often assigned to nuns even of this period. To survive, a young woman had to put aside any perceived disabilities of her sex and combine skilled knowledge with physical endurance, thereby becoming a unique form of frontierswoman.

Nor did class position automatically give the women the confidence necessary to control their volatile surroundings and prevail under those circumstances. Only a few of the *hospitalières* were daughters of the colony's leading families. Others were of diverse backgrounds. Marie-Ursule Cherron, who professed immediately before Mary Davis, was of an upwardly mobile "marchand bourgeois" family. The father of another young hospital sister, Mary-Anne Gauvreau, is listed as an armorer and maker of guns. His standing in the skilled artisan caste is similar to the more modest backgrounds of the Congrégation sisters in Montreal.[74] A few, then, might have expected—or demanded—respect from those around them because of their upbringing. Most, however, earned their identity as controllers of their environment through their own professional work.

Barlow, "Louis," and "Jean" also bound themselves to the hospital sisters by the shared danger of work in the wards. Late-seventeenth- and early-eighteenth-century medical practice proved especially hazardous to its practitioners. Deaths might partly explain why many of the hospital captives do not appear on the redeemed or returned list. What is certain is that young sisters tragically died in clusters from epidemics that first struck their patients. Over the last two months of 1708, for example, the Hôtel-Dieu lost three young sisters to disease. On November 28 of that year thirty-five-year-old Louise Soumande died, followed closely by thirty-four-year-old Marie-Françoise Denis on December 20 and twenty-six-year-old Catherine Gauvreau the very next day.[75]

Mary Anne Davis entered this milieu in January 1710. Father Bigot had been successful in his mission with the young Anglo-Indian woman. There is no extant baptism record for Davis, suggesting that the baptism took place at Saint Francis, since all such records were burned during the final phase of the Seven Years' War. Although Davis had already become a Catholic convert at Saint Francis, Bigot had something else in mind for her than a continued life among the Abenaki. The Jesuit had kept the Sisters of Saint Augustine apprised of the life of the *petite sauvagesse*. The sisters were further attuned to the desirability of attracting young female converts because of their recent, but heartbreakingly unsuccessful, attempt to bring up young Sarah Gerrish of Dover, New Hampshire, as one of their own.[76]

Whatever three-way negotiations ensued, they culminated in Davis's dramatic entrance into the Hôtel-Dieu in Quebec's upper town. Having debarked at the lower town shore, Davis and Bigot had trod the winding path up the steep slope dividing the settlement, before entering the modest stone building. The sisters reportedly marveled at the appearance of the pale woman dressed in buckskin and a white cloth robe, her long blonde hair falling freely about her shoulders and back.[77] The official account of this entrance is probably idealized, but the humble petition of Davis to enter the community, uttered on her knees, must have at least been close to what actually occurred.

Davis lived as a novice among the Sisters of Saint Augustine for almost eighteen months, engaged for most of that time in learning the French language. Doubtless the sisters also introduced her to the basic work of the community, caring for patients. Davis took her final vows on July 16, 1711, taking the name of Soeur Sainte-Cécile.

A religious name is one of the few surviving expressions of individual identity for early modern *religieuses* left to us. Because no annotations exist to explain why one adopted name was chosen over another, the reason for the choice is speculative. But in the case of Mary Anne Davis, the appropriation of the Roman Christian saint is suggestive. Saint Cecilia remained popular in northern France as elsewhere in Europe throughout the premodern era as one of the foundational women in the Christian faith. Two themes dominate her story. First, Cecilia was above all an active converter of nonbelievers. As a young Roman matron, she succeeded in converting her husband to Christianity and then expanded her mission to include her husband's influential circle of friends. For these efforts the Roman authorities put her to death by drowning her in her own household bath. The first efforts to accomplish the execution failed. The failure created the second theme: the miraculous, if temporary, survival in the face of mortal danger imposed by one's religious enemies.[78]

The similarity of Davis's life to that of Cecilia was probably apparent to Davis's superiors because of Davis's known affinity for riparian meditation at Saint Francis as well as her survival of wilderness dangers. The most compelling connection to Cecilia is as an agent of religious conversion. And Saint Cecilia was, after all, a converter of men.

But the problem of language raised in the John Williams narrative remains. Whether she spoke English or not, she had as much contact with the Anglophone patients and captives as any other sister, for English prisoners comprised a significant portion of the community's workload for the first three years following Davis's arrival. If she did not yet know English in 1710, she probably learned quickly from her orderlies.

As in Montreal, the plan of the hospital building reveals much about daily life within the community. When Davis and Barlow worked there, the hospital building measured about 180 by 200 feet, with most of the square footage occupied by a large central courtyard. The south passage was the patient care area with the women's ward directly adjoining that for the men. The pharmacy area was continuous with both rooms. The soldiers' ward held the wartime prisoners in a twenty-by-twenty-foot space, which would have been quite crowded in years such as 1709. The room was secured by its location behind the main men's ward, which offered the only access. The east and north walls enclosed a corridor and various workrooms and storage areas. The *domestiques* probably slept here as well, it being common for servants in colonial Canada to sleep where they worked. The west passage consisted of an entranceway, a covered area jutting into the courtyard where patients could take in fresh air, the choir, the sacristy, and finally, at the southwest corner of the building, a large chapel. The sisters' living quarters occupied the second floor. This building made up part of the outer wall that enclosed the entire property, which also included a small kitchen building and a large garden.

On becoming integrated into the daily life of the frontier hospital, Mary Anne Davis lived out a second and altogether new chapter in her captor's narrative. Sister Sainte-Cécile perhaps remained interested in the possible conversion of her charges, but she certainly realized at some point that these charges were not girls like herself and Sarah Gerrish, amenable to the life and message conveyed by the hospital sisters. They were men, some perhaps as proud as John Williams, all perhaps as resistant to their captivity as this Deerfield minister. The sisters never recorded any but deathbed conversions.

But in the professionalized atmosphere of the Hôtel-Dieu, where women pharmacists and women providers of medical care practiced and consulted, the nature of the coercion had changed. Some factors remained the same, of course. Captain Edward Barlow probably drew his share of water from the Saint Lawrence, as had the Jordan brothers. But now a more complex dynamic was added to the simple hierarchical relationship of owner and slave at the Hôtel-Dieu, in which captor and captive were bound together by reciprocal and mutually dependent professional responsibilities. Captive *domestiques,* like captive patients, depended on the Sisters of Saint Augustine for their survival; the sisters provided a reliable source of food and shelter in this winter-besieged town surrounded a hundred miles in any direction by forest-savvy enemy warriors. And the sisters depended on the captive *domestiques* for the survival of their professional mission, which underlay and formed the living heart of the religious calling that marked their ultimate collective goal.

And the sisters and patients also lived symbiotically. The sick and wounded soldiers and civilian captives depended on the women citizens of the enemy society for their lives—and Sister Sainte-Cécile and her colleagues would respond. She would save their lives—and later if necessary appropriate their healed bodies—because through them she would achieve the success of her community and her ultimate salvation. But the hierarchy defining her life at the Hôtel-Dieu in Quebec could not have failed to impress her. She, like Sarah Gerrish, and for that matter Mary Silver, the Sayward sisters, and Lydia Longley, had been raised where home was a family house, and that house was ruled, at least in theory, by a father. In French Canada there were still fathers: God, the Holy Father in Rome, the king and cardinal in Paris, the intendant and bishop in Quebec, the father confessor of their own community. Yet those fathers were far away—they certainly did not physically reside in the larger house, a women's house.

To the Reverend John Williams, Mary Anne Davis had been the English maid rendered mute by savagery. She had no name in the *Redeemed Captive* only because Williams had failed to give her one. The Jordan brothers and Stephen Williams had similarly failed to name her. And whether Mary Anne Davis was what her parents had christened her or whether it was reflective of what the Father Bigot thought she should be called, the time would come when men would call her Sainte Cécile, a name that she had chosen for herself. Her captor's narrative was written in the wards where she answered only to that name. There, it would be free-born Englishmen who were renamed Jean, Louis, or Edouard in the French style.

John Williams had been too valuable a prisoner to be kept anonymously behind the walls of the Hôtel-Dieu of Quebec, where the refuge was a prison and the prison a refuge. In starkest and simplest terms, Williams's military counterparts in the New England mission, like Captain Edward Barlow, were unmanned in New France. Barlow was an active frontier soldier made passive by being treated by women in a hospital, a passivity that only grew more acute as he recovered and was transformed from a leader of men to a follower of women. Could he see anything beyond this transformation? Would anything, even gratitude, cause him to grant Soeur Sainte Cécile the validity of her own transformation? Were the demands of the wartime frontier enough to create a fellowship between sister and servant?

Williams, a captive in motion, could keep recasting his short-lived encounters into a narrative of Puritan redemption with his unredeemed daughter Eunice as the victim of the other's agency and purpose. But Barlow was caught in a place from which there was no physical or rhetorical escape. The redemptive aspect of the sisters' attentions to him certainly existed. He recovered physically and would have been welcomed as a convert. But as one who wished to return home, the ultimate reality of the situation remained. Before the arrival of Davis, Barlow had experienced his first training and ongoing supervision exclusively at the hands of the French-Canadian sisters. He then watched as these same women enslaved other recovered men. He was present as the sisters leased still more men who would arrive at the gate, delivered by their masters and mistresses from the town and country. Later, he observed as the white *sauvagesse* entered the house, received a new name, and made herself into yet another of his captors. Those men, made passive in one place for so long, simply could not gather the narrative strength to render their mistresses passive. The service to Sainte Cécile and her mission left captives powerless to unname her—except through silence.

CHAPTER THREE

The Hospital: Paradoxes of the Grey Sisters

> The count of 1758 mention five prisoners that the sisters put to work
> in the Mother House while twenty-one others were employed at the
> farm at Pointe-Saint-Charles. One was placed at the Chambly
> farm. . . . Another English prisoner is mentioned working on our
> walls and keeping our grounds. It is very probable he was often
> placed at this employment with the other prisoners.
>
> —Soeurs grises–Montréal, *Ancien Journal*

During the last phase of the New England captivities before the British conquests of 1759 and 1760, a basic captivity paradox—women religious of Canada making themselves servants of God by becoming the mistresses of men—turned inward. After 1744, these women's provision of hospital care and poor relief to the nation at war expanded and transformed. Although teaching and missionary work in the frontier areas continued, these activities no longer preoccupied and defined the economically diverse and militarily besieged colony of French Canada. The hospital sisters acted more diligently than before to heal the bodies of soldiers and citizens—and did so by utilizing the necessary amount of unfree labor. As the history of New France moved into its final phase, the feminine component of this colonial mission became less inclusive of cultural outsiders and at the same time more important to the larger society.

In the changing conditions, the *hospitalières* continued to create their own realm of service. But in the last years of the French-Canadian colony, even a generally recognized social need for charity work did not necessarily move entrenched authorities to allow it. An instructive case is that of Marie-Marguerite Dufrost de LaJemmerais, the widow of François You d'Youville, who through her force of will took control of a defunct and bankrupt general hospital for the poor and transformed it into a prosperous complex of social services vital to Montreal's welfare. She drew on her twin cultural heritages—early Canadian female merchants and members of the women's religious communities—and reinvented both. More precisely, she combined these two heritages in a unique reconfiguration of what may seem a paradox: offering services through the exercise of authority.

Marguerite d'Youville built a refuge for the poor, the chronically ill, the displaced, and those without hope. But for the colony's unfortunates, the price of physical redemption was subjection. D'Youville did not permit idle hands among patients and inmates who could help the community become self-sustaining. As the foundation of the physical support of her institution, she assembled an impressive variety of unfree laborers: female and male convicts, Indian slaves, self-indentured Canadians, and at least twenty-seven British soldiers taken prisoner in the Seven Years' War. Though the Hôpital-Général in theory existed as a women's community, its charter limited it to twelve professed sisters. The dozen women and their handful of novices formed the apex of a pyramidal structure of over a hundred individuals, mostly men, in various states of dependency. The tension between spiritual redemption and the necessity to coerce work from bodies, which had occupied the leaders of the Congrégation Notre-Dame before 1713, was recast by Marguerite d'Youville according to the demands of the colony at mid-century. While maintaining the ultimate goal of serving God's purpose, the tension experienced by d'Youville would be between physical coercion and physical rescue from chronic sickness, destitution, and abandonment.

❀

By 1744, when the intercolonial warfare and extensive captive taking resumed, the women's religious communities had long settled into various peacetime routines.[1] Though no longer the center of outwardly directed transculturation that it had been before the turn of the century, the Congrégation Notre-Dame de Montréal found itself in a productive and relatively placid period. Now a ruled community, the lay sisters had become true women religious. They concentrated their efforts at mid-century on the education of Canadian girls, and they were now one of several such providers. The Sisters of Saint Joseph at the Hôtel-Dieu in Montreal and the Sisters of Saint Augustine in Quebec continued to act as the sole providers of institutional acute hospital care in the colony. The Ursulines of

Quebec had consolidated their redoubtable position as the educators of the girls of the colony's elite.

For the town of Montreal, however, an acute gap in the necessary services had been felt for some years. Pierre Le Ber's charitable project, the Hôpital-Général for the benefit of the town's poor and infirm, had by the 1740s become defunct. Founder Jean-François Charon, a layman and moderately well-off Quebec-born former trader, had taken in the first afflicted residents in 1694. The Sulpicians, as seigneurs of Montreal Island, donated the necessary land and Le Ber provided additional land as well as money. Charon sought to bring his project closer to God by founding a community of lay brothers to run the hospital. Clerical authorities took vows from Charon's new Frères Hospitaliers in 1702. In the next decades, however, the day-to-day operations of the Hôpital-Général became continually undermined in a never ending series of distractions.

Charon, understandably, also wished to close the gender gap in primary education so that young boys, especially those too young or too poor to receive education from the priests, could gain access to the basic literacy skills routinely enjoyed by Canadian girls of all social levels.[2] But entreaties to establish a French teaching community fell on deaf ears in France and Canada. In the end this ambition only served to divert attention from the primary mission of the hospice. By 1707, support for even the hospice had ended. The French naval minister Louis Pontchartrain revoked the vows and status of the Frères Hospitaliers, citing burdensome royal subsidies to other Canadian communities.

The loss of status made it difficult to win new recruits for the brothers, and the refusal of royal money led gradually to a ruinous debt. Charon and his successor, Louis Turc Castelveyre, *dit* Chrétien, managed the farmlands and investments badly; income never came close to meeting expenses. The history of the community, especially after Charon's death during an Atlantic crossing in 1719, became principally an edifying lesson in the techniques used by eighteenth-century Montrealers to keep creditors at bay. By 1725, affairs had reached a state of desperation sufficient to cause Chrétien to flee to the Spanish part of the island of Hispanola in the Caribbean in order to avoid arrest. At the beginning of the 1740s, the house built by Pierre Le Ber was a physical ruin, inhabited only by two remaining Frères Hospitaliers, one of them senile, and four male residents—all in a condition of destitution.[3]

The growing consensus of concerned authorities in Montreal was that Madame d'Youville was the obvious choice to replace the Frères Hospitaliers at the Hôpital-Général. D'Youville, a widowed young shopkeeper of noble origins, had begun in the 1730s to gather around her like-minded women who had begun boarding poor women in several houses she owned in succession. D'Youville also took on a spiritual guide for the community, the Sulpician Louis Normant de Faradon, to help the charity-minded women work toward the formation of a religious sisterhood.

The arrival of d'Youville's embryonic sisterhood at the general hospital led to a gendered revolution. Female energy swept away the anemic remains of the old, male regime. D'Youville and her sisters employed a hired "corps of women" to clean the decrepit old hospital properly from cellar to attic and ordered necessary structural repairs.[4] One of the two remaining brothers left Canada at once, apparently unwilling to live under the authority of d'Youville and her associates, now known locally as the Grey Sisters. The other died soon thereafter. The four male patients inherited by the Grey Sisters were joined by others, and soon the hospital was caring for a multitude of men, women, and children. During the Charon years, for reasons of choice and propriety, the brothers had cared only for male indigents and chronically ill patients. Women, by contrast, could care for all, and they immediately made the social institution far more responsive to the needs of the entire colony.

Whereas the patient base would now reflect the population of the colony, the authority passed into exclusively feminine hands. Some of Montreal's wayward women became the first to experience the institutional revolution. At d'Youville's instigation, young prostitutes found themselves rounded up from the streets of Montreal and confined in the hospital, ushering in a new era of social rehabilitation for women in the colony.[5] The sisters applied the new social maternalism to male subjects as well. D'Youville's placed the young, "exuberantly healthy" Catherine Rainville in charge of the long-term male residents.[6] The newly arrived destitute men as well as those inherited from the Frères Hospitaliers might have been surprised at the novel requirement that they work for their keep.[7] Rainville soon presided over a small empire of projects that increased the revenue of the houses, from the processing of leaf tobacco for resale (the special province of elderly men) to brewing beer. The price of destitution for Montreal's men would now be life under the direction of a woman. Sweeping away a male experiment in social service, customarily the field of women, d'Youville successfully combined her twin inheritances of a *marchande* and a *religieuse*.

What were the roots of this impulse to institute the role of the public mother in New France? Hagiographers have found them in the early years of the founding mother herself. The story, as drawn from the community annals and later chroniclers, goes as follows: Marguerite d'Youville's father, Christophe Dufrost de LaJemmerais, was a man of prestigious rank by virtue of birth and merit.[8] Possessing a natural authority as the son of Breton nobility, he earned a captaincy in the French Army during the Iroquois wars. The Canadian woman he married added a singularly New World distinction to the family's public presence. Marie-Renée Gaulthier de Varennes was a member of the Boucher de Boucherville family—the epitome of self-made Canadian virtue. Her grandfather, Pierre Boucher, had started as the humblest of French immigrants—an indentured servant in the Jesuit mission in the late 1630s. Enriching himself through trade, by 1661 he had obtained *lettres de noblesse* and by the turn of the eighteenth century had become a living legend—a visible connection with the colony's storied and gloried past with over two hundred living descendants.[9]

Marie-Marguerite Dufrost de LaJemmerais, commonly called Marguerite, was born in 1701, the first child of Christophe and Marie-Renée.[10] Five more children, two girls and three boys, followed in almost annual succession. Christophe Dufrost died on June 1, 1708, a full six months before the birth of his namesake son.[11] He left little money for his family, who fell from social prominence into a genteel but genuine destitution. Their penury, worsened by years of delay in receiving Christophe's military pension, became the subject of correspondence among the colony's leaders, who were nevertheless powerless individually to provide for the family's relief. In response, Marguerite's mother, Marie-Renée, began selling her needlework and subjecting her family to austere economy.

The effects on the girl were several. First, she learned the sting of poverty—that is, poverty for those of noble birth. Second, her mother's preoccupation with finances left Marguerite as the principal caretaker, disciplinarian, and even schoolmistress for her siblings, establishing early the habit of maternal authority (and one that did not discriminate between boys and girls). Third, the chroniclers of the elite school run by the Quebec Ursulines recorded that for Marguerite's Dufrost's two years as a boarder there she possessed an unusually serious mind for a girl of twelve, showing a particular aversion to the wasting of time. If true, this perhaps reflected the response of a financially precarious striver among the relatively inattentive and comfortable rich.

The shame of her family's circumstances caused Marie-Renée Gaulthier to grasp at financial security by marrying a charlatan physician and self-styled Irish nobleman, Timothy Sullivan. Non-French transatlantic immigrants were an extreme rarity in Canada, and for one to marry into a family of such esteem as the Bouchers was considered something of a scandal.[12] The social effects of this marriage ruined young Marguerite Dufrost's first marriage prospects and forced her in the end to leave her hometown of

Varennes to enter the Montreal marriage market. Her mother's actions, then, indirectly caused Marguerite's own disastrous marriage to François You d'Youville. Though of a good family, François possessed a vile character. Officially a furrier, he in fact made his living as a dealer in illicit liquor and occasionally slaves along the exchange routes running from the Saint Lawrence to the upper Great Lakes.[13] Marguerite succeeded in having two sons survive infancy, but her life was marked by her husband's frequent and extended absences. Even when he was present in Montreal, François d'Youville drank excessively and committed acts of inebriated violence— some of them directed at Marguerite. In this experience, according to her hagiographers, her divine testing reached its most painful stage, and her journey toward seeking solace in God began.

The death of François in 1730 after eight years of marriage caused Marguerite, like her mother before her, to depend on her own ingenuity for her family's survival. Swallowing her pride, she opened a dress and fabric shop in her house in Montreal's main market square, marketing her wares to ladies who had formerly been her social equals. But more than physical survival was at stake. Her desperately unhappy marriage, the hagiography claims, had been a final formative trial that had bestowed on her a sensitivity to physical and emotional suffering perhaps unusual in Canadian women of her background. Her trials had also provided her with sufficient authority and strength not only to survive but to widen her activities far beyond shopkeeping. The years of suffering with François grounded her character squarely in religion.

Signs of her destiny supposedly appeared to her. Immediately outside her dress shop in the market square happened to be precisely where local prisoners were forced to stand during the day for the purpose of public humiliation—their necks ignominiously placed into iron collars affixed to raised wooden posts. Marguerite d'Youville's career in charity began with taking food and water to these people. D'Youville's impulse in this regard was apparently unique among well-off Montrealers.[14] It was a start.

❧

The fulfillment, of course, is found in the stories of the prostitutes and destitute men. With the ouster of the Charon brothers and thanks to d'Youville's revolutionary presence, suddenly the homeless found an open door in Montreal. The first and later stages of her life dovetail. This sense of service—and her grateful subjects—complete the received image of the early sufferings of d'Youville.

But what do her subjects tell us? In their reactions we discern elements of coercion beneath the fine veil of redemption—and a counternarrative emerges, contesting the hagiography.

The first subject voices emerging from d'Youville's mission are those of her Indian slaves. The Dufrost de LaJemmerais family, like others of its standing, did not hesitate to subordinate previously free societal outsiders for the advancement of the family interest. Records show that Marguerite Dufrost's father, Christophe, owned a *panise* (female Indian slave) from the Great Lakes region who was also named Marguerite. Christophe probably acquired her as an infant sometime between her birth around 1706 and Christophe's own death in 1708. But though her owner, like most female slave owners, was never recorded, she was in fact owned by the widow Marie-Renée Gaulthier, whom she served until the slave's death in 1736 at the age of thirty. The only clue to the enslaved Marguerite's treatment within the Dufrost household was the date of her baptism—shortly before her death.[15] Whether by choice or by force, she did not participate in that part of the family community made accessible by a common faith.

Marguerite Dufrost's youthful experience with her family's slave no doubt prepared her to deal with slave ownership as the newlywed spouse of a trader in captured Indians. Notaries listed François You d'Youville as actually owning only one slave outright, but others who wrote of him mentioned in passing many more—as would be expected from a man plying the slave trade.[16] There seems to have been some overlap between François's slaving and Marguerite's domestic economy. François spent the last years of his life not up-country but living dissolutely in Montreal. Upon his death in 1730 Marguerite inherited three male Indian slaves, who had in all probability been under her direction for some time—an eleven-year-old boy named Pierre, a Patoca male also called Pierre, and another slave unnamed in the records.[17] Their presence in the d'Youville household partially explains how Marguerite managed her transition from a quasi-abandoned trader's wife to an independent storekeeper with time for the charitable activities of a pious young widow with small children. Hagiographers have her bearing these burdens alone.

The determined pace of the widow's activities put considerable demands on her slaves as well. The unnamed male died in 1733. An Indian slave arrived to replace him upon the death of her stepfather, Timothy Sullivan, in 1738. The counternarrative from d'Youville's subjects begins as a singular, stunning, but doomed lawsuit filed by the replacement Indian male slave, whose name appears only as "Indian slave" *(panis)* in the judicial record. The man contested his transfer from the estate of Timothy Sullivan to the ownership of Marguerite d'Youville. As a slave, he could not hope to win his freedom, but he could attempt to maneuver to prevent himself from being transferred—as part of Sullivan's *biens meubles*—to the stepdaughter. Marguerite d'Youville easily defeated this challenge in court and took possession of the audacious slave on the spot.[18]

The slave's litigation may or may not indicate antipathy toward his mistress-to-be, whom he knew well. But it is difficult to imagine a rival motivating factor—given that the only objective that he could have gained was to have been owned by Marguerite d'Youville's mother. The slave was not recorded to have had a family of his own.

Over time other subjects begin to leave traces of possible antipathies. Upon her takeover of the Hôpital-Général, Marguerite d'Youville enforced public morality through the physical control of young prostitutes and *débauchées*. Hitherto, French Canadians had never placed a project such as this on the list of social priorities. Those very few women who existed outside the protective spheres of family or religious community became an unremarkable part of the rough-and-tumble background of frontier life, particularly in the crossroads settlement of Montreal. But as the town (founded as an outpost of piety by Maisonneuve's Société de Notre-Dame) grew, the economy diversified, women began to outnumber men in the colony, and a new consciousness of public virtue began to take root, d'Youville's idea found its champions . . . and detractors.

Sometime in 1748, patrons of local prostitutes in Montreal suddenly found many of the women missing. Inquiries quickly led to the sturdy wooden door of the renovated Hôpital-Général. The decrepit building that until recently had housed only equally decrepit old men now imprisoned the young women of questionable virtue. The bold actions of the prostitutes' jailers quickly led to reaction. In community legend at any rate, a drunken soldier broke through the locked front door of the community and pointed a pistol at d'Youville, demanding the release of the women inmates. D'Youville successfully got rid of the man with pure force of will, ordering the man in a steady and authoritative voice to "leave this house at once!"[19] Whether or not this event actually happened, it must have reflected a genuine feeling in Montreal. The administrative leader of the French colony, the intendant François Bigot (no relation to the priest at Saint Francis) felt enough pressure to make the issue of "Jericho" (the floor housing the prostitutes) part of his overall campaign to shut down the Hôpital-Général and move the dispossessed in d'Youville's care to Quebec.

What is remarkable about the August 17, 1750, letter from Bigot to d'Youville is the indendant's inclusion of specific complaints from within Jericho's walls. The renovations of the Hôpital included twelve rooms on the third floor specifically designed for the purpose of correction. Here the "libertines" were brought. What clearly surprised official observers, the

prostitutes, and their deprived patrons was the harshness of the regime imposed on the young women. In addition to being confined in cells, the prisoners were subjected to an exhausting schedule of domestic work in other
areas of the Hôpital under the direction of the Grey Sister Marie-Joseph
Bénard-Bourjoli, who—at age twenty-five in 1750—was barely older than
most of her charges. Among the disciplinary practices, Bigot specifically
mentioned this custom: "What has most surprised me is that you have
taken upon yourself to cut the hair of the women who have been sent
there. . . . I am glad to teach you, if you do not know it, that it is the business of the superior court to impose such a shameful penalty."[20]

From the point of view of those who sought the rehabilitation of the
débauchées, Sister Bénard's method could be considered ingenious. Women
wore their hair long in New France; the style defined their femininity.
Short hair sent the unmistakable message that the victims had been
stripped of their status as women. Even had they been able to leave the
building, the stigma of shorn hair would have followed them. As they became rehabilitated, then, their hair could be allowed to grow back, with
further haircutting a threat to backsliders.

Only about half of the individuals who took up residence at the Hôpital
between 1750 and 1760 were listed *paralytiques* or *imbéciles,* leaving the remainder free to be engaged in the constant regime of activity and labor.[21]

The latter entered a disciplined regime designed to correct as much as
to provide refuge. If a family entered the Hôpital, the sisters separated men
from women and children because of the dormitory-style accommoda-
tions. Women inmates furnished various forms of community assistance,
but they generally joined one of the main revenue-producing projects:
needle and fabric work ranging from fine decorative pieces to tents for the
French army.[22]

Able-bodied men who had been impoverished—by bad crops during the
1750s, by the displacements of war, or by the hazards of colonial living—
paid a price when they entered the community: infantilization at the hands
of a fictive mother. Men in Catherine Rainville's dormitory were set to work
in the tobacco and beer-making enterprises or assigned general labor. The
escape from maternal control was an early rite of passage for Canadian
boys. From this perspective the psychological impact of the man's symbolic
return to the control of the mother's house becomes clear.

The captive British soldiers, the next contributors to this counternarrative, occupied a more complex station in the community than slaves or de-
tained offenders of morality. Although they, like the *débauchées,* were true
prisoners, these men perhaps had no better reason to think of their situation in terms of rescue than their bitter fellow inmates of Jericho.[23]

To untangle the coexisting threads of the captive soldiers' lives among the Grey Sisters it is necessary to understand the lines of authority present in the institution as of 1753, when the sisters accepted their first prisoners of war.[24] The apex of the authority pyramid within the Hôpital-Général consisted of the mandated maximum of twelve Grey Sisters.[25]

The sisters managed to offset the considerable expense of feeding, clothing, and expanding the physical plant of the growing institution through revenue-producing activities. In addition to the projects already mentioned, the wheat harvests of two farms just outside Montreal owned by the Grey Sisters—one at Chambly and the other at Pointe-Saint-Charles, near the Congrégation Notre-Dame—provided much of the raw foodstuffs consumed by the community. In most years the harvest also delivered a handsome surplus to sell. Wealthy women boarders on the second floor of the main house provided another source of revenue. These widows and unmarried daughters of the leading families in the colony were attracted to the pious but active surroundings of the Hôpital. It may have seemed incongruous for some of New France's leading women to spend years under the same roof as the colony's criminals, captives, and dispossessed. But all these women apparently found it worth paying the very high rents d'Youville charged for a simple single room in order to experience the piousness and social service of the community without permanent obligation.[26]

But the labor of the dispossessed did not completely fill the needs of the Hôpital-Général. Marguerite d'Youville signed numerous contracts for casual labor. The terms of service indicate that "self-indenture" might be a more appropriate description. The laborers essentially bound themselves to the community for a specific term of service in return for shelter, food, and a small salary. Some destitute or spiritually needy Montrealers even became *donnés*, obligating themselves legally to serve the Grey Sisters in perpetuity in exchange for a guaranteed home at the Hôpital and a small stipend. Unlike the short-term dispossessed or ill boarders, the *donnés*, almost all of them men, were not free to leave the community.[27] Like the actual slaves of the Grey Sisters, *donnés* became their property, their *biens meubles*.

How then did the twenty-seven British prisoners fit into this complex milieu? The answer is clouded by conflicting accounts. The memory of the Grey Sisters concerning the British prisoners revolves around one central story, one of rescue through employment. The prisoners received exactly the same treatment as Montreal's poor and dispossessed. There was officially no shame or coercion involved—they were grateful for the opportunity to earn their keep. In the hagiographic accounts, therefore, the Britons were benevolently employed:

This house was a refuge for the needy, and Mother d'Youville never qualified
the term. The plight of the abandoned English soldiers particularly touched
her heart. She could not turn them away from the hospital unbefriended and
unemployed after they had been restored to health. To whom could they go?
What could they do in a country where there was little enough work for loyal
Frenchmen? Small chance they had in finding their way back to British lines
through gauntlets of French and Indian sentries. . . . Her account books reveal that she employed one English soldier on the farm at Chambly, twenty-
one at Pointe-St-Charles, and five at the hospital itself. Unable to pronounce
the hard Anglo-Saxon surnames, she designated foreign employees by their
Christian names, plus the distinction l'Anglais.[28]

To be sure, this interpretation of the appropriate passages of the community's *Ancien Journal* certainly reflected aspects of reality. The prisoners
were, in a sense, "hired" in that they, like the similarly unfree *donnés,* received a small symbolic salary which was in fact paid to the prisoners' actual
redeemer-owners. (This explains why only some captives were recorded as
receiving a salary; the others were owned by the Grey Sisters saw no need
to pay themselves.) And in a sense, the prisoners *had* been rescued from a
potentially worse fate, whether among the Indians or in the disease-ridden
prison in Quebec's upper town that held some of Canada's war prisoners.
But the men were also as unfree as any slave on the sisters' property, clearly
evident in the details of the raw documentary evidence of captivity if not
in the hagiographies.

The first key to the meaning of captivity among the Grey Sisters is the
manner in which the sisters acquired the prisoners. When the Hôtel-Dieu
in Montreal could not meet the demand for its services during the Seven
Years' War, authorities pressed the Hôpital-Général into service caring for
French and English wounded, even though it was not an acute care institution.[29] The sisters housed some of the French soldiers in the rooms that
had once been Jericho on the third floor of the main building, while holding the British patients in a secure room on the first floor. Most of the pris-
oners-turned-servants of the Hôpital-Général seem to have been recruited
from recovered British patients—much as had been the case for the Hôtels-
Dieu during the wars of King William and Queen Anne.

However, many if not most of recovered prisoners were not so recruited—
the patient records reveal survivor after survivor being released to some
unknown custody, presumably back to prison or into the hands of the Indian or French-Canadian individuals who originally held them. This led to
an unacceptable loss of able bodies, as is demonstrated by the sisters' direct entry into the captive market despite their access to many British patients. Marguerite d'Youville herself purchased a man from the Indians,

conducted him back to Montreal, and put him to work in the English ward as a nurse.[30]

This man, known only as "Jean Anglais," worked in the prisoners' ward for at least two years. In entry after entry, the records of the community maintain his generic surname.[31] This hints at another part of the counternarrative. The claim in the annals that Marguerite d'Youville (and presumably her fellow Grey Sisters) were unable to pronounce the English surnames of their British captives strains credulity. D'Youville corresponded not only with the intendant of Canada but with the colonial minister in Paris—through whom her thoughts became known to the king of France as well as the pope in Rome. That this educated, accomplished, and highly motivated woman could be flummoxed by an English surname or alternatively fail to gallicize it is plainly ridiculous—especially in light of the fact that "Jean" and all the others termed "Anglais" worked in her service for months if not years. The naming custom instead could only have served to establish and continually reinforce the hierarchy with the Hôpital-Général community.[32]

The denial of a slave's name and the master's prerogative to assign a new one is, as Orlando Patterson and others have long noted, a fundamental foundation of the institution of slavery. Such an action, these scholars assert, is the master's act of enslaving his property's sense of personal identity.[33] The names "Jean Anglais," "Pierre Anglais," "Edouard Anglais," and so forth constituted a reminder of the captive's outsider and dependent status. "Anglais" as a national identifier became synonymous with "outsider," "dependent," and ultimately "prisoner."[34] The new surname contrasted with the form of addressing women in the Hôpital-Général. The titles of respect "Mère" (for d'Youville), "Soeur" (for her fellow Grey Sisters), and "Madame" or "Mademoiselle" (for the lady boarders and visitors) became synonymous simply with "mistress" when spoken by an English captive.

In this time of social displacement and intercolonial conflict, no spiritual warfare of the sort that marked the lives of Lydia Longley and the Williams family is detectable. No conversion records exist for any men who might have been captives of the Grey Sisters. No grateful narratives of rescue were written by returned captives. No enraptured New England girls joined the Grey Sisters. In Montreal young captive Protestant females, who in earlier wars would have been eagerly sought out by the religious communities, languished and sometimes died in filthy jails just steps from convent walls. Young men who would have been considered subjects for adoption and resettlement died in the same prisons.

The Grey Sisters fought a battle of survival on behalf of themselves and those in their charge. They did what they could for displaced and dependent outsiders, but also marshaled available captive labor to better their chances of succeeding in their wartime mission. In this context, one understands the Grey Sisters' practicality in dispatching newly enslaved prisoners to work: twenty-one on their farm at Pointe-Saint-Charles, one at Chambly, and five at the main house.

The treatment received by these twenty-seven men was consistent with other kinds of bonded labor within the institution. At the main house of the Grey Sisters, we know, Jean Anglais worked in the semiskilled position of *infirmier;* others were employed in simple but strenuous menial tasks. At least one captive, and probably all of them at one time or another, were recorded to have "worked on our walls and kept our grounds."[35] The "walls" refer to part of the ongoing construction at the main hospital house and property at Pointe-à-Callières.[36] The extra strain of the wartime inhabitants of the Hôpital—and the accompanying increase in available labor—had prompted d'Youville in 1754 to finally undertake a long-desired project: a seven-foot-high stone wall surrounding the entire fourteen-acre property. Chroniclers point out that the constant coming and going of the needy and the curious had concerned the sisters, who desired to regulate inmates and visitors more closely.[37]

In building this wall, the captives worked directly under the supervision of the Grey Sisters. To save precious funds the sisters did much of the work themselves. "[The sisters] were seen," one writer recounts, "carrying stones in their aprons, mortar in pails and heating lime in the hospital." The captives compelled to "keep our grounds" had the seasonal jobs of gardening and maintaining the fourteen acres inside the wall. In winter, servants undertook tasks such as making repairs, shoveling snow, gathering fuel, and hauling water. In all this work the British captives were overseen directly by one or more sisters.

That d'Youville parceled out no fewer than twenty-one British prisoners to Jacques Le Ber's former farm at Pointe-Saint-Charles speaks to the importance of the land's large-scale production and to the dramatic shortfall of labor then experienced by the community. Most of the common British soldiers had been probably raised on farms and needed little on-the-job training.

The Grey Sisters preferred to assign one of their own as overseer. The captives at Pointe-Saint-Charles worked under the direction of Marie-Joseph Gosselin, who, aged twenty-five in 1755, was the youngest of the Grey Sisters. Apparently the only supervisor at Pointe-Saint-Charles until the appointment of a foreman to assist her in 1757, Gosselin came from a farming background—as did her counterpart of a previous age, Lydia

Madeleine Longley, who was still living in Montreal in 1755 at the age of eighty-one. Like many of the early farming sisters of the Congrégation Notre-Dame, Marie-Joseph was born on the peaceful and fertile Île d'Orléans. Her father, Michel, worked his plot at Saint-Jean with the assistance of four daughters, his only children who survived to adulthood.[38]

That all the Gosselin children were girls was fortunate for the Grey Sisters: Marie-Joseph's early farming experience at Saint-Jean must have been varied and considerable. Gosselin assumed a responsibility in her mid-twenties that her peers at the Congrégation did not attempt until they had apprenticed as *soeurs fermières* for years or decades. Further, she took on these challenges at a time of chaos in the colony, when the war with Britain was being fought in desperation. And her charges were not relatively compliant servants, but enemy prisoners, twenty-one young men, and perhaps even some older officers as well, held against their will.

Supervising numerous laborers under any circumstances, and especially on a relatively large farm, was a hard and demanding job. Marie-Joseph Gosselin had to plan the work for the day, week, month, and season, respond quickly and correctly to the vagaries of weather, deal with and pay suppliers and middlemen, and see to the feeding, health, and discipline of the prisoners. The twenty-one British soldiers did not come to Pointe-Saint-Charles all at once but had been acquired gradually. Gosselin continually had to receive new arrivals, orient them in the work at hand, and see that they adjusted productively to their new circumstances. It could not have been easy. Gosselin's life on that farm, more than perhaps any other lived individual captor's narrative, demonstrates the joining of competent professional judgment with the assertiveness necessary to successfully and simultaneously act as a farm manager, caretaker, overseer, and jailer—all performed as the lone woman in an otherwise all-male environment.

And how did the soldiers react to their imprisonment—bizarre even by their own standards? Circumstances had changed radically since the days when John Gillett worked on the Congrégation's farm nearby. These twenty-one men were not captive freeholders, resentful of their captors' religion and longing to reestablish themselves at home. They were for the most part young soldiers, many of them conscripts, simply wishing to survive their captivity. However strange they may have found the community that held them and the woman who supervised them, they were probably relieved to find themselves in a situation that offered a strong possibility of survival. They knew their fellow soldiers to be dying in nearby prisons—places notorious for their exposure to the heat and cold and unchecked pestilence. As hard as they must have worked at Pointe-Saint-Charles, the men could easily have regarded their captivity at least as a partial blessing.

The blessing does not sufficiently explain the soldiers' captivity, however. Why twenty-one mostly young men, regardless of their status of purchased prisoners, would consent to obey a single young woman for months and ultimately years on end cannot be explained solely by gratitude; they feared something worse. Suppose they succeeded in escaping from Pointe-Saint-Charles. Then what? The Saint Lawrence Valley crawled with armed French soldiers and Canadian militia, and at least a hundred miles of forest separated them from home—a forest inhabited by a considerable number of French-allied Indians. Recapture—if they had avoided starvation—would certainly mean greater hardship, if not death, among the Indians or back in a Canadian prison.

The gendered aspect of their captivity had, however, in some ways intensified since the days of John Gillett, potentially adding to the captives' unease with their situation. They were still victims, like Gillett, of a vivid power inversion, whether they were working at Pointe-Saint-Charles, at the farm at Chambly, on the Grey Sisters' grounds, or as *infirmiers* within the Hôpital-Général. But what had been in 1696 the province of frontierswomen had become by 1755 a public spectacle. The rise of a more genteel and separate women's culture in New France—parallel to the one taking hold simultaneously in the British colonies to the south—had made the sight of captured men working for nuns one of the most favored spectacles in Montreal. The concerned Grey Sisters decided to build their wall—but in the meantime the gaze and mockery of the audience must have mortified the workers.

The round-the-clock female supervision conducted by d'Youville's Grey Sisters was even more demanding and austere than that of Bourgeoys's Congrégation sisters of a previous era. And the Grey Sisters offered none of Bourgeoys's welcoming entreaties to cultural conversion. These new public mothers had fully anticipated the need for physical coercion to support their universal social service and had built it into their institution. From their first arrival, the British soldiers encountered women captors who, although badly outnumbered by their subordinates, were more than able to incorporate them within their civic mission. The Grey Sisters offered only survival—provided the prisoner worked for it.

When the British prisoners are considered, the gulf between the hagiography and counternarrative is fully exposed. The *Ancien Journal* of the community concludes that rescued soldiers repaid their gratitude to Marguerite d'Youville in 1759 by asking British invaders to spare their building.[39] But despite the prisoners' acceptance of the hard bargain, the sisters treated their captives in ways that seem unlikely to have inspired such loyalty. The Hôpital-Général's record of expenses and income from October

1756 to October 1757 includes the receipt for the *sale* of a British prisoner. The Grey Sisters yielded a fairly good *"profit sur l'Anglais acheté."*[40] That the man was listed as "purchased" implies a relatively quick turnaround from purchase to sale. The record indicates that Marguerite d'Youville and the Grey Sisters *engaged in the captive trade*. This revelation puts a new light on the events previously described. When Marguerite d'Youville went to buy Jean Anglais from the Indians, was this a rescue mission or simply part of the trade she felt to be necessary to sustain her community? That a captive could be sold for profit indicates that rescue was not the only motivation in the Grey Sisters' minds. D'Youville represented an era during which French Canada ceased making overtures to cultural outsiders. She saw her mission as assisting the poor of Montreal. To that end, she held both Indian slaves and British prisoners for the same purpose: not for conversion but for work.

❧

This account of the Grey Sisters illustrates more than the clash of hagiography and its countering voices. Beyond it is the captors' narrative. If Marguerite d'Youville and her associates found innovative ways to render the captives' narrative speechless, what was their contribution to a captors' narrative for the new era? Like the capable and apparently fearless Marie-Joseph Gosselin, Catherine Rainville transformed the scope of their own lives and service by their control of male subjects. The harnessing of male labor allowed Rainville and her counterparts to enter the marketplace as the producers of a diverse array of goods they could not have created had they overseen women and children. In a larger sense, Rainville's occupation allowed the Grey Sisters to universalize their service to the colony and produce the goods needed for self-sufficiency.

Beyond these redefinitions of community and the proximate goal of physical survival, there remains the sisters' construction of the role of women religious as public mothers. The stone walls the sisters and captives built together were intended in part to keep away the annoying public, eager to behold the working sisters and their subjects. Nevertheless, all the inhabitants of the hospital remained visible to those visitors who entered through the front door. While the infantilized destitute and captive prisoners may have felt the sting of humiliation at the inescapable public display, such visits proved of intense interest to Montreal's female elite, particularly those who were inspired to become boarders. An unmarried young woman or a widow, by making a simple payment of rent, could go beyond the simple piety and patriotism that chroniclers have always assumed motivated them. As full participants in the maternal roles of the Grey Sisters, the women boarders enthusiastically engaged in the corrective redemption of the fallen men as well as women. And they fulfilled their patriotism by helping to detain and oversee captive enemy soldiers and officers. The Grey Sisters' version of universally applied public motherhood had, knowingly or not, provided an outlet for the untapped energies and purpose of Montreal's wartime women. And by accessing this resource of female energy, the Grey Sisters cleverly extended the reach of women's authority at their institution.

As for the foundress d'Youville herself, there remain two opposing stories—a received hagiography and an assembled counternarrative. Which comes closer to the captors' own conception of their lived narrative? How did d'Youville and her companions understand their own actions?

Marguerite d'Youville accessed and modified—to the point of redefining—the cultural form of a redemption/coercion complex in a way that suited her times. Like Marguerite Bourgeoys, she did not seek power by rendering service; she sought service through the exercise of the authority she had created. But where Bourgeoys had sought to unify the spheres of service and authority into an organic whole, and the culturally inclusive "little life" of her community remained seamlessly and mutually dependent on its teaching mission, d'Youville demonstrated by her actions that service and authority were separate and culturally exclusive. More precisely, d'Youville regarded her service in what seems to be Augustinian terms—ultimately serving the City of God by exercising her power in the City of Man. In this way she found a singular resolution to the paradox inherent in the lives of the hospital sisters. Lastly, as d'Youville appreciated (but her hagiographers did not), the City of Man demanded a stricter type of control than her hagiographers understood. Yet her eyes were more firmly on the City of God than her subjects could see. Her bridge between the two cities was the community of women she formed in her own image—a community that used the redemption and coercion of captives as an instrument to accomplish its earthly purposes.

CHAPTER FOUR

The Seigneury: Obscuring Marguerite and Louise Guyon

I have shown kindness to the English captives as we were capacitated
and have bought two captives of the indians and sent them to Boston
and have one now with us, and he shall go also when a convenient
opportunity presents and he desires it.
—note from Marguerite Guyon to Colonel Hathorne

Canada's women captors obtained captive men mainly to replace contract and indentured male labor in the domestic economy. The women themselves replaced their trader-husbands and soldier-fathers, absent for months on end, in running that economy. But this practice produced a special type of conflict and misunderstanding between captor and captive. An Anglo-American prisoner in a domestic home might hope that his duty would be to perform the economic role of the absent husband or father. When instead his mistress assumed control of the household and property, a captive's account often distorted reality as he reconstructed his memory to affirm his sense of masculinity. Meanwhile his woman captor might seize the opportunity of a captive placed in her path to envisage greater well-being. *Religieuses* managed their material life for the sake of souls, but secular French-Canadian women managed souls in service of their family's material ambitions—whether those ambitions were to prosper or simply to survive. Such would be the case with John Gyles and his two Canadian mistresses, sisters Louise and Marguerite Guyon.

In a colony of town-dwelling noblewomen and soil-tilling habitants, sometimes overlooked in stories of the ancien régime are accounts of the Canadian version of what the early modern English would have termed the "middling sort," that is, skilled artisans and small landholders. The patriarch of the Guyon family of the Beauport seigneury, on the north shore of the Saint Lawrence immediately below Quebec, combined both of these roles, and the fates of his children and grandchildren demonstrate the range of possibilities of lives begun in New France's middle strata.

Jean Guyon, born in 1592 near Chartres, arrived in Quebec around 1634 as one of the first indentured servants in the colony. A master mason by trade, Jean no doubt proved valuable in the new settlement. In addition to his local work as a mason, he managed to acquire from Beauport's seigneur Robert Giffart a small subfief on the Buisson River. With his wife, Mathurine Robin, he raised nine children, seven of whom survived to adulthood.[1]

Some of Jean's sons worked on the holding at Buisson, but Simon Guyon followed his father into an artisan's life. After learning the trade of a carpenter, Simon lived first in Beaupré and later at Château-Richer, settlements along the Saint Lawrence below Beauport. Simon and his wife Louise Racine raised six children.[2] Three of their five daughters—Marie, Charlotte, and Marie-Angelique—married men of circumstances much like their father. The eldest child and only son, Jean, achieved a remarkable upward mobility of a sort more easily accomplished in the less competitive milieu of Canada than in France. Jean Guyon studied humanities at the Quebec seminary and later philosophy and theology in Paris. He returned to Quebec in 1682, aged twenty-three, after suffering an illness in France. Upon completing his studies in Quebec, he was ordained by Bishop Laval. It seems he served as a Quebec canon for only about a year before leaving for France again as the secretary and representative of Laval—a highly visible and responsible position for a carpenter's son. He also received, like Pierre Le Ber, local notice as an artist, specializing in religious portraits and watercolors of indigenous plants and trees. He died in France in 1687.[3]

Simon and Louise's second daughter, Marguerite Guyon, assumed the role of household mistress at an early age, a common characteristic among Canada's women captors. After her brother entered the seminary and her mother died, Marguerite assisted her older sister, Marie, in running the household. Marie's marriage, followed closely by her father's death, left the seventeen-year-old Marguerite as the head of the household with the responsibility of raising three younger sisters: Louise, age fourteen; Charlotte, eleven; and Marie-Angelique, nine. She had the advantage, though, of having Marie's family and her Guyon relatives nearby.

Perhaps because of her responsibilities, Marguerite delayed her marriage until two years after that of her younger sister Louise. At only sixteen, Louise married a local Château-Richer man named Charles Thibault, the brother of Marie Guyon's husband, Guillaume.[4] Marguerite herself married in January 1686. Although her two youngest sisters were still dependent on her, perhaps the pressure of providing for them was relieved by her making a brilliant match. Unlike Marie and Louise, who had married local men of modest means, Marguerite wed Louis Damours de Chaffours, the holder of several seigneuries and a descendant of French nobility.[5]

Although Louis's father, Mathieu Damours de Chauffours, claimed ancestors among the nobles of Anjou, the name "Chauffours" originated from a family holding in Brittany. Mathieu arrived in Quebec in 1651 and was appointed a charter member of the Sovereign Council in 1663, where he served until his death thirty-two years later. Taking full advantage of the Canadian waiver on the French law preventing the nobility from engaging in commercial affairs, Mathieu took advantage of his fur-trading license granted in 1681 and ruffled the feathers of some of his fellow oligarchs in the pursuit of his profits.[6] His principal legacy to the colony, though, was probably a series of highly energetic sons, many of whom left their mark as leading merchants, soldiers, and landholders/developers.

Four of these sons—Louis, Mathieu *fils*, René, and Bernard—decided to try their fortunes in Acadia, an area that presented opportunities and hazards different from those faced by the inhabitants of the Saint Lawrence Valley. The slightly milder Atlantic climate offered a longer growing season, and the Saint John and Annapolis Rivers gave direct access to the Atlantic—a substantial advantage over the Saint Lawrence, which was choked with ice for six months of the year.[7] But the disadvantages more than outweighed these favorable factors in the eyes of most. Acadia's remoteness from the main fur-trading routes would relegate the area to a permanent backwater of New France—fishing being the more promising industry. Most potentially troubling was the military menace represented by the English colonies. Until the 1750s the English were either unable or unwilling to mount a successful direct attack on the Saint Lawrence region, whether via the forests of Abenaki or Mohawk country or up the great river itself from its mouth to Quebec. Acadia, on the other hand, offered an inviting target for official or private shows of English force, sometimes in response to French and Indian raiding. The English undertook occasional military expeditions into Acadia in the decades before its fall to British control in 1710.

Although mindful of these factors, the Damours brothers decided that the large grants of land they received were worthy of their full attention.

As seigneurs, both of them made land grants to new settlers. Unlike France, however, where seigneurial dues could be a source of significant income, the pittance asked by Canadian landholders reflected the abundance of available land and the paucity of willing habitants. Seigneurs in frontier areas instead expected the principal advantage in making grants to be mutual protection: a seigneur's habitants usually made an effective militia force.

Louis, Mathieu *fils,* and René settled along the rivière Saint-Jean (today the Saint John River) in what is today south-central New Brunswick—Louis and Mathieu on adjoining tracts on the Jemseg Peninsula about sixty miles inland and René on his extensive holding at Medoctec at least eighty miles further upriver. All three men worked as serious farmers—the remoteness of their location demanded no less—but they also each engaged profitably in the local fur trade with the Maliseet Abenaki and Micmac. Each man also introduced illegal liquor sales into this local trade, at least according to officially recorded allegations made by rivals.[8]

The ceremony in which Louis Damours married Marguerite Guyon on January 10, 1686, proved highly distinctive. It was, in fact, a double ceremony, with Louis's brother Mathieu marrying Marguerite's sister Louise. (Louise's first husband, Charles Thibault, had died the previous September; they were childless.)[9] Wasting no time, Louise Guyon joined her sister in the social sphere of the Quebec noblesse. The Damours brothers were quite taken with the Guyon sisters, despite the women's modest backgrounds. (Accounts of Louise after her second widowhood indicate that she was strikingly attractive.)[10] The two couples, married in Quebec on that January day, left together to seek their fortunes in Acadia at Jemseg.

❖

The details of how a young Puritan man from Maine named John Gyles would come to be in the hands of Marguerite Guyon seem tragically familiar. Gyles had been born into a family of comparatively greater wealth and prominence than that of his future mistress from Château-Richer. Years later, he described his origins:

> The flourishing state of New England (before the unhappy Eastern wars) drew my father hither whose first settlement was on Kennebeck River at a place called Merrymeeting Bay, where he dwelt for some years till, on the death of my grandparents, he, with his family, returned to England to settle his affairs. This done, he came over with design to have returned to his farm, but on his arrival at Boston the Eastern Indians had begun their hostilities. He therefore began a settlement on Long Island. The air of that place not

so well agreeing with his constitution, and the Indians being peaceable, he again proposed to resettle his lands in Merrymeeting Bay, but, finding that place deserted and that plantations were going on at Pemmaquid, he purchased several tracts of land from the inhabitants there. . . . [At Pemaquid] he was [later] commissioned chief justice of the same by Governor Duncan. He was a strict sabbatizer and met with considerable difficulty in the discharge of his office from the immoralities of the people who had long lived lawless. He laid out no inconsiderable income which he had annually from England on the place and at last lost his life there.[11]

Thomas Gyles lost his life in the summer of 1689 during one of the first raids of King William's War. Although the spot in Maine he had chosen for resettlement suited his constitution better than Long Island, it was also perhaps the most exposed of all English settlements in North America. The settlers had founded Pemaquid on the Muscongus Bay at the western edge of the wide Penobscot River estuary.[12] Whereas places like Groton, Deerfield, and Haverhill certainly lay at the edge of the English-speaking world, about two hundred miles of Indian territory separated them from their rivals on the Saint Lawrence. But the Penobscot region had long been claimed by the French as their own. Jesuit missionaries, most recently Louis Pierre Thury, had been active on the upper Penobscot for years, and the French civilian settlements of Acadia had by that time reached the lower rivière Saint-Jean.

It was almost inevitable that the French authorities in Quebec and Paris, along with their Abenaki allies, would set their sights on the offending English settlements on the Penobscot once North American hostilities began in 1689. Accordingly, on August 5 of that year a mixed group of French and Eastern Abenaki attacked the houses of Pemaquid. One of the first English captives taken reportedly revealed the presence of the "principal citizen" of Pemaquid, Mr. Gyles, and the Abenaki quickly translated this intelligence into tangible results. The Gyles family at that time consisted of Thomas, his wife (whose Christian name has not survived in the records), and at least six children: Thomas Jr., then about seventeen years old; James, fifteen; John, eleven; Samuel, nine; Mary, eight; and Margaret, five.[13] Thomas Jr., then outside of Pemaquid working with a late-summer haying party, did not encounter the raiders. Samuel also managed to escape. The rest of the family was captured in the attack, Thomas Sr. having been wounded during the fighting.[14] Gyles wrote later of his last encounter with his father:

[The party of captors and captives] marched about a quarter of a mile and made a halt and brought my father to us. . . . My father replied that he was a dying man and wanted no favor [of the Indians] but to pray with his children which, being granted, he recommended us to the protection and blessing of God Almighty; then [he] gave us the best advice and took his leave for this life, hoping in God that we should meet in a better. He parted with a cheerful voice but looked very pale by reason of his great loss of blood which boiled out of his shoes. The Indians led him aside. I heard the blows of the hatchet, but neither shriek nor groan. (I afterwards heard that he had five or seven shot holes through his waistcoat or jacket and that the Indian covered him with some boughs.) (97)[15]

The captors then separated the surviving members of the family, who, after traveling a few days through the Maine forest, encountered one another briefly before a final parting. Perhaps it was the faith of his father that caused John Gyles to have kept his religious beliefs through the nine years of captivity to come. That he emerged from those years with a clear conscience is further testament to the hold of the father on the young mind of John Gyles. Soon after the final encounter with his family, John wrote of the influence of his mother as well. At that reunion, Gyles met a Jesuit, perhaps Thury, with "a great mind to buy" him:[16]

The Jesuit gave me a biscuit which I put into my pocket and dare not eat but buried it under a log, fearing that he had put something in it to make me love him, for I was very young and had heard much of the Papists torturing the Protestants, etc., so that I hated the sight of a Jesuit. When my mother heard the talk of my being sold to a Jesuit, she said to me, "Oh my dear child! If it were God's will, I had rather follow you to your grave, or never see you more in this world than you should be sold to a Jesuit, for a Jesuit will ruin you, body and soul." And it pleased God to grant her request, for she never saw me any more, though she and my two little sisters were, after several years' captivity, redeemed; she died before I returned. And my brother who was taken with me was, after several years' captivity, most barbarously tortured to death by the Indians. (99–100)

Despite Gyles's phrasing, he was never "owned" by this or any other Jesuit. The Maliseets instead took him to one of their settlements in the vicinity of what is now Woodstock, New Brunswick (very near the current New Brunswick–Maine border about 120 miles directly inland), a place that would serve as a base for the sporadically mobile life of his captors. The frontage on the rivière Saint-Jean in this area, within a few years of John Gyles's arrival, would lie within the seigneurial grant of René Damours. John Gyles lived among the Maliseet Abenaki during the balance of his adolescence, from his capture at the age of eleven until he was seventeen or eighteen, when the Indians sold him to the French. His liminality as a

captive is evident in the way he describes his treatment. Returned male captives writing during the mid and late eighteenth century have discussed
how being adopted promoted them from fictive females to males. Gender
metaphors describe their transition from "drudgery" (women's work) to
"freedom" (activities of men).[17] However, John Gyles's attempt to describe
his activities in captivity to his family (the original readers of his narrative)
allow us today, armed with at least some knowledge of Abenaki ethnogra-
phy, to reconstruct his fictive female status. Unless Gyles otherwise informed his readers of the gender divide among the Abenaki, it is unlikely
that his audience would recognize the significance of his work within the
community. The first work Gyles told of doing was during the winter hunt,
when his captors employed him "carrying burdens"—commonly women's
work on extended seasonal migrations (103). Gyles also mentioned in
passing how women and captives worked together in ceremonial as well as
practical ways on the hunt. Upon the arrival of the hunters with meat, Gyles
explains that "an old squaw and captive, if any present, must stand without
the wigwam, shaking their hands and body as in a dance, and singing, '*We-
gage oh nelo woh*,' which if Englished would be 'Fat is my eating'" (104). The
next summer, his first full planting season in captivity, his detailed description of planting, tending, and processing corn clearly indicates that
early in his captivity he functioned economically as a female. He continued to do so for the next year, when his principal employment was carrying water and cutting wood (105–6, 108, 111–12). The sole exception to
his consignment to the female sphere was fishing, in which he was accompanied by Indian boys and men. Although he describes the men's activities of hunting, trading, and war making, Gyles never actually states that
he participated in them.

While the meanings of the routine work with Indian women might have
escaped Gyles's original audience, the author did present women as actors
in his narrative more often than men. He presented women most often as
an archetypal revenge-obsessed, monstrous female. In his account of life
among the Maliseets he made no attempt to assess the cultural meanings
of the participation of "squaws" in adoption-like rites. But he did include
an account of a "barbarous" old squaw "who ever endeavoured to outdo all
others in cruelty to captives. Wherever she came into a wigwam where any
poor, naked, starved captives were sitting near the fire, if they were grown
persons, she would privately take up a shovel of hot coals and throw them
into their bosom, or the young ones she would take by one hand or leg and
drag them through the fire" (113).

Despite its obvious resort to the stock character of an old female tor-
mentor, the passage indicates that Abenaki women had free access to cap-

tives and greatly affected their lives. Some women, of course, sought to ease the captive's burden. Gyles himself, when describing Abenaki religious rites, notes that the woman who introduced him to these customs was "an old squaw who was kind to captives" (114).

During his six years of captivity, Gyles became accustomed to see his female captors as agents. No Pocahontas-style maiden of salvation appears in the narrative, but Gyles does describe an instance in which a young woman saved him from drowning—not the gesture of a love-struck maiden but a simple utilitarian act saving a captive, related without ornament by the grateful author (111).[18]

Whereas his relationship to women remained wary, resigned, formal, or at best ambivalent, Gyles made it abundantly clear that he enjoyed comfortable relationships with other young men. At one point during his captivity, at least two other New England captives lived at the same Maliseet settlement as Gyles:

> But my most intimate and dear companion was one John Evans, a young man taken from Quochecho. We, as often as we could, met together and made known our grievances to each other, which seemed to ease our minds. But when it was known by the Indians, we were strictly examined apart and falsely accused that we were contriving to desert, but we were too far from the sea to have any thought of that, and when they found that our story agreed, we received no punishment. An English captive girl about this time (who was taken by Madokawando) would often falsely accuse us of plotting to desert, but we made the truth so plainly appear that she was checked and we released. (108)

We do not know the identity of the "English captive girl," but it seems that a potentially fatal tension existed between Gyles and his only female counterpart. As readers of the narrative had learned a few pages earlier, the torture and execution of James Gyles, John's brother, had been caused by his attempted escape from the Indians. In the mind of John Gyles, then, the false accusations laid by the English girl essentially amounted to attempted murder. We do not know the cause of these events—whether they resulted from the girl's maliciousness, from her mistaken impression that Gyles had transculturated and represented a threat, or from a narrative distortion on the part of Gyles.[19] But it is likely that Gyles accommodated his captors' wishes only to keep alive; he apparently never considered marrying among the Maliseet or accepting the form of Catholicism that most of them practiced.

Gyles's retention in the female economic sphere is one indication of his continuing liminal status. Another is the story of the events leading to the

end of his sojourn among the Maliseet: "When about six years of my dole-
ful captivity had passed, my second Indian master died, whose squaw and
my first Indian master disputed whose slave I should be, and some mali-
cious person advised them to end the quarrel by putting a period to my
life. But honest father Simon, the priest of the river, told them that it
would be a heinous crime and advised them to sell me to the French"
(124).

Gyles described himself as a "slave" to the end. (And he recounts matter-
of-factly that he stood an even chance at ending up permanently enslaved
to a woman on the cusp of his adult years.) At first, Gyles, now seventeen
or eighteen years old, was horrified to the point of tears at being sold to
"people of that persuasion which my dear mother so detested" (125). But
his initial aversion to the religion of the French Canadians (perhaps Gyles
did not take the nominal Catholicism of most Maliseets as seriously) soon
waned, once he was restored to the sphere of European civilization.

At some point very early in 1696, Gyles's first "Indian master" and the
solomonic Father Simon de la Place accompanied the young Englishman
to a French house on the rivière Saint-Jean (124–25).[20] The young couple who owned the house entertained John warmly. After spending the
night, the Indian and the priest remained while the captive was sent upriver about eighteen miles to a second house. Father Simon joined Gyles
later that day and then informed him, kindly, that he now belonged to the
French husband and wife with whom he had spent the first night. This couple was Louis Damours de Chauffours and his wife Marguerite Guyon.[21]
The second house, at which Father Simon broke the news to John, was certainly that of Mathieu Damours de Chauffours and Louise Guyon.[22] The
two French couples had been establishing their adjoining places on the
river for just over a decade.

❀

After the transfer of John Gyles to Damours and Guyon, the tone of his
captivity narrative suddenly changes. Gyles's fictive female status among
the Maliseets helps us comprehend the exultation evident in his characterization of his new employment: "My French master had a great trade
with the Indians which suited me very well, I being thorough in the languages of the tribes at Cape Sable's and St. John's. I had not lived long with
this gentleman before he committed to me the keys to his store, etc., and
my whole employment was trading and hunting, in which I acted faithfully
for my master and never knowingly wronged him to the value of one far-
thing. They spake to me so frequently in Indian that it was sometime be-

fore I was perfect in the French tongue. Monsieur generally had his goods from the man-of-war which came there annually from France" (126).

In this section Gyles fully restores himself to the male sphere and the narrative figure of himself to the active voice. But this transition comes at the price of a sharp decline in his forthrightness about the conditions of his captivity. His master, Louis Damours—the "monsieur" of the passage above—seems to have sole direction of Gyles's new employment. But the passage also indicates that Marguerite Guyon as well as her husband spoke to Gyles in the Indian tongue. The only reason she would have learned "Indian" herself would be to conduct business with the Natives as did her husband. This admission casts doubt on Gyles's characterization of Monsieur Damours as the sole operator of the stores and the trade that supplied them.

At this point the captivity narrative of John Gyles began to divert attention from the life and interests of Marguerite Guyon. The Damours-Guyon farm at Jemseg, the rented lands of the seigneurial grant, and the fur-trading stores were not the enterprise solely of Louis Damours but very much a partnership of husband and wife. The life of a rural seigneur, especially in settings this remote, demanded skills in land management, settler affairs, and trade. Louis and Marguerite are a classic example of a seigneurial couple functioning as an optimal economic unit.

The captor's narrative begins with this economic function. Marguerite's signatures in the notarial records of the family business signify her partnership with her husband and prove that by the time of Gyles's arrival she had extensive experience acting as her husband's agent in his absence.[23] Seigneurial wives often compensated for disruptions in the lives of their husbands. For men such as Louis Damours, business, politics, and military service required them in some years to be absent from home for many months. Such absences were common in the caste to which Damours belonged, that of enterprising traders and ambitious soldiers.

Gyles was correct when he emphasized that he had "not lived long" with Damours before being entrusted with the store. He must have made a remarkable and immediate impression on his new owners; Gyles could not have lived at Jemseg more than two or three months before Louis Damours had to leave. He had joined a French and Indian military expedition aimed, coincidentally, at Gyles's birthplace—a garrison established at the site of the 1689 Pemaquid attack.

Gyles mentions the participation of Louis Damours in the campaign, which began in June and reached its climax in mid-August, in matter-of-fact terms and almost in passing. In view of Gyles's loyalty to the place and faith of his birth, there is no reason to suspect he provided intelligence to his French master. The high regard Gyles held for Damours before and after the Pemaquid expedition strongly suggests the latter did not exert undue pressure on the captive for possibly helpful information. Whatever thoughts Gyles might have had about the fate of his surviving relatives, after this new raid in the summer of 1696, are buried in the laconic early New England narrative form (126, 126 n. 50). In fact, the Pemaquid expedition proved successful for the French, who took the garrison (but no civilian captives).[24]

During the summer of 1696, John Gyles and Marguerite Guyon experienced their first period of sharing the Jemseg house. Gyles's portrays Guyon as conforming to an Indian captor archetype adjusted to fit Canadian captivities: that of the benevolent mother. The first test for benevolent mothers in the eyes of their fictive sons is often the gift of clothing. The failure of Canadians to properly clothe New England captives recently arrived from life among the Indians could become the focus of a bitterly contentious power struggle. But Marguerite Guyon passed this test brilliantly: "A few days [after arrival at the house] madam made me an osnaburg shirt and French cap, and a coat out of one of my master's old coats. Then I threw away my greasy blanket and Indian flap" (125).

Gyles clearly wished to present Guyon in the maternal role, and there was some basis for this characterization. Marguerite Guyon's life was punctuated by pregnancies and childbirth. The couple had their first daughter, named Louise after Marguerite's sister, around 1683. A second daughter, Madeleine, followed in 1687.[25] Gyles turned eighteen sometime during 1696, and Marguerite Guyon was thirty when the New Englander first arrived. Although too young to be Gyles's mother, the *Canadienne* must have seemed maternal to the young man so long removed from European culture. First, she was, in fact, a mother. Her first two daughters, Louise and Madeleine, had, though, in all likelihood died by 1696. But by the early fall of that year the family had two little girls, two-year-old Marie-Josèphe and the newborn Marie-Charlotte.[26] Second, because Marguerite was his mistress, Gyles would consider her a fictive mother. By conflating the roles of mistress and mother, a servant could legitimize the authority of the woman he served, no matter the age difference.

Later that year Louis Damours was once again the absent seigneur. The veterans of the Pemaquid expedition could not have returned to their Acadian homes much before September, but by early October Gyles was writing that "the gentleman whom I lived with, was gone to France" (128). The occasion for this notation was the English raid up the rivière Saint-Jean, mounted in retaliation for the Pemaquid attack.[27] The objective of the commander, Colonel John Hathorne (who four years earlier had achieved renown as a judge in the Salem witch trials), was Fort Nashwaak, also called

Fort Saint-Joseph. Located about fifty miles upriver from Jemseg, Fort
Nashwaak then served as the seat of French government in Acadia.[28] Louis
Damours had chosen an inopportune moment to attend to business in
France. His entire seigneury lay in the direct path of the attacking English
force, which numbered three ships and about two hundred men.

John Gyles described his actions and those of Marguerite during the attack:

> Madam advised with me. She desired me to nail a paper on the door of the
> house containing as follows: "I entreat the general of the English not to burn
> my house or barn nor destroy my cattle. I don't suppose that such an army
> come up this river to destroy a few inhabitants but for the fort above us. I
> have shown kindness to the English captives as we were capacitated and have
> bought two captives of the indians and sent them to Boston and have one
> now with us, and he shall go also when a convenient opportunity presents
> and he desires it." This done, madam said to me, "Little English, we have
> shown you kindness, and now it lies in your power to serve or disserve us as
> you know where our goods are hid in the woods and that monsieur is not at
> home. I could have sent you to the fort and put you under confinement, but
> my respects to you and your assurance of love to us has disposed me to con-
> fide in you, persuaded you will not hurt us nor our affairs. And now if you
> will not run away to the English who are coming up the river but serve our
> interest, I will acquaint monsieur of it on his return from France, which will
> be very pleasing to him, and I now give my word that you shall have liberty
> to go to Boston on the first opportunity (if you desire it) or that any other
> favor in my power shall not be denied you." I replied, "Madam, it is contrary
> to the nature of the English to requite evil for good. I shall endeavor to serve
> you and your interest. I shall not run to the English, but if I am taken by them
> shall willingly go with them and yet endeavor not to disserve you either in
> your person or your goods." (128–29)

While the gallantry remembered at a distance of three decades may
bring a smile to readers today, the passage exposes some of the power dy-
namics in their relationship. Here, the captor's narrative struggles to
emerge from these inscribed memories. Marguerite Guyon conveys an el-
egant mercy. She makes her captive at once her human shield and her
helper, and we learn that Gyles was not the first prisoner to serve Marguerite and Louis's interests. Gyles himself casts the role of a captive into
an altogether new light. The question is not whether to submit or resist but
whether to serve or disserve. It was a profoundly new question in the history of the captivities. Gyles resolved it by choosing here to transition from
the passive Indian captive to an active agent among the French:

This said, we embarked and went in a large boat and canoe two or three miles up an eastern branch of the river that comes from a large pond, and in the evening [we] sent down four hands to make discovery. And while they were sitting in the house, the English surrounded it and took one of the four; the other three made their escape in the dark through the English soldiers and came to us and gave a surprising account of affairs. Again madam said to me, "Little English, now you can go from us, but I hope you will remember your word." I said, "Madam, be not concerned for I will not leave you in the strait." She said, "I know not what to do with my two poor little babes." I said, "Madam, the sooner we embark and go over the great pond the better." Accordingly, we embarked and went over the pond. . . . Hearing no report of the great guns for several days, I, with two others, went down to our house to make discovery, where we found our young lad who was taken by the English when they went up the river. For the general [Hathorne] was so honorable that, on reading the note on our door, he ordered that the house and barn should not be burned nor their cattle or other creatures killed, except one or two and the poultry for their use. And at their return [he] ordered the young lad to be put ashore. Finding things in this posture, we returned and gave madam an account. (129)

During the Hathorne raid, as he relates it, Gyles never overstepped Guyon's authority, but his use of "we" places him on a par with her as the director of the household's servants—which is somewhat credible, given the trust Guyon has in him. But putting Guyon in the passive role of the infant-laden and relatively helpless female would be unwarranted. The note on the door and the dispatch of servants leave little doubt that this self-reliant seigneuress would not surrender control over her situation. Convincing Gyles—a captive for seven and half years—to forego freedom and serve her interests was masterful. Changing the captive's question into whether to serve or disserve was ultimately more a part of the captor's narrative than Gyles's own.

Marguerite Guyon's sister Louise and her brother-in-law Mathieu Damours were not so fortunate in the wake of the English campaign up the Saint-Jean. We do not know whether Louise weathered the attack with her servants at the seigneury or joined her husband at Fort Nashwaak, where Acadia's governor Joseph Robineau de Villebon was organizing the fort's defenses. Fort Nashwaak was a dubious refuge, since it was the ultimate target of the English.

Whether Louise was in the vicinity or not, without a convenient captive she would have been unable to plead for the sparing of her house. Accordingly, the English proceeded to burn it—further evidence that Hathorne had in fact responded to Marguerite Guyon's playing of the captive card. Far worse, Mathieu Damours fell seriously ill during the bombardment and siege of the fort, which the English abandoned shortly in advance of the winter freeze. Despite his illness, Mathieu earnestly sought to return immediately to Quebec by sea before the ice closed the entrance to the Saint Lawrence. Mathieu had succeeded his father on French Canada's Sovereign Council almost a year before. He had spent most of 1696 in Quebec attending to affairs of state and had rented out his seigneury on the Saint-Jean, the lease to take effect the next year. When Hathorne and the English attacked, Mathieu Damours had by chance been back in Acadia settling his affairs in preparation for the move. After the attack and the burning of his property he set out for Quebec again—but apparently circumstances had changed sufficiently so that Louise and the children did not go with him. He died shortly after the boat left the landing at Jemseg.[29] Louise then took refuge with her sister. The two young women were now on their own for the winter.

After less than a year at the seigneury, John Gyles found himself in a unique situation. He now served two French seigneuresses, who to a not insignificant degree depended on him as well. With the annual freezing of the Saint-Jean and the retreat of the local trading Indians to their winter hunting camps in the Saint Lawrence Valley, work at Louis Damours's pelt-trading store would have ground to halt. During the winter the focus of Acadian families, regardless of their circumstances, turned to the basics of survival. Gyles's previous seven winters among the Maliseets prepared him well for the tasks ahead. He wrote in his narrative about the esoteric art of winter moose hunting as practiced among his Indian hosts. Although he was probably marginalized from such activities as a slave of the Abenaki, the Guyon sisters would have certainly encouraged an attempt to supplement the household food supplies with moose meat or venison. The more pedestrian work engaged in by all servants included routine building repairs, insuring the health of the farm animals, endlessly procuring fuel and water, keeping the fires going, and, of course, cooking—most seigneuries claimed their own bakehouse.

John Gyles makes no mention of Louise Guyon at all in his narrative despite the close proximity in which they lived, not only during the winter of 1696–97 but also the previous year when Louise had run the neighboring seigneury on her own. By later descriptions Louise might be considered a person unlikely to be forgotten: she was determined, engaging, and physically beautiful. Yet her omission is understandable, given the tenor of Gyles's descriptions of his life among the French on the Saint-Jean. Gyles proceeded immediately from his account of his gallantry and self-sacrifice on behalf of his mistress Marguerite and her children during the English campaign to the return of his master Louis and the way in which the latter managed his release.

Had Gyles given a detailed account of his domestic service during that winter with the Guyon sisters, he would have retreated to the relatively passive self-representation characteristic of his life among the Maliseet. Further, it would have been comparatively difficult to portray Louise Guyon as a benevolent mother figure. Louise turned twenty-eight in 1696, only about nine years older than Gyles, and though as far as is known she had two young surviving sons as of that year, they were young enough not to have been a factor in Gyles's day-to-day life.[30] To convey what were virtually certain to have been the raw facts—that he worked as a domestic during the long winter under the direction of two female seigneurs—would have been a jarring disruption to his self-portrayal as the young trustee of the house in his master's absence in all but name.

Ultimately, Gyles chose to emphasize how his own actions brought him closer into the family fold, underlining the gratitude his master expressed to his captive for saving his house and protecting his family. The sieur de Chauffours told young Gyles he would do for him "as for his own" (130). The prospect of adoption clarified Gyles's position within the household. Proffered adoption served as an effective captors' tactic of control, a no-lose strategy that offered an advantage no matter what the captive decided. Louis Damours either won an heir and loyal son or a willing if temporary worker. But in this last stage of Gyles's stay along the Saint-Jean, the captive's calculation also proved an effective and complementary balance. Gyles succeeded in obtaining the advantages of his potential adoption without committing the betrayal of committing permanently to his hosts.

Religion too was a factor that would determine one's fate. When he was eleven, Gyles had feared the supernatural effects of the Catholic biscuit given to him by Father Thury. By age eighteen, Catholicism in his eyes had become semi-comical and no longer threatening. Gyles's almost light-hearted representations of his last contacts with the religion of his captors stand in stark contrast to the grim portrayals of former captives like Hannah Swarton, who had experienced "many threatenings and sometimes hard usages" at the hands of the woman she served because of her failure to convert.[31] In a passage preceding his account of the Hathorne raid, Gyles gave this version of his captors' attempt to convert him:

> A friar who lived in the family invited me to confession, but I excused myself as well as I could. One evening he took me into his apartment, in the dark, and advised me to confess to him what sins I had committed. I told him that I could not remember a thousanth part of them, they were so numerous.

Then he bid me remember and relate as many as I could, and he would pardon them, signifying that he had a bag to put them in. I told him I did not
believe that it was in the power of any but God to pardon sin. He asked me
whether I had read the Bible. I told him that I had when I was a little boy, so
long since that I had forgot most of it. . . . Thus he dismissed and never called
me to confession more. (127)

Gyles portrays himself as not taking the meeting seriously (the "numerous" sins he could not remember a "thousanth part" of) and keeping his
interlocutor at bay with what he could muster as refutations of the priest's
customs. But lest there be any doubt about Gyles's use of humor to deflate
the Catholic faith and highlight his own resistance, he related this remarkably detailed story:

The gentleman whom I lived with had a fine field of wheat which great numbers of black birds visited and destroyed much of. But the French said a Jesuit would come and banish them, who came at length at all things were
prepared, *viz*, a basin of what they call holy water, a staff with a little brush to
sprinke withal, and the Jesuit's white robe which he put on. I asked several
prisoners who had lately been taken by privateers and brought hither, *viz*. Mr
Woodberry, Cocks and Morgan, whether they would go and see the ceremony. Mr. Woodberry asked me whether I designed to go. I told them that I
did. He said that I was then as bad a papist as they and a damned fool. I told
him that I believed as little of it as they did, but I inclined to see the ceremony that I might rehearse it to the English. They entered the field and
walked through the wheat in procession, a young lad going before the Jesuit
with a basin of their holy water, then the Jesuit with his brush, dipping it into
the basin and sprinkling the field on each side of him, next him a little bell
tingling and about thirty men following in order, singing with the Jesuit, *Ora
pro nobis* [Pray for us]. At the end of the field they wheeled to the left about
and returned. Thus they went through the field of wheat, the birds rising before them and lighting behind them. At their return I said to the French lad
[that] the friar hath done no service; he had better take the gun and shoot
the birds. The lad left me awhile (I thought to ask the Jesuit what to say) and
when he returned he said the sins of the people were so great that the friar
could not prevail against those creatures. The same Jesuit as vainly attempted
to banish the mosquitoes from Signecto, for the sins of that people were so
great also that he could not prevail against them but rather drew more as the
French informed me. (127–28)

Holding the folk religious practices of his hosts to benign ridicule served
to convey his opinion of the faith, but humor could serve as a strategy of
self-defense as well. Conscious belittling of the captor's religion could

serve as a narrative device to defuse the actual threats of conversion. The hero at all costs had to portray himself as unwavering in his original allegiances and unceasing in his physical movement forward. The way he resolved the conflict between his faith and his captivity depended on how these impediments were represented. Gyles himself need not have been obscuring experiences such as ill-treatment—Damours and Guyon clearly wished to adopt Gyles rather than rule with the stick. But Gyles's use of humor and ridicule in the narrative suggests the possibility that his resistance to conversion had in fact been more complex than his self-assured account offers.

However, Gyles's accounts of his misadventures in religion do continue to reveal something of the captor's narrative. In the main story line of the narrative, Gyles creates a small domestic world in which he works for his master, saves his mistress and her babies, and has more or less agreeable relations with the "French lads" who work for the family. But in the course of conveying his anecdotes, he illuminates the complexity of the lives and property of Louis Damours and Marguerite Guyon. We learn from Gyles that their seigneury featured a priest in residence and a small army of servants, field workers, and settlers of various descriptions. All these charges give us a sense of the remarkable scale of Marguerite Guyon's responsibilities, whether or not her husband was present at any given time. She did not live as a fictive mother so much as a feudal lady—albeit a New World version, one who directed her own house and fields. By 1696, at the age of thirty, Marguerite had been learning and performing her job for ten years.

Considering the scale on which they lived, that the seigneur and seigneuress would choose to take on the direction of enemy prisoners would not be a matter of significant consequence. No matter how the couple employed them, the men would have simply blended into the large corps of dependents working in support of the frontier establishment. By 1696, procuring Englishmen had become routine for Damours and Guyon. Gyles was, as his writings tell us, not their only prisoner. The note on the door that had saved the house from Hathorne stated that Damours and Guyon had, previous to his arrival, purchased and ransomed two other English captives. The names and circumstances of these captives elude us, but there can be little doubt that Damours and Guyon profited on the ransom and took advantage of their labor in the meantime, and that the New Englanders resisted conversion and transculturation, if offered.

The further revelation of the presence of the three men identified as "Woodberry, Cocks, and Morgan," however, is singular. No such names appear on extant lists of captives at that time and place. Although Gyles's narrative is the only source of information on these men, that is not so unusual: the identities and fates of captives taken by privateers at sea or along remote coastlines are often lost to us.

Why were these men at Jemseg? The casual nature of Gyles's invitation to witness the invocation of divine intervention in the wheat field indicates with little possible doubt that the three prisoners were then residing on the Damours-Guyon property. The only nearby place of formal confinement would have been at Fort Nashwaak, fifty miles upriver.

The question then becomes whether the prisoners were just passing through while being conducted to or from Fort Nashwaak or alternatively had been purchased by a rivière Saint-Jean settler. That Gyles mentions these three Englishmen before he relates the story of the note on the door suggests they may have been just passing through. In the note, of course, Marguerite Guyon explained to the English attackers that she had held only two other captive Englishmen before Gyles—both of whom had by then gone on to Boston. But more telling is that Gyles remained at Jemseg for two years after Hathorne's expedition and that he told the wheat field anecdote strictly to amplify his view of the Catholic faith. So this story and that of the raid were not necessarily related in chronological order. Therefore, a strong possibility is that that the privateers sold their captives directly to settlers along the rivière Saint-Jean. It is unlikely that the privateers could have gained much monetarily from the French authorities at Fort Nashwaak—who would in any case be hesitant at best to devote scarce resources to holding, feeding, and caring for such prisoners over the long term with little prospect of receiving compensation from authorities on the Saint Lawrence or ransom from England or communities in New England.

If the privateers were seeking a private sale, then there is the chance that Woodberry, Cocks, and Morgan were sold to Louise Guyon. She would have had great need for the three captives in the absence of her husband during most of 1696. The failure of Gyles to reveal the owner of the men would have been consistent with his failure to mention Louise at all in his narrative—despite her ubiquity in his life. Of course, Louise may have simply retained the men after the Hathorne raid or brought them to the farm afterward, when she was struggling to maintain a presence on the Saint-Jean in the wake of her husband Mathieu's untimely death. (Since there is no record of Louise's house being rebuilt, it is virtually certain that she continued to run her seigneury and manage her lands from her sister's house until 1700.) Between 1697 and 1700 (when both the Damours-Guyon families would abandon their Acadian lands), circumstance forced Louise to hire help to work her land upriver, but a seigneuress would certainly have also kept some personal servants to maintain her sister's household. If

Louise had chosen Woodberry, Cocks, and Morgan for such employment, this would explain the three men's presence on Marguerite's property with Gyles while also accounting for the men's single appearance in Gyles's narrative. And such captives could also prove a long-term and profitable investment yielding both labor and eventual ransom.

But the strongest explanation is the simplest: that Marguerite Guyon, possibly in concert with her husband, sister, or both, had bought the captives and employed them in her own household. This would account not only for the three prisoners' presence on Marguerite's land but also for various subtleties in the Gyles narrative.

First, the identity of the men. Gyles refers to them as *Mr.* Woodberry, Cocks, and Morgan. This suggests that the three men were older than Gyles and that, since they had been taken at sea, at least Woodberry was in fact an English naval officer. This would also explain why the men appear on no New England captivity records, being Englishmen proper. Second, Gyles admits to a degree of tension between the three new prisoners and himself, the former calling him "as bad as a papist" and "a damned fool." This seems to confirm the three men's age and military status as demonstrated by their license to refer to Gyles in this way. The manner of Woodberry, Cocks, and Morgan perhaps also speaks to their resentment of the relatively privileged treatment afforded to the young storekeeper from Maine—a position that no doubt kept Gyles suspect in the newcomers' eyes. That resentment must have been fed by the inherent shock of being plucked from a Royal Navy ship and deposited in a situation where they faced the prospect of long years of domestic servitude in the hands of two hardened and determined French-Canadian sisters. The men would soon perceive that these noblewomen belonged to a caste which they had yet to encounter in the English-speaking world—women possessing between them considerable experience in extracting labor and profits from captive men, regardless of previous rank or privilege.

The encounter with Woodberry, Cocks, and Morgan, though, tells as much about Gyles's narrative. A full explanation of the disposition and treatment of the three naval prisoners would have challenged the essential presumptions and tenor of the persona Gyles constructed for himself. A description of how Marguerite and Louise engaged in the trade of English naval personnel or, more vividly, trained them for domestic service would have shattered the image of Marguerite Guyon as a benevolent fictive mother. Such a damaging portrayal would have imperiled Gyles's self-representation as a male agent doing masculine business. Whatever the precise circumstances of the captivity of Woodberry, Cocks, and Morgan, there can be little doubt that a feature of their captivity at Jemseg had been a radical social emasculation. A portrayal of this emasculation would have put Gyles's own transition to manhood in doubt—leaving readers to think of him as either a raw youth or an apostate traitor.

As for the captors, their livelihood as managers of seigneuries speaks to the issue of women's ability to control male prisoners. Louise had begun overseeing a seigneury at the age of eighteen, Marguerite at twenty-one. By 1696 the sisters had spent ten years perfecting their skill in supervising and disciplining workers, the majority of whom were men. Incorporating prisoners into their work force would hardly seem a daunting prospect. If the women encountered resistance on the part of English captives, they had at their disposal several mechanisms of control. When their husbands were absent, the Guyon sisters held the loyalty of numerous other servants and settlers capable of assisting them in keeping order. And there were outside authorities to help as well. Gyles records that Marguerite had thought of placing him under confinement at Fort Nashwaak. And Marguerite showed a flexibility in dealing with foreign captives that went beyond simply subordinating them. She treated Gyles with kindness. Gyles had decided at a critical moment not to walk away to freedom, and thereby consigned himself to an indefinite period of further servitude. For the seigneuress, kindness had indeed proved an effective means of control.

The final example of the captor's narrative, discernible in what the captive's written narrative omits, concerns the events relating to Gyles's final release. Upon his return to Acadia in the late spring of 1697, Louis had "said that he would endeavor to fulfill what madam had promised to me," meaning, according to Marguerite, that Gyles "shall have liberty to go to Boston on the first opportunity" if he so desired (130, 129). Yet Gyles remained at Jemseg for two full years after Marguerite's initial assurance. Why?

Word of the Treaty of Ryswick reached New France in early 1698, ending official hostilities between France and England in the New World for a time.[32] Legally, captives were still—in the words of the future Governor Duquesne—"slaves fairly sold." In theory at least, peace between nations would not necessarily free the captives—debts of redemption knew no borders and were matters of individual settlement. The circumstances of 1698 proved exceptional. French officials in Canada, reluctant to inflame New Englanders by the continued presence of involuntary captives, bound civilian captors to a prisoner exchange. Perhaps they assumed that captors had already received their money's worth, if not more, from the work extracted from their unconverted prisoners. The final decision rested with the captives themselves, and New Englanders proved understandably suspicious

about the large numbers of their mostly young countrywomen who remained voluntarily in the land of the enemy.[33]

Accordingly, Gyles writes: "In the year 1698, the peace being pro-
claimed, and a sloop come to the mouth of the river with a ransom for one
Michael Cooms [another rivière Saint-Jean captive] I put monsieur in
mind of his word. I told him there was now an opportunity for me to go
and see the English" (130). Suddenly, then, Gyles seized the initiative and
returned to New England. Damours and Guyon seem not to have been in
a particular hurry to assume an active role in freeing Gyles, since the sloop
had been arranged by the owners of another man. By all appearances,
Damours and Guyon held out rather strongly, not so much for retaining
Gyles in the capacity of a servant as for fully adopting him. "He would do
for me as for his own," Gyles had written of Damours (130).

The strategies of captor and captive reached a stalemate in the last year
and half of Gyles's captivity. Gyles's good work and evident loyalty only increased his captors' desire to keep him in the family. Louis and Marguerite's initial offer of freedom had not led Gyles to take the final step. So the
uneasy circumstance continued until the Peace of Ryswick forced the Acadians' hand. Louis and Marguerite wanted to give John his freedom, but
not the form of liberty John desired.

Gyles did not write about these calculations, but the simple story he told
is also not entirely convincing on the role of the peace treaty. The ceasing
of hostilities no doubt allowed the sloop to sail to the mouth of the Saint-
Jean, but the argument that the treaty led to Gyles's freedom seems incomplete. Damours and Guyon had previously held two captives and later
sent them to Boston; this had certainly happened during a period of war.
The two formal prisoner exchanges during King William's War, the Phips-
Frontenac exchange in 1690 and the Matthew Cary mission in 1695, produced no captives whose circumstances closely fit those of captives held by
Acadians at that time on the Saint-Jean.[34] Therefore, Louis Damours, as familiar with unofficial contacts along the New England and Acadian coastlines as anyone, could have certainly found a way to return Gyles in 1697
in the same manner he had arranged for the return of the previous captives during wartime.

Perhaps in the end the final relinquishment of Gyles had as much to do
with the Damours-Guyon family as with the declaration of peace. The couple's first and only son, Louis, who unfortunately did not long survive, was
born around 1698. If this male heir arrived before the sloop at the mouth
of the Saint-Jean, it might have softened the blow of losing the young man
who might have been an adopted son.

Extracting a captor's narrative from the relationship between a written captive's account and the context of that captivity raises more possibilities than certainties—yet the story of Marguerite Guyon and John Gyles shows unambiguously the aspect of redemption in the replacing of absent men. Guyon and Gyles each assumed part of the role of the itinerant Louis Damours, even when Damours was at home planning the next expedition of war or trade. Marguerite's own signature recorded on notarial documents reflected this authority, her bold, grandly written *Marguerite Guyon* eloquently symbolizing her identity: at once independent and complementary to her husband.[35]

And in the end, that signature tells much about Gyles's representation of his own place at the Jemseg seigneury. He fashioned himself into a capable young man, his master's steward, the protector of his master's wife, children, and property. Yet, it is the name *Marguerite Guyon* that is inscribed on all the important documents of trade and transaction at the seigneury, signed by the hand that held ultimate authority at Jemseg.

But though the captivity of John Gyles was more a part of the captor's narrative than it was intended to be, there is also no doubt that the captivity was an arrangement of mutual benefit. In this sense Damours and Guyon effected a true redemption of the young man from Maine. The captors did not obtain their ultimate objective, but, in the end, their house still stood and their family enterprise still functioned. Gyles emerged from what he termed "slavery" among the Maliseet and was able for the first time to live as a productive individual in the European frontier world, and he had acquired a respectable tale with which to assert, or reassert, the male prerogative of the hero.

Events were not kind to French settlers on the Saint-Jean after Gyles's departure. In 1701 the Acadian governor Joseph de Brouillan made the decision to move the seat of government and center of defense in Acadia to Port Royal in Nova Scotia, leaving the settlers unprotected and vulnerable to English attack. This meant that the two adjoining seigneuries at Jemseg lost their real value overnight: no one could sell such exposed properties. Louis, Marguerite, and Louise did not even enjoy the benefits of one more harvest, for intense flooding on the Saint-Jean ruined the crops. The three left Jemseg for the protection of Port Royal, abandoning fifteen years of constant hope and unceasing effort.

Other catastrophes followed in rapid succession. Soon after arrival in Port Royal in 1701, Marguerite Guyon died in her mid-thirties of unknown causes. Louis Damours at this point placed his two surviving young daughters in the custody of his sister-in-law Louise—who at that time was raising at least two slightly older sons.[36] As early as 1703, at the outbreak of Queen Anne's War, Louis Damours left on another military expedition. He was soon captured in action against the English and confined in the Boston jail for two years before his release in a prisoner exchange. It is unknown whether John Gyles, then living mostly on an outpost along the Maine coastline, knew of his former master's presence and sought to alleviate his suffering in Massachusetts. Damours, weakened by his confinement, died back at Port Royal, aged fifty-three, on May 9, 1708.[37]

Gyles's younger sometime mistress, Louise Guyon, lived the longest of his former captors, in memory as well as in life. After her arrival in Port Royal she quickly became one of the most talked about—that is, notorious—women in New France. The loss of her seigneury had certainly been a blow, but Louise was far from destitute. She received a generous regular pension from Denis Riverin, the man who ascended to the lucrative Damours seat on the Sovereign Council at the unexpected death of Mathieu *fils*.[38] So situated, she began an earnest love affair with the king's lieutenant in Acadia, Simon-Pierre Denis, sieur de Bonaventure. Denis was already married, but together they had an illegitimate son, Antoine, in 1703. The affair cost both parties dearly. Denis was denied his long expected appointment as governor of Acadia, and Louise Guyon was ultimately expelled from Port Royal by order of the French Ministry of the Marine in 1708. She returned, however, to that town in 1711, some months after its conquest by the British.[39] Reputed by some to be a spy, she disappeared from the records immediately thereafter, her captor's narrative eclipsed both by larger events that had swept over her life and by John Gyles's omission of the role she had played in his.

The redeemed captive fared the best of all. After his arrival back in Boston and the reunion with his surviving brothers in 1698, Gyles made good use of the skills he had acquired in captivity. The crown, country, and faith to which he had remained loyal lost no time in turning Gyles's knowledge of the Abenaki and French languages to their benefit. By all accounts a companionable man as well as something of a self-starter, Gyles served variously as a translator, diplomat, and soldier on a number of missions along the northeastern coastline.[40] Like Lydia Longley and the Sayward sisters, he turned the circumstances of his captivity into requisites of his profession. But because he was, unlike them, a man, he was able to return home and put his skills to use.

Marguerite Guyon was dead and gone by 1701, but John Gyles and Louise Guyon lived, separately, along the far northeastern coast of North America through the first decades of the eighteenth century. Did something of the narratives of captive and captor remain with them? Where else had Louise Guyon acquired the language and cultural knowledge to move easily in English-controlled Acadia if not under the involuntary tutelage of

Gyles, Woodberry, Cocks, and Morgan? Gyles, too, put his encounters to good use. But in recording them, he was more inclined to assign his Indian women captors a measure of illegitimate authority, because that ultimately signified savagery to the English-speaking world. French Catholic women's authority, still under the rubric of Christendom, struck too close to home to be revealed.

CHAPTER FIVE

The Household: Captive
and Canadienne

I could not Discover not Even in Those of ye Femanine Sex, any
thing that Looked like Commissaration or Pity But ye Contrary.
—WILLIAM POTE JR., *The Journal of Captain William Pote*

The lives of Marguerite Guyon and John Gyles demonstrate the essential tension between French captor and English captive when
factors of gender complicated both the relationship itself and its
later representation. Other examples of such relationships show variations
of this tension. This chapter examines the contrast in the basic perspective
that captor and captive brought to their experiences. French Canadian
women took a transatlantic view, whereby male captive servants would be
brought into household management or more ambitious projects according to French practice as adapted to the frontier. Captives, on the contrary,
took a frontier perspective, regarding the French Canadian women as a
continuation of the inherent "savagery" they first encountered in the Indian stage of their captivity.

In the marketplaces of Montreal and Quebec, a newly arrived captive of
the Indians would discover familiar arrangements of gender. In the central marketplaces of both towns, an active, engaged female culture of petty
merchants held sway.[1] And along the riverbanks, local and transatlantic female traders conducted their business alongside their male counterparts.[2]

These sights would certainly have impressed themselves upon the Reverend John Williams of Deerfield as he traveled under guard through the
French colony. But Williams's first mention of Canadian women's involve-

ment in the captive trade is in reference to the purchase of the Puritan minister's four-year-old son Warham:

> My youngest child was redeemed by a gentlewoman in the city as the Indians passed by. After the Indians had been at their fort and conversed with the priests, they came back and offered to the gentlewoman a man for the child, alleging that the child could not be profitable to her, but the man would, for he was a weaver and his service would much advance the design she had of making cloth. But God overruled so far that this temptation to the woman prevailed not for an exchange.[3]

Once a captive had been conducted across the threshold, though, and the door had been closed, a new reality took over. This reality was framed by the captors, not the captives, as a simple function of the arrangement of power. And it was no less contested than any other part of the frontier—contested on the grounds of religion, culture, age, and gender.

The redeemer of Warham Williams, and the woman who would shape the realities of several more New England captives, was Agathe Saint-Père, the seigneuress Legardeur de Repentigny, who is regarded as the founder of the Canadian textile industry. Restlessly inventive and possessing great energy, she ultimately created new woven materials from plants native to the Saint Lawrence Valley as well as originating new dyeing techniques.[4] Though she walked a fine line between establishing domestic Canadian textile production and undermining the profitable French mercantile export trade, royal authorities lifted their objection in her case, perhaps because of the disruptions in transatlantic trade caused by the ongoing war with England.

Saint-Père's writings reveal a far greater involvement with the influx of New England prisoners than the John Williams narrative indicates. In a letter to the colonial ministry in Paris dated October 13, 1705, Saint-Père wrote: "The perfect understanding that I have of the care you take of this country flatters me that you will suffer this detail, and find pleasing that of my own initiative I have raised the manufacture of cloth, wool fabric, and serge. To this effect, Monseigneur, I have redeemed nine English from the hands of the savages at my expense. I have put them to work and have placed them in convenient lodgings."[5]

So begins the captor's narrative of Agathe Saint-Père. Nine Anglo-American captives were employed by one of colonial French Canada's foremost woman entrepreneurs for the purpose of turning native fibers into fabric to make New France more self-sufficient in the manufacture of textiles. But until now the captives themselves have not been identified. Four captives among the nine New Englanders mentioned by Saint-Père can be named with certainty. One other can be linked to Saint-Père by circumstantial evidence.

The discovery of the identities of the New Englanders allow us to place Saint-Père's efforts within the colonial development of French Canada. The background in weaving of at least two of the New Englanders establishes the critical link in the transference of weaving knowledge from New England to New France. By accessing the skilled captive labor then available in the colony, Saint-Père established not so much her social role—long since established by the force of her personality—but her professional identity as an agent of intercolonial technical exchange.[6]

Agathe Saint-Père matched if not exceeded the early experiences of Lydia Longley, Marguerite d'Youville, and Marguerite Guyon in the amount of responsibility she shouldered as a girl. She was born on February 27, 1657, in the new settlement of Ville Marie into a family of original settlers, thereby becoming one of the first French girls born in Montreal. But when Agathe was only eight months old her father and maternal grandfather were killed by a raiding party of Iroquois. Agathe's mother, Mathurine Godé, remarried the following year to Jacques Le Moyne, whose family was rapidly accumulating wealth and seigneurial titles through participation in the fur trade.

Agathe was the only child Mathurine Godé brought to her second marriage, an older son having died in infancy.[7] Mathurine proceeded between 1659 and 1672 to give birth to ten more children. The day after giving birth to that tenth Le Moyne child, a son named Louis, Mathurine died from complications at the age of thirty-five. This event left fifteen-year-old Agathe the mistress of her stepfather's now extensive household. Jacques Le Moyne never remarried.[8]

For the next thirteen years, until she was twenty-eight, Agathe Saint-Père took primary responsibility for raising her half-siblings and running the households maintained by her stepfather. Documents point to her de facto maternal role. In 1701, for example, she demonstrated her continued power over her half-brother Nicholas by successfully preventing his marriage to a woman outside the caste of the Canadian noblesse. The bitter young man then departed Montreal permanently to work as a trader in the comparatively less status-conscious Mississippi Valley.[9] So in addition to maternal authority, she acquired in the Le Moyne house an ironclad sense of her own acquired status as a noblewoman—an identity that explains much of her formidable presence.

Legal documents from these years indicate that the large family of Jacques Le Moyne resided principally in a farmhouse at Pointe-Saint-

Charles rather than in the town of Montreal itself.[10] Instead of managing a house in town, Agathe learned a different and potentially more useful set of practical managerial skills by directing a working farm. Life at Pointe-Saint-Charles also brought Agathe closer to the land, where she gained a knowledge of native plants and animals that proved useful in her future textile projects. The proximity of the Le Moyne house to the farm run by the lay sisters of the Congrégation Notre-Dame must have helped nourish the close relationship between the family and Bourgeoys's sisterhood that was to last many decades. Two of Agathe's younger stepsisters, Françoise and Marguerite Le Moyne, became sisters of the Congrégation. Marguerite began her long term as the community's *superieure* during the last years of Bourgeoys's life.[11] Bourgeoys, of course, as one of the very few residents of Ville-Marie in 1657, had known Agathe Saint-Père from birth.

The most pertinent part of Agathe's training at Point-Saint-Charles was in the management of the property itself. The supervision of nine New England captives would have been familiar to one who had begun directing servants during her teenage years. And the continuous example of Catherine Crolo of the Congrégation and her associate sisters overseeing their *engagés* on the neighboring farm would have dispelled any doubts about a woman's ability to manage large numbers of men—if Agathe or her stepsisters had any such doubts.[12] Agathe, by the time of her marriage, had armed herself with the experience and the energy necessary to extend her managerial and maternal abilities into entrepreneurship. The responsibilities of her youth had taught her not only the management of human beings but the techniques of trade and ways to manipulate the law to her advantage. These responsibilities did, however, lengthen the transition into the next phase of her life. Agathe delayed marriage beyond the usual age, finally wedding Pierre Legardeur at the age of twenty-eight.[13]

A flurry of activity immediately followed Saint-Père's marriage. She moved into the town of Montreal to join her new husband, bringing with her a large bequest from her grateful father—who evidently regarded her as much a business partner as a stepdaughter.[14] Between 1686 and 1698, Agathe had seven children, five of whom survived infancy. Four of these, including the two eldest, were daughters.[15] Despite the demands of almost constant pregnancy, during these years Saint-Père assumed control of or started a number of family businesses, to the evident satisfaction of her affable but decidedly relaxed husband Pierre. These included trading in land, fur-trading licenses, and moneylending.[16]

The wartime shortage of imported textiles inspired Saint-Père to become, in her own right, a noted presence in the French colonial economy. Louis XIV was aware of her activities in this area, and personally inspected samples of her experimental fabrics as well as—in legend at any rate—Canadian maple candy of her own recipe.[17] The 1705 shipwreck of the *Seine*, which carried much of the colony's dry-good supplies for that year, has been cited as the origin of Saint-Père's recruitment of Anglo-American prisoners. It may also have encouraged colonial authorities to permit Saint-Père to replace some of these lost goods through her own ingenuity.

Saint-Père, however, had been acquiring captives for at least a year before this shipwreck. The first two were James and Catharine Adams, a married couple from Wells, Maine, who had been carried into a world markedly different from the one they had previously known. Before his Canadian captivity beginning in 1703, James Adams had already lost his freedom once. At eleven, Adams had been convicted and briefly imprisoned for luring two neighbor boys into the forest and confining them in a makeshift stockade deep in the woods—luckily for all, the victims managed to escape. That James Adams emerged later as a working weaver suggests that the young convict might have been apprenticed to a man in that profession.[18]

On August 10, 1703, the same James Adams was captured along with his wife Catharine (née Ford) when a group of Abenaki and French Canadians attacked Wells and the surrounding area. The raiders killed the Adamses' two children—Mary, age three, and James, age one—and marched their parents to Montreal. The birth record of their first son born in captivity positively places the Adamses within the Saint-Père household. This baptismal record dated November 9, 1704, was signed by Agathe Saint-Père and her husband, in whose service the Adamses are listed.[19]

James Adams's profession as a weaver confirms him as one of Saint-Père's nine; it also supports the notion that Agathe developed her entrepreneurial ambitions prior to the wreck of the *Seine*. Catharine Adams might be counted in this number as well, although she is unlikely to have contributed directly to the weaving activities, as weaving fabric was largely men's work in northern New England around the turn of the eighteenth century. From Adams's correspondence with other New Englanders we know that when Agathe wrote, "I have put [the captives] to work and have placed them in convenient lodgings," the lodgings were her own house in Montreal. That James was not housed apart from his wife is further indicated by the birth of her two children in captivity.

James Adams's writings also help to identify the other weavers. In 1705 he wrote to the Massachusetts emissary John Sheldon, then in Quebec negotiating for the release of New England prisoners, that one of his sons, Ebenezer, was being held in the Saint-Père household with him.[20] The name of another of Saint-Père's prisoners is revealed in John Sheldon's letter to his son, John Jr., which he replied to a previous letter from James Adams. This communication contains the emissary's greeting to a man named Judah Wright. Wright, twenty-six years old at the time of the 1704 raid on Deerfield, had been made captive at the same time as the family of the Reverend John Williams. Like James Adams, Judah Wright was an established weaver. Wright joined Adams and others and was compelled to apply his expertise to Saint-Père's undertakings.[21]

The correspondence between the captives and John Sheldon Sr. suggests that most, if not all, of the nine prisoners resided in Saint-Père's household along with the Adamses. We can form a good idea of the living arrangements for the numerous residents under the roof of Legardeur and Saint-Père. Saint-Père established a workshop attached to the main house, and since servants in Canada customarily slept where they worked, the workshop probably served as well as a sort of dormitory, not only for the men but also for at least one woman and two infants. The house itself was crowded enough, serving as the home of Pierre, Agathe, and five children ranging in age from six to eighteen in 1704. Other *domestiques*, whose names and circumstances we do not know, probably resided there as well. The labor patterns that made up the day-to-day life of the New Englanders is also fairly clear. Catharine Adams was not a weaver, yet her pregnancies probably did not spare her from other work in the house. She would have seemed ideally suited, for example, to care for the ransomed Warham Williams.

In addition to those captives who can be definitively placed with Saint-Père: the Adamses, Judah Wright, and Ebenezer Sheldon, another captive can be linked by circumstantial evidence to the Saint-Père establishment. The decidedly colorful Pendleton Fletcher Jr. had been captured in Saco, Maine, in 1703. This young man, probably no older than his late teens, seems to have been something of a jack-of-all-trades, a quality that must have appealed to the energetic Agathe Saint-Père. Fletcher and Adams are linked by the fact that in 1705 or 1706 they began to clandestinely manufacture counterfeit Canadian card money, called *monnaies de carte* by the locals. This inflationary form of currency originated as a way to pay soldiers and consisted of nothing more than signatures and seals printed on ordinary tavern playing cards.[22]

Circumstantial evidence indicates that Fletcher lived in the Legardeur–Saint-Père household along with Adams. It seems unlikely that, given the demanding nature of Saint-Père's enterprise, Adams would be allowed to stray from the workshop area long enough to forge the *cartes* elsewhere. Moreover, the workshop, equipped with various inks, dyes, and waxes, would have been one of the best places in Montreal to attempt such a project. Since Fletcher collaborated with Adams in the forgery, we can conclude that both were probably living under the same roof, as two of the nine New Englanders in the Saint-Père household.

It turned out that Agathe Saint-Père had recruited her involuntary helpers a bit too well—the combination of Adams and Fletcher proved dynamic to a fault. The same creative impulses that had once led Adams into a Maine courtroom were now being used to finance his redemption. Adams's and Fletcher's skills, however, evidently had limits. In 1706 they were caught and convicted of forgery by the Canadian authorities.

Harnessing the skilled labor of captive New Englanders was clearly the captor's main concern, not converting or adopting them. Adams's and Fletcher's illicit activity illustrates how desperately these men wanted to escape this coercion. A forgery conviction carried the possibility of severe punishment, which might include banishment with penal servitude or even death.[23] Ironically, the punishment Fletcher and Adams did receive accomplished what their false *cartes* could not. Governor Vaudreuil banished them from the colony (and presumably reimbursed Saint-Père). Adams and his wife, and probably Fletcher as well, returned to Boston on the ship *Marie* in 1706.[24] But why had the men risked so much?

Two events that help explain James Adams's desperation were the Catholic baptisms of his short-lived infant sons, both named Clement. These baptisms expose the degree of coercion experienced by the Adamses. In New England Congregational practice, baptism was one of only two sacraments practiced by the church. This sacrament represented the parents' presentation of their infant to God and the church community. It was also a naming ritual in which the parents symbolically assumed guardianship of the soul of their child.[25] The details of the Catholic baptism imposed on the Adamses by Agathe Saint-Père impart a vivid image of the extent of the physical and spiritual defeat that captives could experience under the power of their captors—a defeat that resulted in an extreme violation of family integrity and subordination of the individual.

Father Meriel, the ubiquitous proselytizer of captives, conducted the baptism of the first Clement on November 9, 1704. Agathe Saint-Père herself took the primary active parental role as Clement's godmother. The child, however, perhaps gravely ill already, died the next day. At the baptism of the second Clement the next November, ten-year-old Marie-Isabelle Rocbert performed the baptismal duties of the godmother.[26] But this son lived only three months after his baptism. At the second Clement's death, James and Catharine Adams, servants in a Canadian family, had lost all four of their own children due directly or indirectly to their captivity. Their powerlessness was most evident in the baptismal ritual. Agathe Saint-Père, the couple's mistress, and later Marie-Isabelle Rocbert, a young girl acting as the agent of their mistress, had usurped James and Catharine's most crucial function as parents: the safeguarding of the infants' souls.

The captors apparently appropriated the naming ritual as well. "Clement," the male analogue of "Mercy," was an unusual, but not unknown, given name in both New France and New England. If chosen by Agathe Saint-Père rather than the Adamses, the name might have served as a commentary on what she saw as her contribution to the merciful act of the infants' spiritual salvation—the pope during those years was Clement XI. ("Clement" had, in fact, been the name of no fewer than four popes since 1592.) In this light, the choice of "Clement" by Agathe Saint-Père may have been a direct assault on the Adamses' Protestant background. "Clement" as a French Catholic name must also be understood within the context of the conversion aspect of baptism. English names virtually never survived the sacrament of Catholic baptism.

That Saint-Père, and not the captive parents, chose the name is further suggested by its use by another Canadian mistress, Marguerite Bouat (Madame Pacaud), who later became related to Saint-Père by her older brother's marriage to Saint-Père's second daughter.[27] The year before the first Adams baptism, the name "Clement" was given to the newborn son of Anne Odiorne, Madame Pacaud's captive New England servant. That the name was chosen by Marguerite, not her captive, is supported by the 1704 baptism of the family's twelve-year old Indian slave, who Marguerite christened Daniel-Clément. It was Madame Pacaud rather than Monsieur who assumed sole responsibility for the naming: Marguerite signed all the baptism records, since her husband was in France during much of this period.[28]

Whether the name itself suggested "mercy" in the sense of spiritual salvation or emphasized the conversion process by the invocation of the name of the reigning pope, what is clear is that at least two Canadian mistresses of mutual acquaintance called forth this mercy on their young male dependents born outside the Catholic faith. "Mercy," as conveyed by Agathe Saint-Père or Marguerite Pacaud, did not, however, include the conferral of physical freedom. The appropriation of the naming ritual served as a stark indicator of the captors' power.

Ironically, the woman captor with perhaps the least interest in redeeming captives for conversion proved skillful in using religion as an instrument of control—although her Catholicism and desire to see the two Adams infants baptized in the faith was no doubt genuine. It is uncertain, however, whether even Agathe realized how deeply James Adams would react to her demonstration of power. And, of course, other factors intensified the sense of alienation and rebellion among the captives. Their situation instead more closely resembled a form of workshop enslavement familiar across early modern frontiers—and Saint-Père's nature precluded amenities or a break in discipline.[29]

Saint-Père also introduced a form of gender power inversion familiar to male captives elsewhere in Canada. Agathe's oldest daughter, Marguerite, was married in 1705, just as the workshop started production, and probably had little to do with the continually arriving captives after that time. But the family's second daughter, Agathe *fille*, remained at her mother's side until her very late marriage in 1723 at the age of thirty-five. She must have assisted fully in the family enterprises, including the all-important workshop. The supervisory presence of the young woman, sixteen years old when James and Catharine Adams arrived and eighteen when the *Marie* departed down the Saint Lawrence, reinforced the inverted authority under which captive New Englanders suffered.

But to the members of the Repentigny family, by virtue of their class status alone, the arrival and incorporation of these modest, English-speaking rustics hardly challenged their sense of legitimacy as authority figures. Young Agathe's mother, who as a young mistress had demonstrated an imperious and fearless control of her father's property and siblings, would have raised her daughter to feel no hesitation in facing a workshop full of captive English colonists. For mother and daughter alike, the weavers were simply skilled craftsmen to be exploited.

Weavers, regardless of place of origin, were a novelty in New France. The status of textile production in both colonies in the year 1705 differed greatly from what would develop by the middle of the eighteenth century. In northern New England, weaving had not yet become a cottage industry practiced by women as well as men; men were the professional weavers.[30] The lack of weavers in the town of Montreal was probably in part due to the high demand for men in agriculture, trading, and military service. The mercantile economy as enforced by Louis XIV was doubtless a critical factor as well. As late as 1704 the king had discouraged and ultimately vetoed a Canadian call for hemp weavers from France on the grounds that France's monopoly would be broken.[31] It was fortunate for Saint-Père that her capitalizing on the unexpected supply of weavers from New England was not condemned by the king, even in light of the war with England. On the frontier, ordinary skills became extraordinary. Saint-Père herself originated the fabric and dyeing innovations of her workshop, but the New England weavers made possible the technical transference of loom construction and operation.

Apart from her canny use of native raw materials and her skillful sidestepping of the French colonial mercantile system, little sets Agathe Saint-Père apart from other Canadian women entrepreneurs who advanced their family's wartime interests through the influx of cultural outsiders.[32] English colonists found Agathe Saint-Père's capabilities especially impressive, however. In addition to the mention of her in the Williams narrative, John Sheldon, writing in reply to the letter of James Adams, asked if he "wod do all you can with your mistres that my children mite be redemed from the indanes."[33] That the word "mistress" was used instead of "master" is significant in its recognition of a woman's authority within a family structure, especially since Saint-Père was not a widow but a married woman.

But such letters reflected a realism that contrast to how Saint-Père's captives came to be remembered in New England. After his release Ebenezer Sheldon, who had served in the workshop from age twelve to fourteen or fifteen, became a tavern keeper who, as a survivor of the 1704 massacre, became known as "the old Indian fighter."[34] That he at least allowed and perhaps even cultivated this image of himself indicates the kind of stories that were expected of male captives upon their return. Sheldon certainly would have attracted less business and won less respect had he advertised himself as "that old resistor of the French lady-weaver."

Similarly, in Deerfield's old graveyard the headstone of Judah Wright offers this succinct captivity narrative: "In memory of Mr Judah Wright who died August 30th 1747 in the 72nd Year of his Age. He was one of the unfortunate persons who was captured by the Indians Feb 29th 1703/4." The Indians, of course, did not serve as his principal captors any more than they did for Ebenezer Sheldon. Wright's and Sheldon's actual custodian, Agathe Saint-Père, would die and be buried the year after Wright, somewhere in the Saint Lawrence Valley.[35] The story binding Wright and Saint-Père would then rest secure for two and a half centuries.

The clash between the two Agathes and the desperate Adams-Fletcher team finally indicates that the captors' identities as women were inextricable from their caste and their religion—factors that did the most to grant and justify their power. And in the minds of captive men, as during the days of Marguerite Bourgeoys's *engagés*, female figures personified the puissance of the French colony and the Catholic faith. And once again, the men rebelled against these tiny, isolated female states that obliterated all other realities.

❖

From modest farms to the wealthiest of households, French-Canadian women lived captors' narratives that were variations on the theme set by

Agathe Saint-Père. To their captives as well as free travelers, the women's dynamic public presence may have suggested that different arrangements of domestic power were found in this colony. But these arrangements, such as they were, became apparent only when one entered into the interior of a Canadian home. As one traveler, the Swede Peter Kalm, observed: "In their domestic duties [Canadian women] greatly surpass the English women in their plantations. . . . The women of Canada on the contrary do not spare themselves, especially among the common people, where they are always in the fields, meadows, stables, etc., and do not dislike any work whatever."[36]

Kalm does not encounter, or does not mention, the individuals on the receiving end of this implied supervision. One captivity that illuminates this description is that of "Jean L'Anglais." "Jean," eleven or twelve when captured in Maine, no doubt remembered his own given English surname. We do not know whether his new surname represented his liminal status, as was the case with the "Jean Anglais" employed by Marguerite d'Youville (see chapter 3), or was the result of a series of lazy scribes at work in parish archives. At any rate, a militia captain named Noël Gagnon of Château-Richer (near Quebec) purchased "L'Anglais" and placed him in household as a *domestique*.[37]

The denial of the boy's surname was only the beginning of the heavy-handed treatment of Jean L'Anglais in the Gagnon household. His conversion to Catholicism, recorded to have taken place in December 1691, could not have taken place more than a few months after his arrival in the Saint Lawrence Valley. This, combined with his youth (he was thirteen in 1691) and ongoing servitude after becoming nominally Catholic, raises the distinct probability of a forced or fictive conversion. He worked for the Gagnon family for at least fifteen more years. How this family managed to keep him during the period of peace between 1698 and 1703, when there were supposedly no involuntary captives left in New France, is not known. Perhaps L'Anglais honestly wanted to remain as a servant among the Gagnons and continue to work toward establishing himself in Canada. Or alternatively, the family used his boyhood conversion to mask his eligibility for release during the 1698 prisoner exchange.

But that his freedom was not forthcoming until 1707 makes a benign explanation (involving a form of adoption or conversion) extremely unlikely. A domestic captivity of seventeen years duration is at least three times longer than any endured by a sponsored captive who became a Catholic Canadian settler. Further, the Gagnons were not a seigneurial family, nor holders of extensive property—and therefore somewhat below the status and means of those who usually ransomed a New England captive. This may explain the tenacity with which they held on to L'Anglais—his labor represented a true and substantial investment. L'Anglais came to the Gagnons at about age thirteen and was not set at liberty until he was on the verge of thirty—a span representing his most productive years as a manual farm laborer. And, again, there is his assigned slave name.

The structure of the family also illuminates the Gagnons' need for a long-term male captive. During Noël Gagnon's military obligations, his wife Geneviève Fortin and later their eldest daughters took control of the household for long stretches of each year.[38] Clearly this family required someone to assist the mother with her work in the fields, especially in light of Geneviève's frequent pregnancies. Marie, born in 1689, was the first to survive infancy. She was joined over the next thirteen years by four sisters and two brothers. The four eldest were girls. Marie was only two years old when Jean L'Anglais came to Château-Richer, but he remained there long enough to see her grow to assume the role of mistress of the household and fields—and of Jean L'Anglais himself—upon the death of Geneviève Fortin. Lest there be any doubt that a fourteen-year-old girl could assume such responsibility, Marie Gagnon married the very next year, becoming the mistress of her own household.[39]

But the gender balance of the children did not necessarily affect the family's decision to acquire a male captive. The records reveal circumstantially that Canadian families who purchased young single men tended to have a frequently absent father and a predominance of female elder children. But this might reflect the interplay of several factors. The acquisition of a male captive really only reflected the fact that males were generally more available than females, and the added physical strength a male conveyed to the captors was an incidental advantage. And even in families in which boys and girls were somewhat balanced, or boys were the eldest, a need for a male captive might still be perceived. Canadian boys tended to find other occupations than farm work, which they found monotonous, and apparently, like the Indians, worthy of only "squaws and slaves." Even the boys who didn't go with their peers in their middle teens to the West or into the militia found other diversions. As Louise Dechêne describes, "Their lack of discipline, their vagabondage, their contempt for regulations worried the authorities: it was said that the youths of the country would not obey; children do not respect their fathers; parents give them too much freedom; as soon as they can carry a gun, fathers lose all control over them."[40] Evidently, girls were entrusted with the governance of servants because they could better govern themselves.

Wealthy households in town were yet another theater of encounter and conflict. The purchase of the young Dutch captive Peter Kerklass by the wealthy widow Marguerite-Renée Denis offers additional clues about the desire to acquire male captives. Denis is more typical of redeemers of captives than Geneviève Fortin, as she was firmly ensconced in the Canadian nobility.

Marguerite-Renée Denis, like Marguerite d'Youville and Agathe Saint Père, was the eldest daughter of a large family and had acquired the skills to manage others at a comparatively early age. Her father, Pierre Denis, sieur de la Ronde, was a successful businessman, trader, and landowner who later received the lucrative title "Grand-maître des eaux et forêts en Nouvelle-France." He and his wife Catherine LeNeuf had twelve children, all of whom married into illustrious French-Canadian families or joined prestigious religious orders.[41] In 1672, at the age of sixteen, Marguerite-Renée married Thomas Tarieu, sieur de LaNouguère, the Gascony-born son of a French *counseiller de roi* (royal counselor) who had arrived in Canada as a French military officer in 1665. Though a holder of large seigneurial grants, Thomas made the military his principal career, serving as the commander of French troops in Montreal in the mid-1670s.[42]

Thomas Tarieu died in Quebec in May 1678, leaving Marguerite-Renée a rich twenty-two-year-old widow with three young children. Despite the ubiquitous custom of rapid remarriage among seigneurial widows of child-bearing years, Marguerite-Renée elected to remain single, and quickly immersed herself in her late husband's business affairs and landholdings. She succeeded over time in advancing the family's financial and real property interests substantially—enlarging, for example, the landholdings at the seigneury of La Pérade, which she later passed on to her son Pierre-Thomas.[43]

Marguerite-Renée raised her children in the manner of the seigneurial noblesse as well. As was customary she probably arranged for one of her tenant families to care for her infants during their first few years of life—seigneuresses were generally not hindered in their work by nursing or related demands. And certainly, Denis followed the custom of setting her children on their career paths early in their lives.[44] Louise, her eldest child and only daughter, entered the elite Quebec Ursuline convent as a novice in 1688 at the age of fourteen. Louis, the older son, received a commission as an ensign in the French army in 1689 at the not uncommon age of thirteen. Pierre-Thomas, the youngest child, followed his brother into the service the very next year at the age of twelve. By 1690, then, Marguerite-Renée, at thirty-four, was a *commerçante* completely on her own.

But New France was now at war with the colonies of England. The impact on the labor supply was immediate. Judging from the loud complaints about the situation from those elites in regular correspondence with France, the supply of domestic help was hit particularly hard.[45] Not only had seagoing traffic across the Atlantic diminished, but those men available for free contract labor now had their hands full with fighting and getting their own crops in and harvested.

Therefore it is not surprising that a person of considerable means such as Marguerite-Renée Denis would seek to procure a household servant from an alternative source. She found this servant in Peter Kerklass, a fifteen-year-old New Yorker of Dutch ancestry from Corlear (now Schenectady) in the Hudson River valley. Kerklass came in the service of Denis shortly after his capture in the spring of 1692, at about the time Irish-born John Lahey, also from Corlear, was purchased by Jacques Le Ber in Montreal.

The installation of Peter Kerklass as a personal servant *(serviteur)* raises the question of the ultimate intentions of Marguerite-Renée Denis with regard to the young man.[46] No answers are forthcoming, for soon thereafter the trail goes cold. Only one additional detail is known of Peter's life. In the autumn of 1694, after only about two-and-a-half years in captivity, Kerklass converted to Catholicism while still in the service of Denis.[47] No more is known of him—he may have died in captivity, settled in Canada, escaped, or returned in a prisoner exchange sometime between 1695 and 1713. It is certain only that Kerklass lived as a captive in the Denis household between the ages of fifteen and eighteen. But the most likely scenario is that he returned to Corlear in the wake of the poorly documented general release of 1698 at the end of King William's War, when he would have been twenty or twenty-one years old.[48]

Almost certainly Denis did not intend to adopt Kerklass in the strict sense. That Peter Kerklass was approximately the same age as Denis's younger son does not, of course, imply that Kerklass was intended to fill the empty nest. The prospects that might result from Kerklass spending his late teens and early twenties as a widow's *serviteur* stand in sharp contrast to the expectations of a noble French ensign like Pierre-Thomas Tarieu. Marguerite-Renée clearly steered the two young men toward their very different destinies. Nevertheless, her involvement with other captives suggests that Denis cared more for Kerklass and his future than she would have for an Indian slave in an identical employment. About a year after acquiring Kerklass, Denis agreed to serve as the godmother to two of the very few married women converts from New England—Mehitable Goodwin of Salmon Falls, New Hampshire, and Abigail Willey of Groton, Massachusetts.[49] (Goodwin's conversion, made after she mistakenly believed herself to be widowed, proved ephemeral; she chose to return to New Hampshire in 1695. Willey has received some attention from historians as a married woman who used conversion to escape a physically abusive husband back in Massachusetts.) Had Kerklass gone on to live in Canada as a free settler, his fate would no doubt have resembled that of John Lahey—who, after his period of compelled service to a wealthy Montreal patron, married another freed captive and lived thereafter as an ordinary habitant.

From the captor's point of view, then, the calculus determining the short-term fate of Peter Kerklass proved rather commonplace. The high social status of Marguerite-Renée Denis precluded adoption. The noblewoman was less dependent on the long-term labor of her captives than had been the relatively modest Gagnon family. Denis instead stood ready to profit from the labor of the young man until a ransom paid even more. If at the end of this period of personal gain she sponsored a soul for her church and an able body for her country, so much the better.

Denis's purchase of Kerklass also expressed the preference of noblewomen in New France for captives in their mid-teens (John Gyles was about sixteen when he was acquired by Louise Guyon). Male captives in their teens and early twenties proved useful to women whose husbands were often absent and who had both businesses and children to manage; these young captives arrived in New France unattached either by marriage, children of their own, or substantial property holdings back home. In theory at least, they were easier to hold in captivity and were more amenable to marrying and settling in their new surroundings—if not to becoming both Catholic and French. *Canadiennes* also regarded them as old enough to perform heavy labor but young enough to adapt to French-Canadian culture and to a subordinate role within a fictive family. Since every group of captives taken from New England included numerous militiamen, such young men were more or less constantly on the market.

But a wealthy woman of the noblesse such a Marguerite-Renée Denis had the ability and the means to acquire other servants. That she chose a teenaged young man instead of a woman to train as a *serviteur* is instructive. The preference for male servants by families such as the Gagnons, who had an obvious need for someone to perform heavy labor, is understandable, but why didn't Denis avail herself of an older New England woman such as Goodwin or Willey? Or why did Denis not seek a young woman who would (in theory) by virtue of her sex be presumably more religiously and culturally vulnerable? Captives fitting all these descriptions would have been readily available on the captive market in 1692—and easily within Denis's financial means.

The final advantage of male servant as opposed to a female was his ability to perform a greater variety of duties. Male servants possessed a combination physical strength and experience in outdoor labor that few female captives could match. Further, Frenchwomen, unlike the English

Puritans, did not discriminate about the sex of the servant who attended them personally. As one historian of French Canada has noted, "for aid with their toilette, noblewomen did not blush to employ *hommes de chambre* rather than maids."[50] This practice stood in contrast to New England custom at that time, where a woman by convention of propriety "did not undress before her male servants."[51] Because servants in New France worked indoors or outside according to season, with a single purchase a Canadian woman could procure someone suitable for almost all duties required in a Saint Lawrence valley household. We do not know what, if anything, Puritan men made of this potentially unsettling flexibility of service. As with so many other aspects of female orchestration of captivity, the returned men maintained a resolute silence on the subject.

A similar case reveals that, like Agathe Saint-Père, a woman did not need to be a true widow to operate independently in the captive market. In 1705 a thirty-one- year-old noblewoman, Marie-Gabrielle-Elisabeth Dumeny de Vincellotte, purchased sixteen-year-old Joseph Philips and trained him as a household domestic. That her name and not her husband's is entered in the records is an indication, as with Saint-Père, of her perceived autonomy as an economic agent. Indeed, she would have needed to operate autonomously, as her husband, Charles-Joseph Amiot, sieur de Vincellotte, worked away from Montreal much of each year as a fur merchant and militia captain. But Madame de Vincellotte cannot be considered a fictive widow. The married couple lived together for sufficient time each year to ensure that Marie-Gabrielle-Elisabeth was frequently pregnant. Though only two of her children survived to adolescence, one had reached an age to become a supervisory presence in the household: Marie Geneviève, aged seventeen and still unmarried at the end of Philips's captivity.[52]

The strain of an elite household overflowing with children led to the another purchase of a young captive. "François-Phillipe" is listed as captured in 1690 and served the Viennay-Pachot household until about 1696.[53] During his service, however, his mistress, Charlotte-Françoise Juchereau, added eight surviving children to the two born before the captive's arrival. But when her husband, François Vienney-Pachot, died in 1698 at seventy, his relatively youthful widow (referred to in documents as the *veuve* Pachot) succeeded in purchasing a twenty-three year old-Frenchman, Sieur Antoine Lagarde, as an indentured servant the very next year.[54] Because New England captives were generally unavailable between 1698 and 1703, the indentured servant trade seems to have revived somewhat. This rare acquisition of an actual gentleman as an indentured servant (perhaps because of recent impoverishment or a minor criminal conviction) was a coup for the *Canadienne*. Lagarde's title indicates he was unsuited, or at least untrained, for manual or skilled labor. The presence of Madame Pachot's ten surviving children provides the most probable rationale for this purchase. The thirty-nine-year-old widow needed a tutor and caretaker for her children more than the companionship of the younger gentleman.

Women in their thirties and forties seemed to prefer the acquisition of younger men able to work and perhaps amenable to conversion. Like their Abenaki and Iroquoian counterparts, these mostly wealthy women did not seem to be worried about issues of physical control or servant rebellion, for they often could rely not only on a husband but on able-bodied older children, other servants, and up to two decades of experience directing household subordinates. Conversely, the evidence suggests that when younger women needed male domestic assistance they preferred to rely on more experienced help, much as did the women's religious communities. The acquisition by the noblewoman and entrepreneur Louise de Ramezay of the convict Jacques Huet in the late 1730s is an indication that *Canadiennes* could even benefit from the practice in mid-eighteenth-century France of exiling countrymen found guilty of evading the salt tax. Ramezay's choice of a more mature and experienced domestic servant reflects the interests of a younger, internationally engaged businesswoman continually preoccupied with saving her family's teetering and far-flung enterprises. She did not have the extra time, perhaps, to train a potentially troublesome younger novice servant.[55]

There were, of course, exceptions. When Claire Jolliet, Madame de la Georgendière, twenty-two, entered the captive market along with her husband to purchase seventeen-year-old Benjamin Muzzey in 1707, she had just had an infant son; she was to have three or four more children during Muzzey's period of service.[56] The investment in a young, ransomable *domestique* was certainly attractive to those couples expecting their labor needs to grow with their families. But Jolliet's motivation had much in common with her older female counterparts—the simple acquisition of able-bodied domestic labor in a tight market. Such was also the case with the young women of the Celeron family. The captive Elisha Searls, purchased at age fifteen by the Celerons at the beginning of what was to be a seventeen-year captivity, seems to have served a series of his master's wives and daughters. These include his third wife Gertrude Legardeur (who may not have lived long enough to witness the arrival of Searls) and his eldest daughter by his first marriage, Hélène-Françoise, seventeen when Searls was acquired.[57] Hélène-Françoise no doubt assumed the managing role in the life of Elisha Searls, and when she married five years later passed the role of mistress on to a series of younger sisters. Younger women in New

France demonstrated clear ability to act in the stead and after the example of their mothers and older sisters.

❧

Most of what can be known about the contested worlds of female captor and male captive becomes visible through the reassembling of individual circumstances of contact. But collective cultural trends illuminate some broader narrative contests. The clothing fashioned by French-Canadian women, no less a feature of the captors' narrative than their household authority, illustrates how their practices became hostage to men's written representations.

In the wake of his visit to New France, the Swede Peter Kalm, writing with the detachment of the naturalist scientist he was by training, linked the industry and energy of Canada's female population to their distinctive casualness of dress: "Upon the whole," Kalm continues, "[the women] are not averse to taking part in all the business of housekeeping, and I have with pleasure seen the daughters of the better sort of people and the governor himself, not too finely dressed, going into kitchens and cellars to see that everything was done as it ought to be."[58] In defining "not too finely dressed," Kalm links Canadian women explicitly to the Indians: "Every day but Sunday [the women] wear a little neat jacket, and a short skirt which hardly reaches halfway down the leg, and sometimes not that far. In this particular they seem to imitate the Indian women. . . . [Canadian-born women] are accused by the French of being contaminated with the pride and conceit of the Indians. . . . Their hair is always curled, even when they are at home in a dirty jacket and coarse skirt that does not reach to the middle of their legs."[59]

These descriptions establish another dimension to the public and private presence of women in New France. A visitor landing on the banks of Quebec's lower town, or on the south shore of Montreal Island, might almost take the women there to be *sauvagesses*. Their dress, like the Indian clothing they imitated, allowed them to work comfortably in a variety of tasks. Short skirts provided freedom of movement and kept one cool in the stifling heat and humidity of Saint Lawrence summers. In cooler weather, woolen leggings ensured warmth while allowing freedom of motion. More generally, the styles of dress reflected the Canadian women's ability to adopt comfortable dress to a degree not possible in New England or Europe.

Local authorities resisted these sartorial preferences. On Sundays, when legs were covered but plunging necklines were substituted, priests harangued their congregations on the sinfulness inherent in the exposure of women's bodies. Their targets simply ignored these exhortations.[60]

But practicality did not completely hold sway over other types of self-expression. Kalm also reports that, along with their practical skirts, for example, *Canadiennes* favored shoes that would hardly be comfortable while working: "the heels of their shoes are very high, and very narrow, and it is surprising how they can walk on them."[61] Women's clothing accommodated aspects of their working life while expressing their femininity.

Outsiders gave predictably mixed reviews of female self-expression through fashion. Louis Franquet, a visitor from France, confirms Kalm's observation but with a slightly different emphasis. "The [Canadian] women possess a happy and beautiful countenances, have a strong constitution, well-formed legs, small bosoms, and walk and carry themselves gracefully. They carry men away with their spirit . . . they wear good shoes, quite a short bit of skirt held by a tight sash which they wear instead of a dress, and on top they wear a short jacket. It is their pleasure to show that with this clothing all their movements become most pronounced . . . and they captivate many hearts."[62] The same dress styles in which Kalm had found hints of the savage frontier Franquet thought endowed with an enticing feminine grace.

But after the fall of Quebec, free Anglo-American travelers began to offer their own commentary on French-Canadian work and dress. John Lambert wrote that "the [Canadian] girls, from manual labor, become strong, bony, and masculine . . . yet their constitutions remain robust and healthy."[63] George Heriot took a slightly more negative view, stating that "many of the women are handsome when young, but as they partake of the labors of the field they expose themselves upon all occasions to the influence of the weather, they soon take on a sallow hue, and masculine form."[64]

Even allowing for the new genteel sensibilities of the end of the eighteenth century, and recognizing that the women Lambert and Heriot seem to be describing are what would have in the ancien régime been referred to as *habitantes* (Kalm and Franquet note they are referring to women generally, across the spectrum of social class), the difference in the Anglo-American perspective is crucial. Lambert and Heriot both use the word "masculine" in their descriptions of the women's bodies, focusing on the musculature resulting from outdoor work. Like their captive forbears, they do not mention the short skirts (that allowed to make their accurate observations about the women's figures). Whereas Kalm retained the neutrality of the scientific observer, Franquet claimed that "strong constitutions" and "well-formed legs" contributed to a distinctly feminine grace and attractiveness. Yet this same physique led the two Americans to tag the women as "masculine."

The men who wrote about women's work and clothing did not themselves have to live under women's authority. If Canadian women adopted novel forms of dress in part to emphasize "pronounced movements" and to "captivate hearts," Anglo-Americans received another message entirely. Their captive status seems to have prevented them from being captivated.

A captive received conflicting messages when confronted with Canadian women's dress, especially after captivity among the Abenaki or Iroquois. Puritan captives would have associated the Canadian affinity for colorful dress with illegitimate power. Puritan women were restricted in the colors they could wear, and extra finery worn by a woman not of the elite could be considered a criminal matter. Colors and frills, combined with bare legs, signified to a Puritan male captive the illegitimate power and savagery of the French-Canadian woman.

The second set of messages, conflicting with the first, conflated a strong physique with the "masculine" authority of women in the household, market, and field. But to a captive, the revealed bodies of Canadian women graphically emphasized that the individual keeping him captive was female. The narrative silence on the part of the captive men indicated not only that they found their mistresses lacking in propriety but that the *Canadiennes'* fashion preferences assaulted the prerogatives of manhood. The casual display of females, clothed in their "dirty jackets" and "coarse skirts" and engaged in managing "fields, meadows, and stables," as Kalm described them, informed a captive that he—as a man—did not warrant the respect and restraint of female modesty. His masculinity had been made void.

The multiplicity of expression embodied in the dress of *Canadiennes* puts the conflict between captor and captive on a larger stage. These women, although performing what would be in Anglo-America the male roles of working in the fields or trading in a market, hardly saw themselves as becoming men. Nor did they see themselves as becoming savage. The clothing achieved the effect of appealing to those free men to whom they wished to appeal. It simultaneously asserted offhand authority to male subordinates. In the presence of captives, such dress carried no meaning to women other than their own comfort. In the end, the views of traveling free observers or even their own husbands mattered no more than the opinions of the scandalized priests. The opinions of servants, slaves, or foreign captives mattered least of all. This was the essence of the captors' narrative—and the beginning of men's counterattack through strategic silence.

❖

The narrative of Thomas Brown illustrates other aspects of how Anglo-Americans linked captivity among Indians to experience among French Canadians. By the time we read about his delivery into Canadian hands, (see introduction) Brown has impressed us with his high opinion of his ability to manipulate women captors. However, following the success of his clever repartee, which had induced his Indian escort to release him from the sledge he had been compelled to draw, Brown's relative privileges among the Indians were short-lived. Shortly afterward he was interviewed by Governor Vaudreuil *fils* and then sent to live in a "French merchant's house." The merchant's wife is first portrayed as an angel of salvation who hides Brown when the Indians come looking for their property.[65]

After further intervention the governor at Montreal intervened and returned Brown to his Indian captors. In the company of two other prisoners he was taken far from the Saint Lawrence Valley. As Brown recounts:

> My Indian master's home was on the Mississippi. . . . Finally on the twenty-third of August [1757]—having passed over thirty-two carrying places since we left Montreal—we reached the Mississippi. Here I was ordered to live with a squaw, who was to be my mother. I stayed with her through the winter, and hunted, dressed leather, etc. In the spring a French merchant came from Montreal, bringing his goods in bark canoes. When he was ready to return he needed hands to help him and persuaded my mistress to let me go with him. (71)

The "squaw" in question, who is not described, characterized, or humanized in any way, was intended to be his "mother." But this particular mother had no compunction in selling her "son" as a slave at the first opportunity. The woman selling Brown is quickly transformed in the narrative from a "mother" to a "mistress," a term that is more in accord with her actions. His enslaved status is quickly confirmed in the next sentences: "After we got to Montreal, I was sent to work on his father-in-law's farm. Here I fared no better than a slave" (71).

The farm family in which he worked as a "slave" is immediately revealed to have a distinct female presence. These women evince the religious component of the six decades of struggle between captor and captive that had been a constant feature of pre-1713 narratives:

> The family often tried to persuade me to be of their religion and made many attractive promises if I would. Wanting to see what change this would make in their conduct towards me, one Sunday morning I came to mistress and said: "Mother, will you give me good clothes if I will go to mass?" "Yes, son," she answered. "As good as any in the house." She did indeed, and I rode to

church with two of her daughters. They gave me directions on how to behave, telling me I must do as they did. When we came home I sat at the table
and ate with the family, and every night and morning I was taught my prayers.
Thus I lived for more than a year. (71)

At first glance Brown has returned to his established manipulation of
women. But the captive also raises here the specter of religious conversion
that had so bedeviled the Puritan captivity experiences and representations before 1713. In this narrative, however, seemingly rushed to press for
public consumption, he offers without hesitation a forthright and distinctly casual admission of a Protestant's willing participation in Catholic
rites and sacraments. The wink and nod that the clever prisoner conveys
to his readers contains no fear that his actions will be misconstrued as sus-
piciously veering toward apostasy. That captivity encounters had now been
drained of much, if not all, of their religious significance is evident in the
unquestioned public success of Brown's narrative upon its appearance in
1760—when the citizens of Boston were preoccupied with a military,
rather than a spiritual, battle.

But if the clever Brown enjoyed the privileges of membership in a quasi
family, why, if not out of hidden desperation, did he choose to submit himself to the following ordeal?

> At the next house was an English lad, also a prisoner. One day we decided to
> run away together through the woods and try to get home to our families.
> We traveled twenty-two days. For the last fifteen we had no food except roots,
> worms, and the like. We were so weak and faint that we could scarcely walk.
> At last my companion gave out and could go no further. He asked me to leave
> him but I could not. . . . The next morning he died. I sat down by him. At
> first I intended to make a fire and eat his flesh and if no help came, to die
> with him. But finally I came to this resolution: I would cut as much flesh off
> his bones as I could and tie it up in a handkerchief, and then continue my
> journey as well as I could. I did this and then I buried my companion and
> left. I got three frogs more the next day. Being weak and tired, about nine
> o'clock I sat down, but could not eat my friend's flesh. I expected to die soon
> myself and began to commend my soul to God. (71)

Thomas Brown, like Martin Kellogg Jr., half a century before, knew the
implications of trying to walk home through the forest without support.[66]
As Brown and his accomplice also knew, the chances of recapture and, fail-
ing that, starvation were high. Allies were few between the Saint Lawrence
and a long semicircle of English settlements looping southward from Al-
bany to southern New Hampshire. The image of a comfortable captivity is
at odds with Brown's desperate act.

Thomas Brown clearly delights in revealing to his readers how he managed to manipulate his women captors. But the first hint that he hides the reverse—how women manipulated and controlled him—is apparent in the obvious gaps in his tale at the precise times when he lived under female authority. Brown explains in considerable detail the first phase of his captivity, but his story comes to a conspicuous halt when he is placed with the "squaw" on the Mississippi. We see something similar at the French farm: the only aspect of life there he mentions is his false conversion. But his selective admissions and omissions do reveal patterns of authority present in that Canadian farm household.

First, he appeals to his mistress, not to his master, to ameliorate the conditions of his captivity. Then, the particulars of his instruction are carried out by his mistress's daughters. It is possible that Brown intended to convey religion as an unthreatening province of the women of his family, but it is telling that he appealed to the woman who would, according to free observers like Peter Kalm, be responsible for domestic workers, especially in wartime. And he was instructed in religion by precisely those individuals most likely to have supervised his farm work—the daughters of the family. He says nothing about the nature of his work on the farm. Details of his captivity only emerge when he has moved somewhere and has left his French mistresses many miles behind.

As it turned out, however, Thomas Brown's escape attempt failed shortly after the death of his companion. He was recaptured by French troops while still far from his countrymen and returned in shackles to the family from which he had escaped. At this point in the narrative, the final two years of his captivity are telescoped into a mere six sentences. He served his captor family until released under an agreement of exchange a few months later. Incredibly, Brown reenlisted in the British military, was captured, and was returned yet again to the same farm and the same family, the name of which he resolutely refuses to relate. He finally won permanent release at the war's end in 1760. The brevity of his final paragraphs is understandable. The French family would not be likely to be fooled into improving Brown's lot a second time. During the second and third phases of his farm captivity there were no ruses for him to report, no movements to record—only the static impotence of captivity among women. His "mother" and "sisters" probably joined Brown's master in abandoning him as a convert and treating him simply as a temporary slave—an untrustworthy chattel who would deceive them no longer and would be kept secured when they were not extracting his labor, which might in time equal the value of the gun Brown had stolen during his escape.

In the narrative of Thomas Brown the vivid presence of captor women is in some part illusory. His deployment of women is highly selective and intended to highlight what agency Brown could claim while in captivity. The lives and interests of the captor women were no closer to being conveyed to an Anglo-American audience than they were in the era of the Deerfield captivities.

Brown, like other captives, found the "comforts" of domestic slavery to be illusory. As late as the American Revolution, other prisoners held that same illusion. Zadock Steele, a captive soldier facing a long term in a military prison in Montreal, wrote as follows: "I often made application for liberty to take quarters in the family of some private gentleman, where I might enjoy the advantages of a common slave, until I should be able to procure a ransom or be exchanged, urging the manner of my being taken and my destitute situation as arguments in my favor, having been stripped of all my property by the Indians and deprived of all my change of clothes."[67]

But those who actually had to endure "the advantages of a common slave" (which Steele never actually experienced) provided very different perspectives. Peter Labaree, a French Huguenot resident of New Hampshire, was taken from the fort at Number 4 on the upper Connecticut River in 1750. Evidently horrified by his hard treatment among the Montreal family who had purchased him, he wrote a letter of protest to an official of New France, probably the governor, asking him "if it was according to Christian law, that a white man should be taken in peaceable times and sold as a slave?" Labaree remembered that the governor's response was that "the laws of the country are what Mr. General said."[68]

Labaree held bitter feelings, no doubt, because of the length of his forced domestic service—seven years elapsed between his capture and his eventual escape. His status as a Huguenot might also have caused the Montreal family to treat Labaree punitively, which would explain in part the severe discipline of which he complained as well as the fact that the family continued to hold him even after ransom was paid—forcing his escape.

That Zadock Steele might have been mistaken in his expressed preference for life as "a common slave" is confirmed as well by North American–born captives. Nathan Blake, also of New Hampshire, escaped his Indian captors north of Quebec and gave himself up to the French at that town. "Offered the choice between farm-work or prison," Coleman notes, "he chose the latter."[69]

Blake had in effect chosen male over female supervision. As in the earlier period, wartime continued to expand the domestic supervisory roles into wider domains than could be generally found in the British colonies. Another captive, Bartholemew Thorn, employed the common practice of describing his purchase as a man, writing later of being "sold to a Gentlman at Montreal." But if, like most, the gentleman in question was married, had daughters, or even employed a female housekeeper, Thorn's actual work, that of a gardener, would certainly have been directed by a woman. After about five years of this "monotonous life" he risked starvation by escaping through the woods back to New England.[70]

Four Anglo-American prisoners—employed against their will during the Seven Years' War to "pick peas" before successfully escaping back to Pennsylvania—must have worked under female supervision, although no mention is made of the fact.[71] Picking peas, even in peacetime, was women's work in colonial Canada. And during wartime it was even more likely that these men worked alongside women who directed them. No mention of the "masters" is made in the account of the pea pickers, nor would we expect them to be.

❧

How, finally, did returned men represent their women captors in response to new and diverse circumstances of captivity characteristic of the post-1744 era? On January 3, 1747, the British schooner captain William Pote Jr., from Casco, Maine, wrote the following in a journal he kept while a prisoner of war in Quebec: "January ye 3d This Day Died Josette Lorain, our Prison keepers Daughter, about 15 Years of age, one that had behavd Verey well to ye prisoners, and abliged them all yt Lay in her power. . . . January ye 4th Buryed monsieur Lorains Daughter, In a Verey Genteel and Decent manner, after having had many Ceremonies."[72]

What was this new manner of contact between the captives and this *Canadienne*, a fifteen-year-old girl in a prison housing almost three hundred British prisoners—from whom she had contracted her fatal fever? Had she understood her role there in the way suggested by William Pote, as a Canadian version of the maiden of salvation?

The approach to these questions is textual, contextual, and circuitous. It begins where it ends, in Pote's journal which he kept daily during two years of captivity and smuggled out, hidden in the underclothes of one of his female fellow prisoners, upon his release eight months after Lorrain's death.

Pote was captured when the *Montague*, a schooner under his command, and the *Seaflower* were boarded by a mixed group of French and Indians on May 17, 1745, while the ships lay near shore on the Annapolis Basin. The schooners had then been in the process of completing a supply run to Annapolis Royal (formerly Port Royal), the main British stronghold in Nova Scotia. The captors separated the party, Pote falling in with a group

of Hurons beginning their journey back to their settlement just north of
Quebec. Compelled to carry a heavy pack of Huron supplies, Pote embarked with his captors on a lengthy journey by foot and boat—at first
heading northeast parallel to the west coast of Nova Scotia and then due
east to the Saint John River at Jemseg before a final turn northwest to the
Saint Lawrence. They made the final section of the journey by canoe upriver to Quebec. Though the Hurons apparently hoped that Pote would be
forced to settle in their village at Lorette, the governor at Quebec intervened and placed the captain in prison, which he entered on July 25,
1745.[73]

Pote's account of the treatment he received from free women along the
path of his journey assumes a surprisingly familiar pattern. His narrative
indicates that gender—not religion or nationality—proved the most formidable barrier separating captor and captive.

Though Pote found furies aplenty along his route to the Saint Lawrence,
he does not record a maiden of salvation among the Eastern Abenaki as
he would soon among the French at Quebec. His experiences on the journey and his turn to Indian men for protection establishes a crucial framework in his writings from the Quebec prison. Like Gyles, he interacts with
men, British as well as French-Canadian, on terms of easy mutual reliance
perhaps reflective of his New England origins and his naval background.
Women, when of the Indian or Canadian captor culture, are distant and
unknowable—whether they are treating prisoners with kindness or cruelty. Even his countrywomen, who comprised perhaps 10 or 20 percent of
the population of the prison, are not described except to record their arrival, sickness, or death—with the exception British females mentioned in
unflattering terms. He complains of the "women Prisoners yt was Taken
with Capt. Salter [who] fought about their honosty which is as Invisible in
Either, as ye North Star in ye Lattd of 50 South, they Being as I Believe as
great whores as Lives."[74]

As he moved into the Canadian segment of his captivity, Pote does actually experience the kindness of a French woman, in the form of several
bottles of "good beer" on the day before he entered prison. Once confined
there, however, he reacts with disapproval and seeming resentment when
such favors are not forthcoming. After a fire in the prison, the Canadians
relocated the inmates to tents erected behind makeshift pickets in an open
courtyard. There the prisoners became something of a public spectacle.
Pote records: "this Day there Came many of ye people of ye Town, to See
us in our New habitations, But Could not Be Admitted in to See us, Except
Some of ye Quallity, who Came in with ye officers of ye Guard to Inspect
how we Looked, in our New Encampment, But I Could not Discover not

Even in those of ye Femanine Sex, any thing that Looked like Commissaration or Pity But ye Contrary." Later, Pote writes that during a period of fine weather, other "Quality" persons visited, joined this time by "Soldiers wives who Came In By Douzens."[75] Pote saw the desire of Indian women he had seen earlier in his captivity to "dance around" prisoners now recurring in the apparent fascination shown by *Canadiennes* to "inspect" the inmates of the prison. The mental gender barrier remains firmly in place throughout the narrative.

Josette Lorrain, the prison keeper's daughter, obviously proved an exception to the pitiless women of the town of Quebec. Another prisoner, who also kept a journal of his captivity in the Quebec prison but whose name is lost to us, corroborates Pote's positive view of the girl, writing that her death "was regretted by all or most of the prisoners as being a faithful friend to the English as far as was in her power."[76] (That this author and William Pote frequently employ almost identical terms when describing and characterizing events such as the death and burial of Josette Lorrain suggests that the unknown officer conferred closely with Pote before recording them. The two men shared quarters with others of relatively high rank in the prison.)[77] But what else can be said of her short life among the prisoners?

It was the job of Josette's father, Joseph Perron, *dit* Lorrain, to see to that the building and grounds were maintained, the supplies procured, and internal security maintained. The prison building itself consisted of two stories and measured 150 feet by 18 feet. The front yard in which the prisoners exercised ran the length of the building and was about 30 feet wide.[78] Small, separated wooden pickets enclosed the yard.[79] At the beginning of 1747, Joseph, a sergeant in the army guard, was probably in his mid or late forties. He was married to Marie-Joseph Roy, then forty-two. Of the seven children born to them between 1731 and 1746, only two were living at the time,—Marie-Joseph, *dite* "Josette," the eldest, and five-year-old Marie-Anne.[80]

Although Joseph worked as the official prison-keeper, he was assisted by his wife and Josette. At the time of Josette's death from "prison fever" in early January 1747, her mother and younger sister were ill as well.[81] All over the European world during the seventeenth and eighteenth centuries the wives, daughters, and widows of the official jailers often acted as keepers and supervisors of the men, women, and children confined in local jails.[82] There is no reason to suspect that the Quebec prison operated differently, since Josette died from direct exposure to them.

All signs indicate that in the prison Josette and her mother played a service role fused with aspects of supervision. Pote's narrative states that the prisoners did their own cooking and laundry.[83] Medical care also stood outside the duties of the warden and his family—care being delivered either by the Hôtel-Dieu or in an outside ward used during the winter of 1746–47 when the epidemic grew ever more severe.[84] The only other task requiring rounds in the prison was managing the prisoners and property.

Of course, a visible armed force backed prison wardens. Pote writes that twenty soldiers began to guard the perimeter, and a sentry box was added outside the fence pickets in response to an early escape attempt by two prisoners.[85] Pote's fellow prisoner noted that the single sentry box outside the fence was replaced by two others established within the pickets in the prison yard to increase security.[86] Though the armed soldiers were mainly concerned with outside security, Pote reports that one of them would count the prisoners twice a day. When the war called the guards away, they were replaced by armed habitants. Eventually, the arrival of Swiss mercenaries in Quebec allowed these farmer-guards to return to their lands and militias.[87]

But internal order was the responsibility of the three Lorrains—and there was much to be done. None of the four captives who left narratives of the Quebec prison—Pote, the unidentified journal keeper, Nathaniel How, or the Reverend John Norton—mention any Canadians within the prison apart from Joseph Lorrain and his small family. The Lorrains required each prisoner to be in their beds or hammocks between eight at night and six in the morning.[88] Before the original building burned, the captives were allowed four hours each day in the yard. The three hundred men, women, and children were all turned out together during this period.[89]

Joseph Lorrain's individual tasks as an overseer also reveal something of his family's work. Despite William Pote's rank as a captain, which allowed him to reside in a separate officer's apartment, he was unceremoniously set to work by Lorrain shoveling the ever present snow from the yard, and later he helped construct a magazine for the keeper after the prison building burned.[90] Although Pote records one episode of kindness in which Lorrain provided the officers with brandy and mutton pies on New Year's Day, 1747, two episodes confirm conflict between the Canadian sergeant and his prisoners. The first was an apparent quarrel between Lorrain and Pote over an issue the journal writer does not identify. In another episode, a British prisoner is placed in the "dungeon" for referring to the keeper by an obscene epithet.[91]

But does the narrative of William Pote and the context of the prison routine address the captor's narrative of Josette? Fifteen at her death, she had only a short time to develop a sense of self-identity. But to the extent that someone of her youth could be said to have a profession, Josette Lorrain was employed by her colony and king on the front line of King George's War. When she made the rounds of the Quebec prison she was much closer to that front line than most: she found herself face-to-face with three hundred of the enemy. These particular representatives of Britain were at a distinct disadvantage—deprived of liberty as well as afflicted physically and mentally. But Josette Lorrain as well as her parents had to simultaneously keep the prisoners alive and keep them under control. Josette may very well have a been "a faithful friend to the English as far as was in her power," but the kindnesses she granted did not primarily benefit her prisoners, however grateful. Ultimately, Josette served her family's interests in doing their military duty, which in turn served the colony's interest in preventing as much as possible discomfort, sickness, and death from accelerating to the point it could become an issue in the war.

Pote's projected image of Josette Lorrain as a tender-hearted girl who acted as an angel of mercy was not only narrowly construed but omitted entirely a primary aspect of the warden's job of control. As part of the Lorrain family she granted what comforts she could, but she also helped ensure that nothing going on in the two stories of the prison escaped proper notice and that all rules were followed. We do not know the particulars of her duties directly, but she would have assessed the health and cleanliness of the building and its residents, reporting, for example, when a female prisoner might need to leave the prison temporarily for her "lying-in" period near the end of her pregnancy and making sure the curfew and exercise routines proceeded without incident.[92] Her role on the front line of the war was by any definition a varied and active one, and it gave her a profession and identity as an agent of French Canada, not as a savior of the enemy.

Although Pote and his anonymous companion convey the quality of mercy in their young captor, they are finally as reluctant as any captive of the previous wars to grant her, at least in writing, the authority she held. It is perhaps telling that neither British journal keeper specifies the work he was assigned before the death of Josette Lorrain in January 1747, although they had been in captivity for a year and a half at that point. Only during the six-month period after Josette's burial does Pote mention the manual work he was compelled to perform: shoveling snow and building the magazine. His counterpart relates that he was made to whitewash the interior of the prison building only after the girl's death.[93] Although it is conceivable that the men did no work through the first three-fourths of their captivity, it is more likely that no journal kept by a British officer for eventual presentation to the outside world would have mentioned shoveling snow or whitewashing walls under the direction of a fifteen-year-old French girl.

Still less would they have included what would have been to their readers the outrageous and ridiculous mental image of ten or eleven of King George's officers being instructed to take to their hammocks for the night, told to carry and empty the communal chamber pots, or shackled for a day's work outside the prison by this same girl. The maiden of salvation aspect of Josette's life was far, far more preferable to convey.

But even by the standards of William Pote's own considerable humanity, Josette Lorrain deserved better. Her profession cost her her life. Pote had granted to Father Chaveleze, who died at almost the same time as Josette and from the same fever, a "Brave Presence" despite his role as a promoter of the enemy faith:

> January ye 5th Died in the City of Quebec ye Reverend Father, Chavaleze, a man of Brave Presence, he was of ye order of Saint francoise, and one of ye Governours Council a Great and Learnd man, about 14 Days past, brought his reasons in writing why ye Roman Catholick faith was preferable to ye Protestant, he Gave it to ye Revernd mr John Norton our minister [and fellow prisoner] to answer, he was Verey Industrious in Visiting ye Sick In this prison, and made Several Converts to ye Roman faith Both of Sick and well, and Caught his Distemper In ye Prison By his frequent Visits.[94]

The presence of Josette was every bit as brave as that of the priest—the girl entering the prison again and again at the height of a murderous epidemic. But the enemy faith that poor Josette brought to the prisoners was not the superiority of the Catholic religion so much as comfort and control dictated by her custodian's job. Her job was neither outrageous nor ridiculous—it was apparently earnestly and faithfully performed. Yet Pote and his companions could not see beyond that final barrier: women remained the aspect of French Canada most foreign and most obscured.

❖

A final echo of the captor's narrative is found during the American Revolutionary War. George Avery was by his own account an "unsteady" and "giddy" youth with "vain expectations to be something in the world."[95] A twenty-one-year-old American soldier employed on a Vermont farm during the summer of 1780, he was captured in a raid led by the British lieutenant Richard Houghton at the head of three hundred Indian warriors. His experience first as an Indian captive of Caughnawagas and then as a diseased and emaciated patient in an unnamed Canadian hospital are familiar to readers of previous captivities, with the exception that the captors were now themselves British.

After recovering from his illnesses Avery fell under the patronage of the unnamed doctor who had treated him. The doctor had in mind two possible masters who might wish to employ the prisoner of war, one in Quebec and the other forty-five miles downriver in the country. For unknown reasons both these potential masters the doctor had in mind were of the Jewish faith. At the doctor's recommendation, Avery elected the rural location, as prisoners at large in the town of Quebec were then under threat of being removed to military prison.[96]

Avery entered the service of a man he initially refers to as Mr. "Lion" and later as "Lyon."[97] Lyon is described as an unlearned but talented Jewish "country trader." His trading must have included the activities of a long-distance latter-day *voyageur*, as Avery tells of the man having had two children in Upper Canada "by a squaw" who he had been "obliged to leave."[98] In order to best assist his successful but illiterate master, he is set to work keeping his master's accounts and, like John Gyles, overseeing his stores.

Soon after Avery's arrival in the country, his existence was altered by his master's marriage to a woman the captive describes as a "jewes[s]." Avery's new Jewish mistress made an immediate impact. Although in all likelihood a young woman, she acted as Avery's benevolent mother by improving the quality of his clothes—his previous shirt being of such poor quality and condition as to have actually produced a state of despair in the captive. She still acted as a mistress, however. When Mr. Lyon returned from Quebec after an extended time, Avery happened to be out at that time on an "arrand" at the behest of his mistress.[99]

By fulfilling some of the tasks of the "absent man" to a working merchant, Avery lived out the economic function of so many of his captive predecessors—facilitating the mobile lives of their masters by providing needed skills. In this way his captivity resembled that of the renowned John Gyles almost a century before. Gyles's master and mistress had been willing to overlook the difference in their respective social classes to try to adopt their servant as their son. Unlike Gyles's case, though, there was no religious dimension to Avery's captivity. His relationship to the Lyons is reflected in the document as one of comparative impersonality. In addition, it is virtually certain that the couple made no effort to convert Avery to Judaism or adopt him as their son. By the late eighteenth century, the calculus of power that defined this type of relationship had more or less been distilled to pure economics. While the religious and cultural definition of Canada had expanded to include those of new ethnicities acting in the familiar social roles of voyageur and domestic mistress, the scope of possibilities inherent in the captor-captive interaction had contracted.

Avery's experiences demonstrate how the cultural, social, and economic aspects of captivities in the latter part of the eighteenth century combined elements of continuity and change. His story was the final chapter, however. When George Avery left Quebec near the end of the Revolutionary War in 1782, the era of Canadian captivities was over. Avery coaxed his earnest tale, meant for his own religious comfort rather than for publication, from his active but exhausted mind in 1846. That year, the direct memory of a cultural phenomenon that had begun in the mentalities of late medieval France, reached fruition at the turn of the eighteenth century, and extended into modern times was extinguished in the men who had lived as captives. But their writings remained—continuing to hide so well the lives of the women who had lived as their flesh-and-blood captors.

Afterword

Born in 1685, Esther Sayward, the little sister of Congrégation Notre-Dame missionary Mary Sayward and friend of Lydia Longley, lived eighty-six years.[1] During that time she witnessed five intercolonial wars and saw New France rise from a rough fur-trading outpost with underpinnings of a medieval French religious *mentalité* to an economically diversified, post-Enlightenment British colony. Born a Puritan on the Maine frontier in the era of the Mathers, seven years before the Salem witchcraft trials, she lived seventy-one years as a *Canadienne*. At her death in 1770, she was a subject of the British Empire, then on the verge of fighting to keep its American colonies.

Esther Sayward's life binds together many aspects of the captors' narrative of Canadian women. As a young student, she had joined the *soeurs fermières* of the Congrégation at harvest time in 1696, when the new captive John Gillett arrived in the community and began his work under Marie Guyon, Marie Gagnon, Marguerite Letourneau—and Lydia Longley.

Esther Sayward never became a sister of the Congrégation. In all probability she worked as a lay teacher for the community before her marriage in 1712 at the age of twenty-seven. During these teaching years, she enjoyed the combination of a secure home among women and a professional station while maintaining the freedom to move around the town and region. She certainly visited her sister at nearby Sault-au-Récollet, seeing for herself the instruction of the young female New Englanders and perhaps even the labors of the captives Joseph Bartlett and Martin Kellogg. She would have played a prominent role the arrival of the future *hospitalière*

Mary Silver, attended her baptism, and must have admired Silver's activities as a nurse and catechist to the captives of the Hôtel-Dieu. Every older
girl at the Congrégation knew their neighbor Agathe Saint-Père, the step-
sister of their *superieure* Marguerite Le Moyne. When Saint-Père established
her textile workshop, Esther lived just steps away and would have been a
frequent visitor as a courtesy to one the community's great patronesses and
her daughters. There she would have met newly arriving English-speaking
captive weavers. It is not hard to imagine what these increasingly disgrun-
tled and desperate men made of their zealously Catholic, and unmistakably free, nineteen-year-old visitor from Maine.

Esther Sayward married brilliantly in Canada, joining the colony's highest social stratum and becoming its most successful businesswomen after
1712. Upon her subsequent visits to Quebec, she had the occasion to meet
Mary Anne Davis, a nurse at the hospital where her sister Mary had died
in 1717. She even journeyed to New England in 1725 to visit her mother,
Mary Plaisted, traveling in the company of Samuel Jordan, the former English slave from Mary Anne Davis's Abenaki village of Saint Francis.[2]

As one of the mainstays of Montreal noblesse, Esther would have joined
the other seigneuresses in the market square and bought cloth and finished dresses from Marguerite d'Youville. In her elder years, Esther must
have marveled with other Montrealers at the rise of the Grey Sisters. If she
visited her old friends living as wealthy lady-boarders at the Hôpital-
Général during the Seven Years' War, the sight of a new generation of Anglo-American prisoners going here and there under the direction of the
sisters may given her a strong sense of the continuity of Canadian life amid
the profound changes she had seen.

But even in witnessing these events, Esther Sayward would make her own
singular contribution to the collective captors' narrative being written by
the lives of her acquaintances and companions. Unlike her peers Marguerite-Renée Denis and the women of the Legardeur–Saint-Père family,
Sayward entered the caste too late to employ New Englanders as captive
servants. Instead, she inscribed her actions into the captors' narrative by
purchasing, holding, and utilizing Indian slaves.[3]

Esther Sayward became, by herself, a sustaining presence in the Indian
slave trade. During the first two years of her marriage, Esther and her husband purchased three enslaved Indian children: Pierre-Marie, a boy about
ten years old; Ignace, about seven; and Marie-Madeleine, also around
seven.[4] Though Ignace died a year after his acquisition, presumably Esther
raised the other two as household slaves.

Over the years that followed, the couple purchased Charles, of unknown
age, around 1719, and then the next year bought a young girl who they

named Marie-Anne. Marie-Anne, like Ignace, died soon after purchase. In 1721 and 1730 the Lestages added two older teenage boys, Louis and Jean-Marie. All these slaves were Great Lakes Indians. After the death of Pierre Lestage in 1743, Esther assumed control of her share of the seigneuries and the multifaceted trading business. She also assumed sole ownership of the human property, which by then included a recently acquired slave of African origin named Valentin. As a widow she acquired a twenty-two-year-old Indian woman in 1744 and an African man of the same age in 1748. Esther Sayward purchased her last two slaves, two young Indian women, when she was eighty-three years old in 1767. At her death she had been a slave owner for fifty-eight years.[5]

All the slaves are listed as residing in Montreal, confirming that the Lestages, like almost all their fellow owners, used slaves primarily as household domestics.[6] In the case of the Lestages, the one possible exception was the African Valentin, whose later contract as a servant on a trading expedition to the West suggest that he may have been employed on similar voyages by Pierre Lestage.[7]

When Esther Sayward's seigneurial peers were filling their houses with children, she filled hers with young slaves. That she began buying young Indian boys and girls several years before the death of her own young children, Marie-Josèphe and Jacques-Pierre, suggests that she did not originally regard the slaves as adoptive replacements.[8] But the conversion element of slavery in New France calls to mind her sister Mary's work at the Sault-au-Récollet mission.[9] Both sought to take in *petits sauvages* and *petites sauvagesses,* effect their conversions, and introduce them to French Christian civilization.

Though Esther may have derived some of the same sort of satisfaction from the baptism of her slaves as had her missionary sister, the similarities end at that point. There is no evidence she acted contrary to the essential customs of her new caste and assisted Indians or Africans in any unusual way. Esther did sponsor the entrance of two young women into the Congrégation Notre-Dame, but these were her own niece Marie-Anne Lestage and another *Canadienne* named Élisabeth Bissonet.[10] An indication of how much had changed in the mind-set of the sisters and the colony is that the "Marie-Anne" present in the Congrégation in the early 1720s was not a sister but rather the community's own fifteen-year-old Indian slave.[11]

When Esther returned to the arms of the Congrégation in the 1750s, she devoted herself principally to the welfare of the other sisters—many of whom were her elite social peers. Her needs and business responsibilities were too great for her to move into a typical boarder's room, so she bought a townhouse adjoining the Congrégation and received permission to cut a door allowing her unrestricted access to the sisterhood. For well over twenty years she acted as a friend and benefactress to the community, donating, among other things, an entire chapel.[12] Her comparatively genteel form of service belonged to an age significantly transformed from that of Lydia Longley, her sister Mary, and Marie Barbier.

Esther Sayward's case is unique and typical. No other New Englander or *Canadienne* took her particular path from being a redeemed student and prospective *religieuse* to a teacher, *commerçante,* and *maîtresse.* But the possibilities and meanings of Esther Sayward's life as a businesswoman and slave owner had been constructed over time by her predecessors and numerous peers, who made different aspects of the collective Canadian captors' narrative with their actions. All these aspects, that she had witnessed with her own eyes, created the social matrix in which Esther Sayward built her own life and chose the others who were to involuntarily assist her.

❧

To the small group of New England–born Catholic female captors who had themselves once been captives, captivity and identity were closely intertwined. For these former Puritan women, captive men and boys were more than a practical solution to the problem of how to accomplish their material and religious missions. Mary Sayward gave spiritual guidance to captive girls who in New England would have received their religious instruction from Puritan men. The only such men in evidence were the captives who worked all around them under the watchful eyes of their Catholic Mohawk mistresses—a lesson no doubt edifying to all. Esther Sayward, for her part, enslaved distant cousins of the people who had been the scourge of her girlhood home. Lydia Longley directed the labor of a man who, in Massachusetts under different circumstances, might have been her husband. Mary Silver and Mary Anne Davis relied on male subjects to an even more fundamental degree. These men were at once the objects of professional service as well as the subjects and constituent elements of their former countrywomen's authority.

Canadian-born and Indian women shared these personal transformations in pursuit of communal service. Marguerite Letourneau, Marie-Barbe d'Onotais, Catherine Rainville, and Marie-Josèphe Gosselin began building their religious and professional lives on the captive and servant trades while still in their late teens or early twenties. Their superiors, such as Marie Barbier and Marguerite d'Youville, faced the larger challenge of reconciling their appropriation of men with service to mankind. But they did not see these choices as being mutually exclusive. To them, slavery could be a form of rescue, and all actions were ultimately redemptive.

Secular Canadian women, married and not, had fewer obligations in the spiritual realm. This is reflected in the captivities they orchestrated. The captives of women like Agathe Saint-Père, Marguerite and Louise Guyon, Marguerite-Renée Denis, and the still mysterious Mrs. "Lyon" did not so much redefine these women as enable them. The availability of men, temporarily enslaved, presented these women not with a crisis in gendered authority but with an opportunity to exercise this authority in pursuit of normal interests and advantages. Very much like their Iroquois and Algonquian counterparts, male captives became part of the wartime culture in which Canadian women played a sustaining role.

❀

For the final story we return one again to where we began—Marguerite Bourgeoys's Congrégation Notre-Dame. Immediately following the death of the Congrégation's foundress in the first days of 1700, the community summoned the artist Pierre Le Ber, the son of the man who had rescued Lydia Madeleine Longley, to paint Bourgeoys's true likeness. Le Ber finished the task quickly and effectively, leaving a stark and striking record of Bourgeoys's features as a legacy for the sisters.

More than two and a half centuries later, one Congrégation sister and scholar, Eileen Scott, began to suspect that the portrait still treasured by the community as a "true likeness" could not, in fact, have been painted by Pierre Le Ber. The painting bore little resemblance to others attributed to Le Ber and, in fact, looked unlike anything painted during the era in which Bourgeoys had lived. In an act of remarkable foresight, the sisters had the painting x-rayed. The results were stunning. Underneath the "true likeness" lay another painting of a face. Soon afterward, the surface layer was removed and the genuine portrait of Bourgeoys by Le Ber restored.[13]

In the mid-nineteenth century, the sisters of the Congrégation Notre-Dame had deemed Le Ber's portrait unacceptable and had commissioned someone to produce an image that better represented their own Victorian-era conception of their founding foremother. They then presented the new portrait as the "true likeness." The actions of the nineteenth-century sisters demonstrate graphically the tendency for each generation to re-create the past in its own image. The women could have easily obtained a new canvas on which to have their new portrait appear, but they understood that in order to create a new past one has to simultaneously obliterate the old.

Partly restored image of the authentic likeness of Marguerite Bourgeoys. Pierre Le Ber's 1700 deathbed portrait emerges on the left, while on the right the nineteenth-century painting by an unknown artist remains. Used by permission, Musée Marguerite Bourgeoys, Montreal.

Pierre Le Ber's vivid representation conveys Bourgeoys the frontierswoman. The Victorian portrait shows the face of a genteel and benevolent mother. In written representations as well, the days of early Canada have been painted over by Victorian-era ideas about gender roles, captivity, race, and slavery. This book has attempted to strip off this veneer and reveal the lived captors' narrative and the responses it evoked.

It took tremendous courage for Sister Eileen Scott and her colleagues to hazard to look anew at the visage of the frontierswoman who had given them their mission so long ago. The captors' narrative challenges us to understand that from Marguerite Bourgeoys to Marguerite d'Youville, from Louise Guyon to Josette Lorrain, women on the Canadian frontier acted according to the prerogatives of their social caste, their religion, and their status as legal holders of heretics captured in events perceived as just wars. Even after religion as a factor legitimizing the holding and utilization of captives faded and gender roles became more sharply distinguished, women continued to ignore the official disabilities of their sex and practiced coercion in a purer form undiluted by what nineteenth- and twentieth-century observers would essentially see as benevolent maternal acts of redemption and conversion. The women of the colonial frontier had not, of course, seen themselves in that way. Devoid of sentimentality, the original frontierswomen, and their daughters and granddaughters as well, believed that redeeming a captive through the exercise of their maternal authority was a service to God, their family and caste, and themselves. And, if circumstances dictated, they acted as the unapologetic mistresses of men.

After the living memory of these encounters ended with the death of George Avery in 1846, what endured? The captivities in Catholic French Canada became, after the fact, the sole province of those who offered representations stripped of the essential conflict between woman and man that had defined them. The returned captives, as well as the later promoters and interpreters of their stories, would in time make Canada's women captors into invisible captives of the written word.

Notes

Introduction: Narratives of Captor and Captive

1. The two defining treatments of the New England captivities in Canada both touch on issues of gender. See Laurel Thatcher Ulrich, *Good Wives: Image and Reality in the Lives of Women in Northern New England, 1650–1750* (New York: Vintage, 1982), chap. 11; James Axtell, *The Invasion Within: The Contest of Cultures in Colonial North America* (New York: Oxford University Press, 1985), chap. 12. On captivity and gender generally, see June Namias, *White Captives: Gender and Ethnicity on the American Frontier* (Chapel Hill: University of North Carolina Press, 1993); Gary L. Ebersole, *Captured by Texts: Puritan to Postmodern Images of Indian Captivity* (Charlottesville: University Press of Virginia, 1995); and Kathryn Zabelle Derounian-Stodola and James Levernier, *The Indian Captivity Narrative, 1550–1900* (New York: Twayne, 1993).

2. The percentage must remain approximate. Alden T. Vaughan and Daniel K. Richter have found in their statistical analysis of New England captives compiled by Emma Lewis Coleman and Charlotte Alice Baker that a little over 60 percent of captives from that region between 1689 and 1760 were male. However, during the last two intercolonial wars, in 1744–48 and 1753–1760, Canadians and their French allies took probably another one thousand captives to New France not from the New England colonies. These prisoners were virtually all soldiers and therefore all male, raising the approximate percentage to 80 percent. The names and origins of these men have never been systematically compiled. See Alden T. Vaughan and Daniel K. Richter, "Crossing the Cultural Divide: Indians and New Englanders, 1605–1763," *Proceedings of the American Antiquarian Society* 90, 1 (1980): 23–99. My thanks to an anonymous reader for pointing out the scope of the non–New England captivities.

3. C. Alice Baker, *True Stories of the New England Captives Taken to Canada during the Old French and Indian Wars* (Cambridge, 1897), 232.

4. John Rutherfurd, "John Rutherfurd's Narrative of a Captivity" (c. 1763, copied in letter form by the author in 1787), in *The Siege of Detroit in 1763*, edited by Milo Milton Quaife (Chicago: The Lakeside Press, 1958), 227.

5. Ibid., 232–33.

6. Ibid., 240.

7. Ibid., 241.

8. Ibid., 244–45.

9. Examples from narrative sources of this phenomenon are ubiquitous. For one example from the French point of view that evokes the complexity of the changeable status of captives marked for torture, see the 1709 letter of Father Antoine Silvey, reprinted in *Letters from North America*, edited and translated by Ivy Alice Dickson (Belleville, Ont.: Mika Publishing, 1980), 134–36 (no. 36). Torture of nonlethal duration would then lead to other fates. William A. Starna and Ralph Watkins suggest that "adoption" among the Northern Iroquoians could assume more complex forms. They maintain that adoption in the context of mourning war was a misnomer, and adoptees remained distinctly subordinate within their new families and communities, a status better described as "liminal incorporation." The idea that captives received full and complete transculturation and acceptance resulted primarily, they maintain, from historians who put too much stock in Euro-American narrative accounts written by observers who had fundamentally misunderstood the process. Assembling an impressive array of linguistic evidence supplemented by alternative written sources, the authors show that "adoptees" undergoing "requickening" in fact assumed a permanent outsider role. They concluded that in many cases this liminality could be called a form of slavery. William A Starna and Ralph Watkins, "Northern Iroquoian Slavery," *Ethnohistory* 38, 1 (1991): 34–53.

10. "J. C. B." ["Jolicoeur" Charles Bonin?], *Travels in New France* (c. 1757), edited by Sylvester K. Stevens et. al. (Harrisburg: Pennsylvania Historical Commission, 1941), 100.

11. *Jesuit Relations* 54:92–94, quoted in Starna and Watkins, "Northern Iroquoian Slavery," 51.

12. See Almon Wheeler Lauber, *Indian Slavery in Colonial Times within the Present Limits of the United States* (New York: AMS Press, 1913), 46 n. 1.

13. My translation. See Roland Viau, *Enfants de néant et mangeurs d'âmes: Guerre, culture et société en Iroquoisie ancienne* (Montréal: Boréal, 1997), 189, 193.

14. Alice N. Nash, "The Abiding Frontier: Family, Gender, and Religion in Wabanaki History, 1600–1800" (Ph.D. diss., Columbia University, 1997), esp. chap. 5. Note that Nash's discussion is more relevant to the New England captivities since she takes as her subject the Western Abenaki, the Algonquian people often allied with the French on the mixed raids. Iroquoian Mohawk were often also involved in these raids, as well as in the captive trade. Generally, Iroquoian and Algonquian practice in regard to the treatment of liminal outsiders was similar except for the use of ritual torture, which the Algonquians usually did not employ. See, for example, the description of Algonquian Huron practice in the 1637 relation of Jesuit Father François le Mercier in *Black Gown and Redskins,* edited by Edna Kenton (London: Longman and Green, 1956), 126–30. For the absence of torture among the Abenaki, see Cornelius J. Jaenen, *Friend and Foe: Aspects of French-Amerindian Cultural Contact in the Sixteenth and Seventeenth Centuries* (New York: Columbia University Press, 1976), 139.

15. Ibid., 263–66.

16. See, for example, Susan Mosher Stuard, "Ancillary Evidence for the Decline of Medieval Slavery," *Past and Present* 149 (1995): 19, 19 n. 58. Stuard cites the complementary work of Drew Gilpin Faust. For the most relevant references see Faust, *Mothers of Invention: Women of the Slaveholding South in the American Civil War* (Chapel Hill: University of North Carolina Press, 1996), 62–69.

17. See, for example, Barbara Olexer, *The Enslavement of the American Indian* (Monroe, N.Y.: Library Research Associates, 1982), 2.

18. Roland Viau, *Femmes de personne: Sexes, genres, et pouvoirs en Iroquoisie ancienne* (Montréal: Boréal, 2000), 176.

19. See chapter 2.

20. Viau, *Femmes de personne.* Viau's conclusion—that the placement of defeated men into women's economic roles ultimately shows the disdain that Iroquois men held for the lives and work of their wives, daughters, and mothers—is correct but incomplete. Describing these

captivities exclusively in terms of male authority ignores the implications and meanings of women's direct control over the lives of captive slaves—as reflected in scores of accounts from the *Jesuit Relations* to the narrative of John Rutherfurd and beyond.

21. William Pote, *The Journal of Captain William Pote, Jr,* edited by Victor H. Palsits (New York: Dodd, Mead, 1896), 57–58.

22. Nash, "Abiding Frontier," 265–66, 266 n. 39, citing *Hubbard's History of the Indian Wars,* vol. 2.

23. Thomas Brown, "A Plain Narrative of the Uncommon Sufferings and Remarkable Deliverences of Thomas Brown" (c. 1760), in *Captured by the Indians: 15 Firsthand Accounts, 1750–1780,* edited by Frederick Drimmer (New York: Dover, 1985), 62–68.

24. Gretchen L. Green, "Gender and the Longhouse: Iroquois Women in a Changing Culture," in *Women and Freedom in Early America,* edited by Larry D. Eldridge (New York: New York University Press, 1997), 14.

25. Emma Lewis Coleman, *New England Captives Carried to Canada* (Portland, Maine: Southworth Press, 1925), 1:289.

26. Ibid., 2:402.

27. Benson J. Lossing, *The Hudson from the Wilderness to the Sea* (privately published, 1866), 72, italics in the original.

28. Starna and Watkins, "Northern Iroquoian Slavery," 48.

29. Henry Clay Alder, *A History of Jonathan Alder: His Captivity and Life with the Indians* (c. 1850), transcribed by Doyle H. Davison, edited by Larry L. Nelson (Akron: University of Akron Press, 2002), 46–48, 52. The journey of Jonathan Alder's verbal narrative into print via his son Henry Clay Alder, Ohio antiquarian George W. Hill, and others was quite complex. Nonetheless, Larry L. Nelson, the editor of the recent critical edition of the Alder narrative, is convinced that the passages apparently originating with Hill, including those relating to "Sally" and the gendered division of labor among the central Ohio Shawnees "represent the story Alder was willing to tell only privately." This might explain why the information regarding the refusal of Sally and others to permit him from assuming a male social role was revealed by Alder's relatives and friends only well after his death.

30. Coleman, *New England Captives,* 2:292.

31. John Demos, *The Unredeemed Captive: A Family Story from Early America* (New York: Knopf, 1994), 83.

32. Coleman, *New England Captives,* 2:312.

33. Governor Duquesne to Wheelwright correspondence from 1753 relating to the captivity of Solomon Mitchell; related in Coleman, *New England Captives,* 2:267.

34. My thanks to an anonymous reader/reviewer for providing a plausible estimate of the non–New England captives of the later eras.

35. Alden T. Vaughan and Daniel K. Richter, "Crossing the Cultural Divide: Indians and New Englanders, 1605–1763," *Proceedings of the American Antiquarian Society* 90, 1 (1980): 23–99.

36. Ibid., 62. Vaughan and Richter's revisionist study challenged the assumption held by several historians that a substantial number of New Englanders had found Indian life more desirable than the rigid, repressive Puritan society into which they had been born. Countering the assumption that "large numbers" of Europeans had "chosen to become Indians," Vaughan and Richter estimated that during the century and a half between 1605 and the end of the Seven Years' War in 1760, a minimum of twenty-four and a maximum of fifty-two individuals from New England became voluntary, permanent, "white Indians." These figures represent only between 1.5 and 3.2 percent of the almost 1,700 known captives taken during the intercolonial wars. When the hundreds upon hundreds of unknown captives are added to the total, the percentages become virtually insignificant.

37. Historians have argued that young female Puritans in Catholic captivity tended to

transcend early conditioning and find their own answers. But why did more females than males convert? Laurel Thatcher Ulrich has offered a convincing if one-sided set of factors: "the primacy of marriage, the influence of religion, and the supportive power of female networks." Ulrich based her assertions on the fact that almost no married women chose to start their lives anew in Canada, on the conversion efforts of Canadian women, and on the presence of mutually supportive women captives in Montreal and Quebec. See Ulrich, *Good Wives,* 208. My thesis explores the converse case: how the actions of the captor society, Canada, pulled captive women in by encouraging their conversion while simultaneously pushing back captive males (with the exception of young boys of fully adoptable age) by denying them a full part in life. See William H. Foster III, "Males Resisted, Female Adapted: New England Captives and Converts in the Cultural and Social Context of New France, 1660–1760" (M.A. thesis, Smith College, 1995). Alice Nash has considered "push" factors to supplement the "pull" factors emphasized by Ulrich. She suggests that the decision for both sexes should be understood in terms of Caroline Walker Bynum's theories of female liminality. Nash points out that New England pushed its inherently "liminal" women away while pulling men back into their privileged positions in their original homes (Nash, correspondence with author, autumn 1995). For the theoretical foundations of these thoughts see especially Bynum, "Women's Stories, Women's Symbols: A Critique of Victor Turner's Theory of Liminality," in *Anthropology and the Study of Religion,* edited by Robert L. Moore and Frank E. Reynolds (Chicago: Center for the Study of Religion, 1984); and Bynum, "'. . . And Woman His Humanity': Female Imagery in the Religious Writings of the Later Middle Ages," in *Gender and Religion: On the Complexity of Symbols,* edited by Caroline Walker Bynum, Steven Harrell, and Paula Richman (Boston: Beacon Press, 1986).

38. The Williams captivity is discussed fully in chapter 2.

39. The so-called "Governor Dummer's War," fought sporadically between 1722 and 1724, only brought about thirty-five civilian captives from New England to Canada.

40. One of the few who have suggested that we see New England captives in terms of available labor is Peter Moogk. See Moogk, "Reluctant Exiles: Emigrants from France in Canada before 1760," *William and Mary Quarterly,* 3d ser., 46, 3 (1989): 463–505, esp. 499–500.

41. Moogk, "Reluctant Exiles," 482–83. See also Louise Dechêne, *Habitants and Merchants in Seventeenth-Century Montreal,* translated by Liana Vardi (Montreal and Kingston: McGill-Queen's University Press, 1992), 31.

42. See generally Moogk, "Reluctant Exiles."

43. A partial review of the names of servants who embarked for Canada at La Rochelle (as well as the names of their contracting masters and mistresses) appears in G. Debien, "Engagés pour le Canada au XVIIe siècle vus de la Rochelle," *Revue d'histoire de l'Amérique française* 6, 2 (1952): 177–233; 6, 3 (1952): 374–407. Though Moogk has suggested that the La Rochelle servants comprise only about 30 percent of the total bound for Canada, the drop-off in the number of contracts after the onset of King Williams' War in 1689 at this port gives a rough idea of the extent of the disruption to the indentured servant trade. Between 1681 and 1689, sixty-three servant contracts were recorded. During the subsequent eight-year period of the war, 1690–97, only eleven contracts were signed. See Debien, "Engagés pour le Canada," 400–404.

44. Moogk, "Reluctant Exiles," 498–99.

1. The Farm: Lives of the Congrégation Notre-Dame

1. The English trading outposts further north on the Hudson Bay would have hardly altered the perception of Grotonians that they perched on a cultural precipice.

2. A monument in a field now owned by the Fitch family marks the approximate spot of the house on the Longley Road connecting Groton and Pepperell.

3. A representative sample of this correspondence culled from the Shattuck Manuscript and the Massachusetts Archives appears in Samuel A. Green, *Groton during the Indian Wars* (Cambridge, Mass.: John Wilson, 1883), 51–59. Green, the chronicler *nonpareil* of the Groton frontier, wrote the first and definitive reconstruction of the events leading to and following from the Groton captivities.

4. *Groton Town Book*, also known as "The Old Indian Record," 5–46.

5. I thank Ray Tolles, a neighbor of the Fitch [Longley] property, whose house stands about two hundred feet from the original Longley house site, for discussing this point with me during my visit to Groton in late August 1998. From what was known of the cellar in the nineteenth century (it is no longer discernible) and the pegs and other small artifacts found around the area, Tolles is confident that the Longley house was a log cabin rather than a frame house. Virginia May, a chronicler of Groton homesteads, shares this opinion. See Virginia A. May, *A Plantation Called Petapawag: Some Notes on the History of Groton, Massachusetts* (Groton: Groton Historical Society, 1976), 127.

6. For the 1691–92 list of garrison houses in Groton, see Caleb Butler and Lemuel Shattuck, *The Groton Herald*, July 3, 1830; Green, *Groton during the Indian Wars*, 58–61.

7. "Old Indian Record," passim.

8. If this version of events is correct, the only possible source was John Longley, the sole member of the family to return to Groton.

9. For the profit motivation, see the "Relation of Villieu," in *Documents relating to France* (Massachusetts Archives), 4:260–61; Green, *Groton during the Indian Wars*, 65. Although there seems to be no documentation that the Longleys contracted for a servant, there remains the mystery of the unaccounted victim—or survivor—of the Longley massacre. Caleb Butler's 1848 history of Groton—an important link between the oral histories of the late eighteenth century and the late-Victorian antiquarians—contains the claim that a daughter, Jemima, survived the raid and lived many more years in Groton. This story seems almost certain to be false as "Jemima Longley" appears in no other account of the raid or any town record. Perhaps the townsfolk of Groton confused the story of the Longley raid with later family history. One of John Longley's sons, Zechariah, married a woman named Jemima, who bore a daughter, her namesake, in 1754. More credible is the story conveyed in 1890 by the local historian Francis Boutwell. A Groton woman named Farnsworth recounted to Boutwell several stories she learned from her grandmother, Lydia Longley Farnsworth, a daughter of John Longley. Farnsworth family lore had it that in 1694 the Indians killed a resident of the Longley house not related to the family by blood. This victim was never subsequently written about or named. Whether this person was a young servant or someone else is unknown. For the Jemima Longley story see Caleb Butler, *History of the Town of Groton* (Boston: T. R. Martin, 1848), 94. For the actual Jemima Longleys see *Vital Records of Groton Massachusetts*, vol. 1, *Births* (Salem: Essex Institute, 1926), 147, 148. For the unknown victim see Francis Boutwell, *People and Their Homes in Groton Massachusetts in Olden Times* (Groton: privately published, 1890), 6.

10. Emma Coleman retrieved this report of Rouse from a contemporaneous document she refers to as "Province Galley." See Emma Lewis Coleman, *New England Captives Carried to Canada*, 2 vols. (Portland, Maine: Southworth Press, 1925), 1:287.

11. For the Swedish perspective on women's dress see Peter Kalm, *Travels in New France* (1770), translated by Adolph B. Benson (New York: Dover Publications, 1987), 403; for the French perspective see Louis Franquet, *Voyages et mémoirs sur le Canada par Franquet* (1854) (Montréal: Éditions Élysée, 1974), 57. This issue is discussed in considerable detail in chapter 5.

12. *Dictionary of Canadian Biography* (Toronto: University of Toronto Press, 1966–76), 3:374–76.

13. René Jetté, *Dictionnaire généalogique des familles du Québec des origines à 1730* (Montréal: Presses de l'Université de Montréal, 1983), 670; *Dictionary of Canadian Biography*, 3:375.

14. The story of the failure of the Charon experiment and its eventual takeover by Marguerite d'Youville and her Soeurs grises is extensively discussed in chapter 3.

15. See *Dictionary of Canadian Biography,* 3:376.

16. Ibid.

17. Coleman, *New England Captives,* 1:206.

18. Marcel Fournier, *De la Nouvelle-Angleterre à la Nouvelle-France: L'histoire des captifs anglo-américains au Canada entre 1675 et 1760* (Montréal: Société Généalogique Canadienne-Française, 1992), 156; Coleman, *New England Captives,* 1:206.

19. For the slave "Jacques" see Marcel Trudel, *Dictionnaire des esclaves et de leurs propriétaires au Canada français* (Ville LaSalle, Québec: Éditions Hurtubise, 1990), 362.

20. "Baptême de Lydie Longley," April 24, 1696, Archives Congrégation Notre-Dame (hereafter cited as ACND); Jetté, *Dictionnaire généalogique,* 387, 710. Note that an incorrect transcription of Lydia's baptism appears in the *History of the Congrégation Notre-Dame,* 2:105, Archives of the Centre Marguerite Bourgeoys, Montreal. Dupont signed an abbreviation of "Marie-Madeleine" on the document of baptism, not "Madame" as in the transcription. Marie Madeleine was the daughter, not the wife, of Nicolas Dupont de Neuville.

21. Jacques Le Ber's deceased wife, Jeanne Le Moyne, was the sister of Sister Marguerite's father, Jacques Le Moyne. See Jetté, *Dictionnaire généalogique,* 710, 711.

22. See, for example, *History of the Congrégation Notre-Dame,* 2:106. The fictionalized biography of Lydia Longley by Helen McCarthy Sawyer on this point is also reflective of the oral tradition of the Congrégation among whom she researched her book. See Helen A. McCarthy, *Lydia Longley: The First American Nun* (New York: Farrar, Straus & Cudahy, 1958), 117–74.

23. *Dictionary of Canadian Biography,* 3:376–77.

24. Ibid. See also Bourgeoys's own description of this event in Marguerite Bourgeoys, *The Writings of Marguerite Bourgeoys* (c. 1658–98), annotated by Sister Saint Damanse de Rome, translated by Mary Virginia Cotter (Montréal: Congrégation Notre-Dame, 1976), 136–37.

25. Mary Sayward preceded Longley as a student, but the latter was the first to take her vows and become a novice.

26. For Vaudreuil and Joybert see Jetté, *Dictionnaire généalogique,* 611, 986.

27. This network is discussed at length below.

28. See chapter 5.

29. Mary Swarton was the daughter of Hannah Swarton, whose influential captivity narrative was co-written by Cotton Mather. Unfortunately, the circumstances of Mary's captivity before her conversion and marriage are not known. It is highly unlikely that Mary Swarton was a resident at the Le Ber household, as her baptism is listed as taking place at Cap-Madeleine, not Montreal. See Jetté, *Dictionnaire généalogique,* 631. In her narrative Hannah mentions only that she was separated from her daughter for two years and that Mary remained in captivity when she returned to New England. See Hannah Swarton, "A Narrative of Hannah Swarton" (c. 1697), in *Puritans among the Indians: Accounts of Captivity and Redemption, 1676–1724,* edited by Alden T. Vaughan and Edward W. Clark (Cambridge: Harvard University Press, 1981), 157.

30. Jetté, *Dictionnaire généalogique,* 631. Lahey's position as a menial servant is further suggested by the identity of his evident replacement, Pierre Resneau, a common indentured servant from France who Jacques Le Ber signed to a three-year term on May 1, 1696. This also suggests that the conversion of John Lahey and his release were almost simultaneous. For Resneau see G. Debien, "Liste des engagés pour le Canada au XVIIe siècle," *Revue d'histoire de l'Amérique française* 6, 3 (1952): 403.

31. For the godparents of Lahey and Swarton's children see Coleman, *New England Captives,* 1:207. The New England-born *religieuse* who does appear on the list is Mary Silver of the Hôtel-Dieu in Montreal. She is discussed in chapter 2.

32. Bourgeoys, *Writings,* 182.

33. Ibid., 69.

34. Ibid., 171.

35. On the *filles de roi* at Pointe-Saint-Charles see Émilia Chicoine, *La métarie de Marguerite Bourgeoys à la Pointe-Saint-Charles* (Montréal: Fides, 1986), 49–74.

36. Chicoine, *La métarie de Marguerite Bourgeoys,* 165.

37. Charles de Glandelet, *Vie de la Vénérable Soeur Marie Barbier: dite L'Assomption* (c. 1706), 1882, 33, ACND (reprint of the manuscript held by the Archives du Séminaire de Québec). My thanks to Patricia Simpson for making the manuscript available to me.

38. Mary Anne Foley, "Uncloistered Apostolic Life for Women: Marguerite Bourgeoys's Experiment in Ville-Marie," (Ph.D. diss., Yale University, 1991), app. B; and Jetté, *Dictionnaire généalogique.*

39. Picard is listed in the census of 1666. See Jetté, *Dictionnaire généalogique,* 911.

40. Ibid. The Picards had twelve children between 1670 and 1694, ten of whom survived to adulthood.

41. See the introduction for the Governor Duquesne quotation on captives' legal status.

42. As discussed in chapter 3, the Grey Sister Marguerite d'Youville herself traveled to Indian villages to purchase captives. Montreal businesswoman Agathe Saint-Père, however, enjoyed the luxury of being presented with captives for her inspection at her own doorstep.

43. "Extract from Rev. Dr. Stephen Williams' Journal" (c. 1720), commonly known as the "Stephen Williams Manuscript," in Stephen W. Williams, *A Biographical Memoir of the Reverend John Williams* (Greenfield, Mass.: C. J. J. Ingersoll, 1837), 115–16. Stephen Williams, who was personally acquainted with the two men, explains the situation as such: "John Gillett worked as a servant to the nuns at their farm, and N. B. [Nathaniel Belden] worked for the Holy Sisters." SWM, 115–16. There can be little doubt that the Congrégation employed Gillett while the Hospital Sisters employed Belden. In addition to Barbier's obvious need for farm labor, which she demonstrated by contracting the labor of Pierre Picard on the exact day Gillett was brought to Montreal, the indication that that Gillett worked *for the nuns* at their farm suggests the direct supervision practiced by the Congrégation—the cloistered Hospital Sisters did not directly operate the farm that they owned. The differential use of "nuns" and "Holy Sisters" implies the men resided in separate communities, and then as now in English usage "sisters" is synonym to "nurses." The further use of the word "Holy" is perhaps reminiscent of the first syllable in the word "Hôtel"-[Dieu].

44. See chapter 2.

45. There are several spellings of this family surname in the records. I have chosen "Gillett" because this is the version appearing in the *New England Historical and Genealogical Register,* 101 vols. (Boston: New England Historic, Genealogical Society, 1880–1947). Other common spellings include "Gillet," "Gillette," "Gillit," and "Gilet." The double *t* suggests that the family placed emphasis on the second syllable.

46. Joseph's father Jonathan Gillett was born in Somerset, England, during the first decade of the seventeenth century. Himself the son of a Puritan minister, Jonathan Gillett immigrated with his brother first to Dorchester, Massachusetts, and then on to the Connecticut valley where he was established with his family at Windsor by 1639. See *New England Register,* 100:274–75.

47. Ibid., 101:43–46.

48. Ibid.

49. Coleman, *New England Captives,* 1:131–36.

50. The affairs relating to the Gillett children's inheritance were fairly complex and can be at least partially traced through the Hampshire County probate records reproduced in the *New England Register,* 101:45 (January 1947), 154–60 (April 1947). What is not entirely clear, though, is the location or locations where John Gillett spent his later childhood and adolescence. Between 1680 and 1682, to be sure, he would have lived with his mother at Nathaniel

Dickinson's house, but thereafter at the age of eleven it is not clear whether he would have remained at Dickinson's house, returned to the Jennings, or perhaps stayed with other Gillett relatives back in Windsor, Connecticut. The latter case is suggested by the deaths of his siblings in 1683 and 1686 having been recorded there. Nor is it clear when he returned to Deerfield (permanent settlement had resumed by 1680)—but that he did so, most likely with one or more brothers, is certain.

51. Stephen Williams, "Stephen Williams Manuscript," 113–15.

52. According to the records of Deerfield the Gilletts and the Beldens must have already known one another—John's father, Joseph, had his house on Deerfield lots 31 and 32, directly across the streets from the Beldens. See Susan McGowan and Amelia F. Miller, *Family and Landscape: Deerfield Homelots from 1671* (Deerfield, Mass.: Pocumtuck Valley Memorial Association, 1996), 157.

53. Daniel Belden was a carpenter by trade and one of Deerfield's leading citizens. He had, for example, been chosen as a Selectman the same year he was captured. See The Deerfield Town Book, March 2, 1696 (transcribed by Richard Melvoin, 1981), Historic Deerfield-Pocumtuck Valley Memorial Library. "Belden" is also commonly spelled "Beldin" and "Belding" in the documents. "Belden" is a derivative of the English surname "Baildon."

54. "Petition of Samuel Partridge to the Massachusetts House of Representatives" (c. June 1698), in "Stephen Williams Manuscript," 113–16; *New England Register,* 101:237 (July 1947); George Sheldon, *A History of Deerfield, Massachusetts* (Greenfield, Mass.: E. A. Hall, 1895), 1:254.

55. "Stephen Williams Manuscript," 115–16.

56. Coleman, *New England Captives,* 2:131.

57. Patricia Simpson, the author of a superb biography of the early life of Bourgeoys, writes that although it is possible the Carmelites turned Marguerite down because of her relatively modest social status, another explanation may be that the leaders of the convent had already discerned the implications of the natural leadership Bourgeoys had assumed among the devout girls of Troyes. The Carmelites may have then benevolently rejected the applicant in order to direct her to the more active life for which she was so obviously suited. See Patricia Simpson, *Marguerite Bourgeoys and Montreal, 1640–1665* (Montreal and Kingston: McGill-Queens University Press, 1997), 43–45.

58. The early-seventeenth-century model for the Canadian wilderness missions included Saint Vincent de Paul's Filles de la Charité. See Leslie Choquette, "Ces Amazones du Grand Dieu: Women and Mission in Seventeenth-Century Canada," *French Historical Studies* 17, 3 (1992): 631–32.

59. "Wandering life." The most comprehensive study of the theological dimensions of the *vie voyagère* is Foley, "Uncloistered Apostolic Life." The historical context that helped create Bourgeoys's vision is dealt with most extensively in Simpson, *Marguerite Bourgeoys and Montreal,* chapters 1 and 2.

60. Bourgeoys, *Writings,* 81–82.

61. Ibid., 48–49.

62. This characteristic in Bourgeoys's behavior emerges from the supremely pragmatic ways she dealt with a wide variety of individuals. Perhaps the writing that best expresses this pragmatism is her critique of ordinary human uses of "love." She writes: "When we learn that a foreign country is pillaged or oppressed, we have compassion for the people, but this touches us only when we know it. We love those who are travelling through because they bring us some profit; we love the poor to whom we give what is superfluous; we love our associates because to lose them would harm us; we love our friends because their conversation pleases and is agreeable to us; we love our parents because we received good things from them or because we fear to be punished." Bourgeoys, *Writings,* 59.

63. Ibid., 54.

64. See generally Simpson, *Marguerite Bourgeoys and Montreal.*

65. See generally Peter Moogk, "Reluctant Exiles: Emigrants from France in Canada before 1760," *William and Mary Quarterly*, 3d ser., 46, 3 (1989): 463–505.

66. Chicoine, *La métarie de Marguerite Bourgeoys*. This remarkable volume is the single best resource on the history of the farm-school.

67. Patricia Simpson throughout her text reiterates the importance of financial and material self-reliance. See especially *Marguerite Bourgeoys and Montreal*, 161–69.

68. *Writings of Marguerite Bourgeoys*, 29.

69. For the work of Crolo see Marie Morin, *Histoire simple et veritable (les annales de l'Hôtel-Dieu de Montréal, 1659–1725)* (Montréal: Hôtel-Dieu, 1979), 74–75; and Simpson, *Marguerite Bourgeoys and Montreal*, 163.

70. Bourgeoys, *Writings*, 177, 179.

71. On the conflict between Bourgeoys and her fellow sisters regarding the appropriateness of taking in female immigrants see Simpson, *Marguerite Bourgeoys and Montreal*, 168.

72. Personal conversation with Patricia Simpson, September 1998.

73. *Recensement, 1667*, Archives Nationales de Québec–Montréal (hereafter cited as ANQ-M). Examples of these contracts appear frequently in the notarial records relating to the religious communities. For one typical example that spells out the terms of becoming a *donné* see the self-indenture of Pierre Picard to the Congrégation. *Greffe* of Adhémar, October 9, 1696, ANQ-M.

74. Bourgeoys, *Writings*, 155.

75. For Crolo see Chicoine, *La métarie de Marguerite Bourgeoys*, esp. 15–83.

76. Conversations with Patricia Simpson, September 1998; and Foley, "Uncloistered Apostolic Life," app. B.

77. Censuses for 1666, 1667, 1681, ANQ-M. For clarity I have not counted the three men with whom the Congrégation signed separate *donné* contracts, although two of them are also listed on the census as *domestiques engagés*. I discuss the special cases of the *donnés* below.

78. Computed from Foley, "Uncloistered Apostolic Life," app. B; and Jetté, *Dictionnaire généalogique*.

79. This conclusion is reached by a comparison of the names of the Congrégation's servants in the 1666, 1667, and 1681 censuses with the genealogical records of compiled by René Jetté in *Dictionnaire généalogique*.

80. Moogk, "Reluctant Exiles."

81. See the case of Pierre Picard below.

82. Bourgeoys, *Writings*, 101. A slightly different interpretation of the Thomas Mousnier encounter is put forth in Chicoine, *La métarie de Marguerite Bourgeoys*, 79.

83. Chicoine, *La métarie de Marguerite Bourgeoys*, 164.

84. Ibid., 44.

85. Bourgeoys, *Writings*, 5.

86. Pierre Picard, the first foreman at Pointe-Saint-Charles, was not hired until 1696. Even after that date, however, the chief *soeur fermière* remained in residence at the farm and served as the principal authority in the fields.

87. Bourgeoys, *Writings*, 177. Bourgeoys goes on to list several aspects of her successors' backsliding in laxity. "Now," she wrote in 1698, "we must have mattresses, sheets, and all sorts of utensils; we want to live in a different fashion from simple people. We want to have all the comforts that the settlers do not have."

88. Bourgeoys, *Writings*, 171.

89. For the family of Vivien Magdelaine see Jetté, *Dictionnaire généalogique*, 749–50. For the indenture see the *greffe* of Adhémar, July 26, 1688, ANQ-M; and Chicoine, *La métarie de Marguerite Bourgeoys*, 82.

90. This finding was originally made by Benjamin Sulte in 1916. Reported by Chicoine, *La métarie de Marguerite Bourgeoys*, 81, 83 n. 28.

91. The ages are computed from the list of early Congrégation sisters contained in Foley, "Uncloistered Apostolic Life," app. B.

92. Jetté, *Dictionnaire généalogique*, 24. A reasonable supposition, based on the premises of Starna and Watkins discussed in the introduction, would be that the Huron father of Marie-Thérèse Gannensagouas remained liminal at the Mountain Mission, and that the marginality reflected as well upon his daughter. See William A. Starna and Ralph Watkins, "Northern Iroquoian Slavery," *Ethnohistory* 38, 1 (1991): 34–53.

93. For Marie de L'Incarnation see Natalie Zemon Davis, *Women on the Margins: Three Seventeenth Century Lives* (Cambridge: Harvard University Press, 1995), 63–139.

94. This yoke has survived and is on display at the Congrégation's Maison Sainte Gabrielle in Montreal, the successor to the original farmhouse built on the original site at Pointe-Saint-Charles. Parts of the present house date from 1698, the oldest complete building on Montreal Island.

95. My thanks to Patricia Simpson for discussing with me the community's collective memory of day-to-day life during the time of Marie Barbier's leadership. This list of duties is confirmed by the later experiences of Nathaniel Belden's father, Daniel. Stephen Williams reported that the Indians at Caughnawaga-Sault Saint Louis did not convey the senior Belden to Montreal until July 1697, when the Sulpicians, perhaps emulating the Hospital Sisters holding Nathaniel, purchased Daniel. Daniel Belden, unlike his son or John Gillett, saw fit to list his duties among his French captors. Among the Sulpicians (Williams mistakenly calls them Jesuits), Belden's "business was to wait upon them, and cut wood, make fires, &c." "Stephen Williams Manuscript," 116.

96. Discussions with the museum staff of the Maison Sainte Gabrielle, Montreal, April 1996.

97. John Cotton Jr. articulated the ungodliness of celibacy in "A Meet Help," a sermon delivered the summer of Lydia Longley's capture. See Edmund Morgan, *The Puritan Family* (New York: Harper & Row, 1966), 29. See also Mary Beth Norton, *Founding Mothers and Fathers* (New York: Knopf, 1996).

98. For the Schuyler-Dellius mission to Frontenac, see Coleman, *New England Captives*, 1:79.

99. According to the petition that Gillett's commanding officer, Samuel Partridge, submitted to the Massachusetts House of Representatives in the summer of 1698, there is no doubt that Gillett was not free in September 1697 when he was transported as a "prisoner unto old france." See *New England Register*, 101:238–39 (July 1947).

100. Ibid.

101. From France and England Gillett sailed back to New England, arriving in Deerfield just before the Beldens. "Stephen Williams Manuscript," 116.

102. Glandelet, *La Vénérable Soeur Marie Barbier*, 13.

103. For details of the farm at Sainte-Famille see Raymond Létourneau, *Sainte-Famille: L'Aînée de L'Île d'Orléans* (Sainte-Famille, Quebec: privately published, 1984), 357–406, esp. 363–64, 370–72, 378. Unfortunately, as of early 2002 the Congrégation Notre-Dame records of the Sainte-Famille mission have been misplaced. The search for them is ongoing. If they are located, they may shed more light on the later activities of Lydia Longley.

104. For Catherine Crolo see Simpson, *Marguerite Bourgeoys and Montreal*, 42–43. For Marie Barbier see Glandelet, *La Vie de la Vénérable Soeur Marie Barbier*, 4–5.

105. Nicholas Barbier was killed by the English at Laprairie on August 11, 1691. See Jetté, *Dictionnaire généalogique*, 47.

106. The respective paths to the Longley and Tarbell farms led in different directions. The two-mile track to the Longley property ran north along what is now Longley Road connecting Groton to Pepperell, Massachusetts, and Nashua, New Hampshire. The Tarbell farm

lay about one mile out of town along a path running west and then south out of town. This is now called Peabody Road connecting the town to the Groton School and eventually to Ayer. By foot, it would have taken over an hour, and perhaps two in less than optimal conditions, to walk between the Longleys' and the Tarbells' via the village center. The more isolated Longley place was slightly more exposed to raiders from the north, but to live west of the town did not guarantee security. There is today a plaque near the farm site along this road recounting the story of the Tarbells. Interestingly, the inscription, circa 1883, reflects well the tendency among nineteenth-century antiquarians to put the actions of male captives in the active voice while female captives are acted upon in the passive voice: "NEAR THIS SPOT THREE CHILDREN SARAH, JOHN, AND ZECHARIAH TARBELL WERE CAPTURED BY THE INDIANS, JUNE 20, 1707 [OLD STYLE DATE]. THEY WERE TAKEN TO CANADA WHERE THE SISTER WAS PLACED IN A CONVENT. THE BROTHERS BECAME CHIEFS OF THE COUGHNAWAGA TRIBE; AND WERE AMONG THE FOUNDERS OF ST. REGIS WHERE THEY HAVE DESCENDANTS NOW LIVING.

107. For the most detailed account of the John and Zachariah Tarbell see Green, *Groton during the Indian Wars*, 109–24.

108. For the Rocberts see the section on Agathe Saint-Père in chapter 5. For Tarbell's placement in the Congrégation, see Green, *Groton during the Indian Wars*, 109–10; and Coleman *New England Captives* 1:293–94. I caution the reader here about the Tarbell account in the *Groton Historical Series*, 3:128–33. This version fills in details between known facts in an unreliable manner. The statement that "[Sarah] was delivered to M. Lamorandiere [*sic*], and was adopted into his family, the event being celebrated by a feast in which many of the French settlers were invited, while the little stranger was a special guest of honor" is a flight of fancy. LaMorandière had no such immediate "family" in which Sarah could be appropriately "adopted." Further, the account claims that Lydia Longley gave Sarah Tarbell the news of John Longley's return, while in fact Sarah Tarbell was certainly already personally acquainted with John Longley. If Sarah and Lydia did encounter one another it would be Sarah who would deliver news of John Longley to his sister. Most important, chroniclers of Groton have universally missed the fact that Tarbell's baptism record clearly indicates that Tarbell had been living with the Congrégation sisters at La Chine, not Montreal. The La Chine mission to the Indians had been established by the Congrégation in 1683 as part of the general expansion of the community. Accounts, then, of the "reunion" of Longley and Tarbell must be put in the context of their physical separation. Finally, the *Groton Historical Series* account claims Sarah definitely entered the novitiate of the Congrégation. Although possible (see below), no direct evidence exists for this conclusion. Thanks to Patricia Simpson for the information on the La Chine mission.

109. Readers should be alerted to an error relating to Sarah Tarbell in Marcel Fournier's recent and generally reliable French-language reference work on the New England captives. His entry on Tarbell states she decided to return to New England following her conversion and returned in a prisoner exchange in September 1712. None of the sources he cites, however, mention Tarbell's decision or the return. I am unaware of any other evidence that might support this claim. See Marcel Fournier, *De la Nouvelle Angleterre à la Nouvelle France* (Montréal: Société Généalogique Canadienne-Française, 1992), 213–14.

110. Sarah Tarbell probably died at La Chine soon after 1710. Had she proceeded further in her career at the Congrégation or married, records of these events would almost certainly survive. Although it is unusual that a certification of death would not be entered into the parish records, such gaps do exist—particularly in outlying areas such as La Chine. The lack of records supports the view that Tarbell died at La Chine.

111. "Extrait du Registre des Baptemes," April 17, 1733, Paroisse Saint-Famille, Archives Congrégation Notre-Dame. One of only two existing signatures of Lydia Longley appears on this document. For the Prémonts see Jetté, *DGCQ,* 944.

112. Francis Marion Boutwell, *People and Their Homes in Groton, Massachusetts in Olden Time* (Groton: privately published, 1890), 5. A special thanks is due here to the late Samuel A. Green for donating this and other rare materials on Groton to the Cornell University Library in the 1890s.

113. Green, *Groton during the Indian Wars,* 75.

114. Esther Wheelwright to her mother, September 24, 1747, AUQ.

115. Coleman, *New England Captives,* 1:286. The translation is presumably Coleman's own.

116. Bourgeoys, *Writings,* 60.

117. *New England Register,* 101:239.

118. The author of the Gillett genealogy raises the possibility that John may have had some previous interest in the Lebanon tract, which had been originally sold by the Indians to four proprietary investors in 1692. See *New England Register,* 101:239–40.

119. Nathaniel H. Morgan, "An Appendix of Historical Notes," in *Early Lebanon,* by Orlo H. Hine (Hartford: Case, Lockwood, and Brainard, 1880), 152–53, 156; *New England Register,* 101:240–41.

120. Coleman, *New England Captives,* 2:66.

121. Ibid., 2:68.

122. At least the Belden property (unlike that of John Gillett, who had been declared legally dead by Pynchon shortly after his capture) had been preserved for the returning captives by the residents of Deerfield. The citizens of the town even released him from paying the town rates during the time he had been in captivity. See The Deerfield Town Book, December 27, 1698 (transcribed by Richard Melvoin, 1981), Historic Deerfield-Pocumtuck Valley Memorial Library.

2. The Frontier: Girls' Own Errand into the Wilderness

1. Joseph Bartlett, "Narrative," in Joshua Coffin, *A Sketch of the History of Newbury, Newburyport and West Newbury from 1635 to 1845* (Boston: Samuel Drake, 1845), 331. Bartlett spelled the surname of his captain "Waindret." The Christian name of Wainwright is sometimes mistakenly listed in other documents as "Samuel."

2. For the Haverhill attack see Emma Lewis Coleman, *New England Captives Carried to Canada* (Portland Maine: Southworth Press, 1925), 1:352–55; Charlotte Alice Baker, *True Stories of the New England Captives* (1897) (Bowie, Md.: Heritage Books, 1987), 318, 319–25; Bartlett, "Narrative," 331.

3. Bartlett, "Narrative," 332.

4. Ibid. See the chapter epigraph.

5. This connection has been made previously by Emma Coleman as well as by Laurel Ulrich. See Coleman, *New England Captives,* 1:359 n. 37; Laurel Thatcher Ulrich, *Good Wives: Image and Reality in the Lives of Women in Northern New England, 1650–1750* (New York: Vintage, 1982), 211.

6. The Gyles narrative is discussed at length in chapter 4.

7. In particular, the timing of the Martin Kellogg captivity and the presence of Father Meriel in Montreal are precisely and correctly rendered.

8. Neither Marcel Fournier, René Jetté, nor Emma Coleman located a certificate of baptism for Ebenezer Nims or Sarah Hoyt. This raises the question of the circumstances of their "marriage" at Sault-au-Récollet. The lack of documentation might reflect their status as "white Indians." Further, the evidence that their son was baptized a Catholic in 1713 does not necessarily reflect the religious status of their parents. The children of captives were sometimes baptized at the sole instigation of the parents' captors, as in the case of the Adams family

discussed at length in chapter 5. Finally, in an astounding coincidence, Joseph Bartlett's second wife, whom he wed in 1721, was also named Sarah Hoyt. The captive Sarah from Deerfield and Mrs. Bartlett from Amesbury, Essex County, were, however, not related.

9. See the discussion of this point in the introduction.

10. Bartlett, "Narrative," 332–33.

11. See the introduction.

12. Bartlett, "Narrative" 332–33.

13. For Martin, Kellogg Jr., see Coleman, *New England Captives*, 2:97–100.

14. Ibid., 1:356. Louis Dupuis, *dit* Parisien, a former *voyageur* and soldier in the garrison of Quebec, is the only man of that surname both from the town of Quebec and serving as a militiaman at that time. See also René Jetté, *Dictionnaire généalogique des familles du Québec des origines à 1730* (Montréal: Presses de l'Université de Montréal, 1983), 391.

15. The baptism record of Mary Silver is found in *Histoire Congrégation Notre-Dame* (Montréal: privately published, n.d.), 3:139. The women of the extended Denis family actively sponsored many captives. The story of Marguerite-Renée Denis (the sister of Marie-Charlotte) and her captive Peter Kerklass is discussed in chapter 5. For the Denis family and the Pécaudy-Contrecoeurs see Jetté, *Dictionnaire généalogique*, 333, 886.

16. John Demos, *The Unredeemed Captive: A Family Story from Early America* (New York: Knopf, 1994).

17. There was a three-year interruption in the leadership of Marguerite Le Moyne. Between 1708 and 1711, Catherine Charly, like Marie Barbier a daughter of the Montreal artisan class, served as *supérieure*. See *History of the Congrégation Notre-Dame*, 3:141, Archives of the Centre Marguerite Bourgeoys, Montreal; Jetté, *Dictionnaire généalogique*, 231.

18. This account is based on the most detailed reconstruction of the York raid. See Charles Edwin Banks, *History of York Maine* (Boston, n.p., 1931), 1:287–97. Thanks to Kevin Sweeney for pointing out that the Oyster River raid also surpassed the fatality total at York.

19. The lists compiled by Banks and Coleman include an unusually high percentage of young male captives who elected to marry and permanently settle in Canada. This might suggest these young men had little to return to relative to a more representative sample of captives. The correlation of social liminality with the tendency to remain in Canada was reinforced by the lack of private ransomers, thus lengthening captivity and perhaps increasing the opportunities to form permanent attachments in New France. Banks also mentions explicitly that his list of named captives include a significant number of individuals with surnames that do not match the known family names of York, suggesting that a number of servants were captured in the raid and then transported to Canada. See Coleman, *New England Captives*, 1:221–30; Banks, *History of York Maine*, 295–96.

20. For the births of the Sayward sisters see *History of the Congrégation Notre-Dame*, 3:274–76.

21. Coleman, *New England Captives*, 1:237–38.

22. See, for example, Madame Pacaud's involvement in the ransoming and sponsorship of the captives Anne Odiorne and Martha French. Coleman, *New England Captives*, 2:7–8, 82–84.

23. The actual baptismal records of both Sayward sisters have been lost.

24. Such a mistake occurred in the captivity of Mehitable Goodwin. See Coleman, *New England Captives*, 1:185–86.

25. Hannah Swarton, "A Narrative of Hannah Swarton" (c. 1697), in *Puritans among the Indians: Accounts of Captivity and Redemption*, edited by Alden T. Vaughan and Edward W. Clark (Cambridge: Harvard University Press, 1981), 153–54. Swarton's mistress was identified by Vaughan and Clark; see 153 nn. 7, 8. For the family of the intendant see Jetté, *Dictionnaire généalogique*, 118.

26. See Louise Dechêne, *Habitants and Merchants in Seventeenth-Century Montreal*, translated by Liana Vardi (Montreal and Kingston: McGill-Queens University Press, 1992), 28.

27. Such was the case of Sarah Gerrish of the Hôtel-Dieu in Quebec.

28. Coleman, *New England Captives,* 1:238–39.

29. Ibid.

30. *History of the Congrégation Notre-Dame,* 3:277; Charles P. Beaubien, *Le Sault-au-Récollet* (Montreal: Beauchemin, 1898), 164–67; Coleman, *New England Captives,* 1:239.

31. Coleman, *New England Captives,* 2:91, 91–97, 102–12.

32. Tarbell's case is discussed in detail in chapter 1. For Martha French see *History of the Congrégation Notre-Dame,* 3:35; Coleman, *New England Captives,* 2:83–85. In addition to these students, Silver had arrived too late to meet another woman taken in by the Congrégation sisters: Elizabeth Price. Price, a marginal figure in Deerfield, had before her capture taken the perhaps unique step among English women in that town of marrying a local Indian man. What happened to this man, called Andrew Stevens, in the wake of the 1704 Deerfield attack is not clear, but after some time at the Congrégation, Price married a master shoemaker in Montreal in February 1706, thereby a achieving some small measure of upward social mobility. That Price had previously held a marginal status is indicated by, in addition to her previous marriage to an Indian, the speculation (by Coleman, based on the signature on her baptismal record) that Elizabeth Price was barely literate, even after some months among the Congrégation sisters. Interestingly, most of the witnesses to her marriage were New Englanders then living in Montreal, including Samuel Williams and Christine Otis. Esther Sayward signed as well. Lydia Longley did not sign. For Price see *History of the Congrégation Notre-Dame,* 3:27–28, 35; Coleman, *New England Captives,* 2:84–85, 113–16.

33. Sisters of the Congrégation Notre-Dame in 1708 are properly called *religieuses* as their status as a lay sisterhood ended with the adoption of a rule in 1698.

34. *History of the Congrégation Notre-Dame* 3:27–28, 35; Coleman, *New England Captives,* 2:84–85, 113–16.

35. It is critical to note here the proper translation of archaic French terms for medical institutions. "Hôtel-Dieu," literally "house of God," denotes a location where acute medical care was provided—it is a term analogous to our current use of the English word "hospital." Two "Hôtels-Dieu" existed in Canada before the British conquest: that in Montreal run by the Hospital Sisters of Saint Joseph and the Quebec institution operated by the Sisters of Saint Augustine. These places are not to be confused with the "Hôpital-Général" of Montreal or its counterpart in Quebec. Hôpitaux-Générals were locations of long-term care for the chronically ill or aged, the dispossessed poor, and sometimes orphans, criminals, or the mentally ill. A "Hôpital-Général" should be understood, then, as a combination hospice, almshouse, nursing home, and jail.

36. Gédeon de Catalogne, "Plan of the Hôtel-Dieu de Montréal," (1695). Courtesy Archives Hôtel-Dieu, Montréal.

37. Ibid.; conversation with Nicole Bussières, December 1998. Due to the community fires that destroyed key documents, we do not know the names of the New Englanders confined at the time.

38. An establishment the size and scope of the Hôtel-Dieu hospital and its farmland simply could not have been run without significant acquisition of labor. We do, however, have information about the labor situation from the period before and after Mary Silver's stay. The census of 1666, for example, lists two male domestic servants and twelve male farm workers, all presumably indentured, belonging to the Sisters of Saint Joseph. Keep in mind, though, that the Hôtel-Dieu existed on a far smaller scale in 1666 than in 1710. We learn as well that the *supérieure* of the Hôtel-Dieu during part of this time, the annalist Marie Morin, was herself the daughter of one of the first male indentured servants of the Hôtel-Dieu, Noël Morin. After Noël was freed and made his fortune, he became a generous benefactor of the community that had once owned him—suggesting the good treatment that could be expected by servants of the women's communities during the colony's first years. When the surviving

records of the Hôtel-Dieu resume in the 1750s, they reveal that the sisters made extensive use of free and contract labor and that they acquired at least one male New England captive as well—a laborer listed without a name. And as discussed in chapter 1, Nathaniel Belden was certainly a captive of the Hôtel-Dieu between 1696 and 1698. For the 1666 servants see *Rapport de l'archiviste de la Province de Quebec pour 1935–1936* (Quebec, 1936), esp. "Estat general des habitans du Canada in 1666"; for Noël Morin see Jetté, *Dictionnaire généalogique*, 634. For the New Englander see Archives Hôtel-Dieu, Montréal, "Depenses," May 1756.

39. Baker, *True Stories*, 319–29; Coleman, *New England Captives*, 1:356–58. Jetté, *Dictionnaire généalogique*, 800.

40. Bartlett, "Narrative," 333.

41. Ibid.

42. For Fourneau and Price see Coleman, *New England Captives*, 2:113–16.

43. Ibid., 116.

44. For the marriage of Hurst and Buraff see Coleman, *New England Captives*, 2:92–93; for the Bouat-Pacaud network, 2:7–8, 83–85.

45. For Jacob Gilman see Coleman, *New England Captives* 1:374–75; 2:91–93.

46. Bartlett, "Narrative," 332–33. See in particular the reported outcome of his debates with Father Meriel and Madame Delude.

47. Massachusetts Archives, 105:59. Reprinted in Baker, *True Stories*, 326–27.

48. As reprinted in Baker, *True Stories*, 328. These sentiments are remarkably similar to the ones expressed by the Ursuline Esther Wheelwright to her mother in 1747. This letter is preserved in the Ursuline Archives in Quebec.

49. Ulrich, *Good Wives*.

50. *Registre journalier des des malades* (1717), 279, Archives Hôtel-Dieu, Québec (hereafter AHD-Q).

51. For the most recent example, see Demos, *Unredeemed Captive*, a remarkable treatment of the tale of Eunice Williams, John's daughter, who chose to remain at Caughnawaga as a Mohawk.

52. John Williams, "The Redeemed Captive Returning to Zion" (1707), in *Puritans among the Indians*, edited by Vaughan and Clark, 185–86.

53. The reprint of the John Williams narrative in the 1981 Vaughan and Clark edition from Harvard is the most authoritatively annotated. A note states in part, "This English maid has not been identified." See Alden T. Vaughan and Edward W. Clark, eds., *Puritans among the Indians: Accounts of Captivity and Redemption* (Cambridge: Harvard University Press, 1981), 184 n. 27.

54. The phenomenon of the two "Mary Anne Davises" is the most mysterious part of this story. What is certain is that two New England-born religious sisters—Soeur Saint-Benoit, of the elite Quebec Ursulines, and the one in focus here, Soeur Saint-Cécile eventually of the Quebec's Hôtel-Dieu—both are recorded to share the name of "Mary Anne Davis." Coleman states, probably rightly, that one of these women was probably the daughter of John Davis of Oyster River, who was taken captive in 1688 and believed to have been placed in "a nunnery." The given name of the Oyster River girl is unrecorded in the New England sources—leading Coleman to the plausible claim that "Marie-Anne" was strictly a French baptismal name. Coleman believes that although descendants of this Davis family as of 1925 claimed the Ursuline as their own, it is more likely that their ancestry traces to the *hospitalière* Mary Anne. See Coleman, *New England Captives*, 1:268–70. For a similar perspective by the Hôtel-Dieu *annalistes*, see "Mere Marie-Anne Davis de Sainte-Cécile," Transcriptions/T12 C500, no. 118.2, AHD-Q.

55. See Ursule des Anges, "Resquiet in Pace—1761," July 12, 1761, AHD-Q.

56. Williams, "Redeemed Captive," 186.

57. Alice Nash has pointed out this aspect of Ruth's story. See Alice N. Nash, "The Abid-

ing Frontier" (Ph.D. diss., Columbia University, 1997), 265. As I stated in the introduction, Nash's excellent chapter on captivity among the Abenaki and her discussion of the Saint Francis mission should be considered the definitive treatment of the subjects.

58. See Jeanne-Françoise Juchereau de Sainte-Ignace, *Les annales de l'Hôtel-Dieu de Québec, 1636–1716* (c. 1716) (Québec: Hôtel-Dieu, 1939), 347–48; H.-R. Casgrain, *Histoire de L'Hôtel-Dieu de Québec* (Québec: Brousseau, 1878), 350–52.

59. For Eastman see Coleman, *New England Captives*, 2:131, 293. I discuss Eastman in the introduction. For Stark see Nash, "Abiding Frontier," 264.

60. Coleman, *New England Captives*, 2:26–27.

61. Davis left Saint Francis for Quebec in 1710.

62. For the physical description of Davis see Casgrain, *Histoire*, 350–52. The mention of the "white robe" is somewhat mysterious here as the winter robes of Abenaki and Iroquois women tended to be made out of either moosehide or beaver pelts. One possibility is that the sisters of the Hôtel-Dieu had earlier made a gift of the white cloth which was then conveyed to her by Bigot. More likely is that a hide robe was decorated with white quillwork, a favored adornment of northeastern Indian women. See Josephine Paterak, *Encyclopedia of American Indian Costume* (Denver: ABC-Clio, 1994), 56.

63. Vaughan and Clark's superb annotation to this passage of "The Redeemed Captive" bears repeating here: "Williams was adhering to a standard Puritan position. William Perkins, a major English Puritan spokesman, asserted that a Protestant servant should not obey a master who ordered him to attend Mass (*The Workes of that Worthy Minister of Christ . . . Mr William Perkins*, 3 vols. [London, 1612–37], 1:758). Similarly, Williams's contemporary, Benjamin Wadsworth of Massachusetts, argued in *The Well Ordered Family* (Boston, 1712) that children and servants should obey their parents and masters only in 'lawful things.' Ordering a servant to blaspheme God by attending Mass did not fit the Puritans' notion of lawful." See Vaughan and Clark, *Puritans among the Indians*, 186 n. 28.

64. Alden T. Vaughan and Daniel K. Richter, "Crossing the Cultural Divide: Indians and New Englanders, 1605–1763," *Proceedings of the American Antiquarian Society* 90, 1 (1980): 23–99.

65. *Registre journalier des malades* (1690), 81; (1693), 148, AHD-Q.

66. Ibid. (1693), 149, 179.

67. *Recettes et dépenses* (1693), 1:292, AHD-Q.

68. This figure is my own calculation using the *Recettes et dépenses* for the calendar year 1694. See ibid. (1694), 1:294.

69. *Greffe* of C.-H. Dulaurant, January 24, 1742, Archives Nationales de Québec–Montréal.

70. *Registre journalier des malades* (1709), 2–3, AHD-Q.

71. For "Jean" and "Louis," whose surnames were not recorded, see *Registre journalier des malades* (1709), 1, 62, AHD-Q. For Edward Barlow, transcribed in the Hôtel-Dieu records as "Eduard Berloe," see Marc-André Bédard, *Les protestants en Nouvelle-France*, Cahiers d'Histoire, no. 31 (Québec: Société Historique de Québec, 1978), 52.

72. Although Barlow does not appear in the conventional records of captives, we do know he was living in Charleston, Massachusetts, in 1688 and was buried, as a militia captain, on December 21, 1738. See "Taxes under Gov. Andros," *New England Historical and Genealogical Register,* 101 vols. (Boston: New England Historic, Genealogical Society, 1880–1947), 34:270; "Christ Church, Boston, Records," 101:162.

73. Computed from the Hôtel-Dieu profession roster as reprinted in Casgrain, *Histoire,* 582–87. The median age for the Sisters of Saint Augustine was twenty-three in July 1711, the date of Mary Anne Davis's profession (she had arrived as a novice in January 1710). The computation did not include Antoinette Du Tartre, then aged 76, who in 1711 was by twenty-seven years the oldest nominal member of the community, but was long retired from active hospital work.

74. For Gauvreau see Casgrain, *Histoire*, 587; Jetté, *Dictionnaire généalogique*, 42. For Cherron see Jetté, *Dictionnaire généalogique*, 245; Casgrain, *Histoire*, 586.

75. See Casgrain, *Histoire*, 584–85.

76. For the story of Sarah Gerrish see Juchereau, *Annales*, 258; Coleman, *New England Captives*, 1:144–45. None of the New England captives were written of more rapturously than young Gerrish. Captured from her Dover home in 1689, she was described by Casgrain as quoted in Coleman's translation as a "beautiful and ingenious damsel of seven years of age." Coleman goes on to state: "Their historian describes her as of such rare intelligence, noble bearing and exquisite tenderness she became the idol of the [Hôtel-Dieu] community." Even the taciturn chronicles of New York allow that she was "somewhat good-looking." Unfortunately for the Sisters of Saint Augustine, Gerrish was from one of the leading families of her New Hampshire town, who succeeded in winning her release after only one year. No doubt to the horror of Sarah's surviving parents in Dover, she had already adopted the Catholic faith, undergoing voluntary conversion at the extraordinary age of eight. Such was the hold of the faith and women's community on the mind of yet another Puritan girl that she swore to the sisters before her departure that she would remain true to her new religion. The sisters took the news of Sarah's early death in 1697 at the age of fifteen as a sign that God wished to take this pure soul from the world instead of allowing her earthly life to continue among the Calvinistic heretics. The sisters must have seen the arrival of the also physically striking Mary Anne Davis as the second coming of their lost treasure.

77. Casgrain, *Histoire*, 350–52.

78. Saint Cecilia's tale is told many places. Perhaps the best introduction to the lives of women saints is the almost century-old effort by the Briton Agnes B. C. Dunbar. See Dunbar, *A Dictionary of Saintly Women*, 2 vols. (London: George Bell & Sons, 1904), 1:167–68.

3. The Hospital: Paradoxes of the Grey Sisters

1. The "Three Years War" of 1722–24, also called "Governor Dummer's War," produced only about thirty-five named captives. See Emma Lewis Coleman, *New England Captives Carried to Canada* (Portland, Maine: Southworth Press, 1925), 2:133–70.

2. The question of female and male literacy rates has been extensively reviewed by Roger Magnuson. He concludes that although signatures in marriage contract records give males a slight edge in absolute literacy measured crudely, it remains undeniable that at the primary level girls enjoyed far more access to education than did boys in French Canada. See Roger Magnuson, *Education in New France* (Montreal and Kingston: McGill-Queen's University Press, 1992), 86–111, esp. 100.

3. More detailed versions of the story of the Charon community exist in every history of the Grey Sisters. Two English-language versions are to be found in Albina Fauteux, *Love Spans the Centuries*, vol. 1, *1642–1821*, translated by Antoinette Bezaire (Montréal: Meridian Press, 1987), 19–64 (originally published in 1915 as *Hôpital Général de Montréal*); Mary Pauline Fitts, *Hands to the Needy: Marguerite D'Youville, Apostle to the Poor* (c. 1950) (Garden City, N.Y.: Doubleday, 1987), 118–39.

4. Fitts, *Hands to the Needy*, 137.

5. See the detailed discussion of the "Jericho" experiment below.

6. Fitts, *Hands to the Needy*, 141–42. For the description of Rainville see p. 111. Although Fitts states she was of noble birth, the Jetté genealogy suggests her father worked as an artisan, see René Jetté, *Dictionnaire généalogique des familles du Québec des origines à 1730* (Montréal: Les Presses de l'Université de Montréal), 963 (family of Charles Rainville).

7. Fitts, *Hands to the Needy*, 141–42.

8. This perspective, and the events described in this section, are drawn mainly from Fau-

teux and Fitts, who in turn drew heavily on the *annales* of the Grey Sisters and community oral history.

9. Boucher's longevity was partly responsible for his fame as a link to the colony's origins. Just before his death in 1717 he celebrated his ninety-fifth birthday. The literature on Boucher is extensive. See, for example, *Dictionary of Canadian Biography* (Toronto: University of Toronto Press, 1966–76), 2:82–87; Jetté, *Dictionnaire généalogique*, 136, and Raymond Douville and Jacques Casanova, *Daily Life in Early Canada,* translated by Carola Congreve (New York: Macmillan, 1967), 21–24.

10. Jetté, *Dictionnaire généalogique,* 378. I use "Dufrost" here as a surname of economy and convenience. Members of the family, including Marguerite, would often use in addition or exclusively one of the seemingly countless spelling permutations of "LaJemmerais," the family's seigneurial title.

11. Ibid.

12. Peter Moogk, writing in the *Dictionary of Canadian Biography,* has done a marvelous job exposing the contradictory nature of Timothy Sullivan. Regarded by the majority of his contemporaries as a charlatan and a quack, he was seen by others, including Governor Vaudreuil, as a remarkably gifted physician. Sullivan possessed obvious personal magnetism that drew people to him, but also had a violent streak that led to several assault charges and to the public awareness that he regularly beat his wife, Marie-Renée Gaulthier. Sullivan clearly falsified his letters of Irish nobility, and Moogk speculates, probably correctly, that the Irishman originally immigrated to New England and then sought better prospects among his fellow Catholics in the Saint Lawrence Valley. He probably crossed the frontier around 1717. See *Dictionary of Canadian Biography,* 3:602–4; Fitts, *Hands to the Needy,* 38–40; Jetté, *Dictionnaire généalogique,* 1058.

13. Fitts, *Hands to the Needy,* 58–59. Fauteux, *Love Spans the Centuries,* 72 n. 9. For the discussion of the d'Youvilles and slavery see below.

14. Fitts, *Hands to the Needy,* 76.

15. Marcel Trudel, *Dictionnaire des esclaves et leurs propriétaires au Canada français* (Ville LaSalle, Québec: Éditions Hurtubise, 1990), 321.

16. Ibid., 429–30.

17. Ibid., 430.

18. Marcel Trudel, *L'esclavage au Canada français* (Québec: Presses Universitaires Laval, 1960), 122–23; Trudel, *Dictionnaire des esclaves,* 392, 430.

19. Fitts, *Hands to the Needy,* 145–46. Fitts also tells the most comprehensive tale of Jericho; see 144–47.

20. Ibid., 147. Fitts's translation.

21. My estimate from the records of "Registre de l'entrée des pauvres à l'Hôpital-Général de Ville-Marie," Archives Soeurs Grises–Montréal, esp. 3–13 (hereafter: ASG-M).

22. See Fauteux, *Love Spans the Centuries,* 137–42.

23. The British prisoners began arriving in 1753, but the last of the female inmates of Jericho were still being mentioned as present in the community late in 1755. The Grey Sisters had stopped accepting new female prisoners in 1750. See ibid., 107 n. 8.

24. Although the Seven Years' War did not begin "officially" until 1756, the Grey Sisters' archives clearly indicate they had purchased captives beginning three years earlier. This might reflect the irregular and ongoing frontier conflicts producing "unofficial" captives between the end of "King George's War" in 1748 and the onset of the final French-English intercolonial conflict. Another possible explanation for the 1753 and 1754 acquisition dates is that these captives may have been held in remote locations by Indian captors at the conclusion of King George's War and never released or ransom until they came to be in the hands of the Grey Sisters. Similar episodes occurred in the more or less continuous warfare from 1689 to 1713.

25. "Noms des Soeurs depuis le commencement de l'Institute jusqu'à nos jours," ASG-M.

26. For the retired matrons see, for example, "Etat des Personnes qui Logeoit dans l'hopital General de Montreal Lors de Lincedie arrivee Le 18 Mai 1765," in Albertine Ferland-Angers, *Mère d'Youville,* 3d ed. (Montréal: Centre Marguerite d'Youville, 1977), 332.

27. For three examples of such self-indenture contracts signed by Marguerite d'Youville see [Danré de Blanzy], "Engagement de François Cazarille et Marie Hust," October 2, 1749; [Danré de Blanzy], "Engagement de François Barret et Jean Barret," March 27, 1753, both in Archives Nationales de Québec–Montréal; and "Engagement de F. Dagenest," March 27, 1757, ASG-M (originally from Archives du Séminaire de Saint-Sulpice, Paris).

28. Fitts, *Hands to the Needy,* 209–10.

29. Even though the community bore most of the expenses of caring for their prisoners, on occasion the Canadian authorities recognized a responsibility for indirectly pressing the Hôpital-Général into medical work. The intendant, for example, paid 727 livres in 1757 to make repairs to the room holding the British prisoners. See *Ancien Journal,* 1:57–58, ASG-M.

30. For the purchase story and the amount paid, 200 livres, see *Ancien Journal,* 1:57.

31. For "Jean Anglais" see ibid., 1:57–58; "Recettes et depenses," September 4, 1747–December 31, 1779, 133, 148–49, 181, ASG-M.

32. For the examples of this naming practice, see the 1753–59 entries in "Recettes et depenses."

33. Orlando Patterson, *Slavery and Social Death: A Comparative Study* (Cambridge: Harvard University Press, 1982), 56–58.

34. According to Governor Duquesne's declaration in a similar case, a "Jean Anglais," purchased outright by a French citizen from the Indians in a just war, would be considered a "slave fairly sold." See the case of Solomon Mitchell, Coleman, *New England Captives,* 2:66–68.

35. *Ancien Journal,* 1:58, ASG-M.

36. The Grey Sisters' property was located directly across rivière Saint-Pierre from the Montreal stockade. The Hôpital-Général was easily reached, however, on foot or by cart in just a few minutes through a gate and across a bridge continuous either with rue Saint Francis-Xavier or, further west, the gate and bridge connecting with rue Saint-Pierre. So although the Hôpital-Général was located outside the stockade, it was not really separate from the town. Today, rivière Saint-Pierre is underground, long since paved over by the growing city. Part of it, however, is still visible to visitors to the lower floor of the remarkable Musée d'archéologie et d'histoire de Montréal.

37. On the wall see Fauteux, *Love Spans the Centuries,* 143–44. The gatekeeper of the property was termed a "porteress," an appointed position which rotated among the more junior sisters.

38. Jetté, *Dictionnaire généalogique,* 517.

39. *Ancien Journal,* 1:309, ASG-M. This story is meant to convey that God found a way to reward d'Youville's kindnesses to the soldiers.

40. "Recettes et depenses," 157, ASG-M.

4. The Seigneury: Obscuring Marguerite and Louise Guyon

1. René Jetté, *Dictionnaire généalogique des familles du Québec des origines à 1730* (Montréal: Les Presses de l'Université de Montréal), 548; *Dictionary of Canadian Biography* (Toronto: University of Toronto Press, 1966–76), 1:359.

2. Their seventh and last child, Barbe, born around 1675, probably died sometime after 1681.

3. *Dictionary of Canadian Biography,* 1:359.

4. Jetté, *Dictionnaire généalogique,* 1074.

5. "Damours" sometimes appears in the records as "d'Amours"—a form many descen-dants of this family favor today. The seigneurial title "de Chauffours" is often spelled without the second "f." The family tree of Mathieu Damours was truly impressive. The genealogist René Jetté traces some of Damours's most illustrious French ancestors, going all the way back to Enguerrand II Le Portier de Marigny of the thirteenth century. See Jetté, *Dictionnaire généalogique,* 300–301.

6. *Dictionary of Canadian Biography,* 1:245.

7. The Little Ice Age, then prevailing over the northern hemisphere, produced ice con-ditions on the Saint Lawrence far more severe than is the case today.

8. For the Damours brothers, see *Dictionary of Canadian Biography,* 1:245, 245–46, 2:166–67.

9. For Charles Thibault see Jetté, *Dictionnaire généalogique,* 1075.

10. Louise's later life is discussed below. See also *Dictionary of Canadian Biography,* 3:681–82.

11. John Gyles, "Memoirs of Odd Adventures, Strange Deliverances, etc." (c. 1736), in *Puritans among the Indians: Accounts of Captivity and Redemption, 1676–1724,* edited by Alden T. Vaughan and Edward W. Clark (Cambridge: Harvard University Press, 1981), 95–96. Hereafter cited by page number in the text. The Gyles residence, at "Merrymeeting Bay," was probably on the eastern shore of the mouth of the Kennebec River near present-day Wool-wich. See John A. Vinton, "Thomas Gyles and His Neighbors," *New England Historical and Ge-nealogical Register,* 101 vols. (Boston: New England Historic, Genealogical Society 1880–1947), 21:353. The proprietor of the lands around Pemaquid, the second Gyles residence in Maine, was Governor Duncan (or Dongan) of New York. The claim of Massachusetts on the Maine coast at that time went effectively only as far as the Kennebec. The entire area to the east of the Kennebec, all the way to the Saint Croix River (the present-day border between Maine and New Brunswick) including the extensive area around the mouth of the Penob-scot, had been granted by King Charles II to the Duke of York and had thereby passed to Province of New York. The area around Pemaquid was officially termed the "County of Corn-wall, New York." It was this county over which Thomas Gyles presided. Vinton also agrees with John Gyles that Thomas was fairly wealthy by New England standards. See *New England Reg-ister,* 21:357, 358.

12. Near present-day New Harbor, Maine.

13. The *Dictionary of Canadian Biography,* 3:272, mistakenly lists Gyles as nine years old at the time of his capture.

14. For the details of the Pemaquid assault see *New England Register,* 21:359–61; Emma Lewis Coleman, *New England Captives Carried to Canada,* 2 vols. (Portland, Maine: Southworth Press, 1925), 1:167–79. Estimates of the number of captives taken from Pemaquid vary from a low of twenty (Vaughan and Clark) to a high of fifty (Coleman). Coleman, however, found records of only nineteen named captives who met the usual variety of fates. Several of the young women eventually married Canadians and settled permanently in New France.

15. In the introductory to this narrative Gyles explains his genuine reluctance to write about his father: "I have been likewise advised to give a particular account of my father which I am not very fond of, having no dependence on the virtues or honors of my ancestors to rec-ommend me to the favor of God or men; nevertheless, because some think it is a respect due to the memory of my parents, whose name I was obliged to mention in the following story and a satisfaction which their posterity might justly expect from me, I shall give some account [of him], though as brief as possible" (p. 95). This admission indicates the external pressure to reveal personal details still antithetical to the Puritan narrative form. This form has con-tinually given rise to the erroneous assumption that settlers of this era felt the loss of loved ones less keenly than did their descendants.

16. Vaughan and Clark link this part of the narrative with Thury. See Gyles, "Memoirs," 99 n. 13.

17. See, for example, John Rutherfurd, "John Rutherfurd's Narrative," in *The Siege of Detroit in 1763,* edited by Milo Milton Quaife (Chicago: Lakeside Press, 1958).

18. Vaughan and Clark note that Gyles himself noted that, lest anyone get the wrong idea, "though both male and female may be in the water at a time, they have each of them more or less of their clothes on and behave with the utmost chastity and modesty" (*Puritans among the Indians,* 111 n. 29).

19. John Evans, Gyles's fellow captive, froze to death while still in captivity. His possible origins in Cocheco (Dover, New Hampshire) are discussed briefly by Coleman. See *New England Captives,* 1:144.

20. De La Place was identified by Vaughan and Clark; see *Puritans among the Indians,* 112 n. 30. The Maliseet parties disputing the ownership of Gyles had earlier given him a remarkable degree of freedom in choosing his next owner. Before coming to the French settlements on the Saint-Jean, Gyles had earlier rejected being sold to the captain of a French ship on the grounds that a seagoing life would give him little chance of seeing New England again. See Gyles, "Memoirs," 124.

21. Gyles identifies his purchaser as "Monsieur Dechoufer."

22. Based on direction and distance.

23. See her signed notarial records in the National Archives of Quebec. Some of the Montreal examples are cited below.

24. The best original source on this campaign from the French perspective is P. F. X. de Charlevoix, *History and General Description of New France* (c. 1715), translated by John Gilmary Shea (Chicago: Loyola University Press, 1870), 5:23–34.

25. Jetté, *Dictionnaire généalogique,* 301.

26. No death records for Louise and Madeleine exist (the Acadian records being less complete than those of the Saint Lawrence parishes), but the combined fact that Gyles does not mention them and the finding of René Jetté that each was a patient in the Acadian outpost of the Hospital Sisters of Saint Augustine leads to that conclusion. For Marie-Josèphe and Marie-Charlotte, see Jetté, *Dictionnaire généalogique,* 301.

27. The circumstances surrounding this retaliation were fairly complex. See Charlevoix, *History,* 5:30–34.

28. Ibid., 30, 30 n. 3. Fort Nashwaak (also spelled "Naxoat" in some sources) was at the present-day site of New Brunswick's capital city, Fredricton. Port Royal, in Nova Scotia, had not yet been designated the seat of government in French Acadia.

29. *Dictionary of Canadian Biography,* 3:681, 1:245, 245–46; Jetté, *Dictionnaire généalogique,* 300, 301.

30. There is some confusion over the birth dates and deaths of three of Louise Guyon's five sons. Of the two sons who certainly survived to adulthood, Joseph is positively known to have been born in 1687 and Mathieu-François in 1692. The birth dates of the others, who apparently died before reaching the age of marriage, can only be estimated. Jetté lists Louis as being born around 1689, Nicolas around 1695, and a fifth son around 1696. See Jetté, *Dictionnaire généalogique,* 301.

31. Hannah Swarton, "A Narrative of Hannah Swarton," in *Puritans among the Indians,* edited by Vaughan and Clark, 154.

32. The September 1697 Treaty of Ryswick ending the "War of the League of Augsburg" in Europe—the New World manifestation of which was known in New England as "King William's War," did not end hostilities between New England and the French-allied Abenaki. The so-called "Second Abenaki War" lasted until 1699. However, recognizing that the Massachusetts and New York authorities would generally fail to distinguish between those civilian captives held by the French and those among the Abenaki, Governor-General Frontenac

urged his Native allies to free their prisoners in 1698. See Ian K. Steele, *Warpaths: Invasions of North America* (New York: Oxford University Press, 1994), 145–47; Coleman, *New England Captives,* 1:76.

33. See esp. ibid., 1:76–78.

34. The Phips-Frontenac exchange did not send any men back to Massachusetts, only "women and children." The only man in the 1695 exchange who might have conceivably been held by Damours and Guyon was James Alexander, who appears briefly in the Indian phase of the Gyles captivity narrative. It is more than likely, however, that Gyles himself would have related the coincidence of his presence at Jemseg to the reader.

35. There are several extant examples of her signature documents pertinent to the management of the joint marital property. See, for example, July 12, 1700, *greffe* of J. C. Loppincot, "Vente de la terre située au Port Royal," Archives Nationales de Québec–Montréal. The summary emphasizes: "La femme de Louis Damours signe Marguerite Guyon."

36. It is impossible to tell for certain how many of Louise Guyon's sons were alive in 1701 and 1702. Because infant mortality was more common than death later in childhood, an estimate of two is probably safer than that made in the *Dictionary of Canadian Biography*, which assumes Louis Damours' daughters joined five male cousins in their aunt's household at Port Royal. See *Dictionary of Canadian Biography* 3:681–82.

37. Ibid., 2:166–67.

38. Ibid., 3:681.

39. Ibid.

40. The appendix to Gyles's narrative in which he outlines his later career does not appear in the Vaughan and Clark collection. See instead Samuel G. Drake, *Indian Captivities, or Life in the Wigwam* (Auburn, New York: Miller, Orton, and Mulligan, 1854), 106–9.

5. The Household: Captive and *Canadienne*

1. See André Lachance, "Women and Crime in Canada in the Early Eighteenth Century, 1712–1759," in *Crime and Criminal Justice in Europe and Canada,* edited by Louis A. Knafla (Waterloo, Ont.: Wilfrid Laurier University Press, 1981), 160; Jan Noel, "New France: Les femmes favorisées," *Atlantis* 6, 2 (1981): 82.

2. See generally Kathryn A. Young, "'. . . sauf les perils et fortunes de la mer': Merchant Women in New France and the French Transatlantic Trade, 1713–1746," *Canadian Historical Review* 77, 3 (1996): 388–407; Jan V. Noel, "Women of the New France Noblesse," in *Women and Freedom in Early America,* edited by Larry D. Eldridge (New York: New York University Press, 1997).

3. John Williams, "The Redeemed Captive Returning to Zion" (1707), in *Puritans among the Indians: Accounts of Captivity and Redemption, 1676–1724,* edited by Alden T. Vaughan and Edward W. Clark (Cambridge: Harvard University Press, 1981), 188. However, John Williams's early-nineteenth-century biographer, Stephen W. Williams, interpreted "youngest child" to mean "youngest *daughter.*" Four-year-old son Warham was the youngest surviving child of the family and therefore is the most likely candidate for redemption by Saint-Père. In addition, Williams's youngest surviving daughter was seven-year-old Eunice, who at that time resided with the Mohawks. Stephen W. Williams's interpretation must therefore be discounted. See Stephen W. Williams, *A Biographical Memoir of the Rev. John Williams* (Greenfield, Mass.: C. J. J. Ingersoll, 1837), 51. Though generations of readers offered commentary on the Williams narrative, the identity of the "gentlewoman" remained a mystery until 1954. That year, Marine Leland, a history professor at Smith College used the correspondence of the most prominent woman textile entrepreneur in Montreal in 1704 to establish with certainty that the Canadienne in question was Agathe Saint-Père, the wife of Pierre Legardeur,

seigneur de Repentigny. See Marine Leland, "Madame de Repentigny," *Le bulletin des recherches historiques* 60 (1954): 75–77.

4. See J.-N. Fauteux, *Essai sur l'industrie au Canada sous le régime français* (Québec: Proulx, 1927); E.-Z. Massicote, "Agathe de Saint Père, Dame Le Gardeur de Repentigny," *Le bulletin des recherches historiques* 50 (1944): 202–7; Albert Tessier, *Canadiennes* (Montreal: Fides, 1946).

5. My translation. The original (reprinted in Leland, "Madame de Repentigny," 75–76) reads: La parfaite connaissance que j'ai des soins que vous prenez de pays, me flatte que vous souffrirez ce détail, et que vous trouverez bon que de mon propre mouvement j'aie levé une manufacture de toile, droguet, serge croisée et couverte. Pour cet effet, Monseigneur, j'ai racheté neuf Anglais de la main des Sauvages à mon dépens. Je leur ai fait faire des métiers et leur ai fait monter dans un logement commode.

6. The primacy of family interests in the pursuits of Canadian businesswomen has been forcefully established by Jan Noel; see Noel, "Women of the New France Noblesse."

7. See René Jetté, *Dictionnaire généalogique des familles du Québec des origines à 1730* (Montréal: Les Presses de l'Université de Montréal, 1983), 1030.

8. Ibid., 711.

9. Madeleine Doyon-Ferland, "Saint-Père, Agathe de (Legardeur de Repentigny)," in *Dictionary of Canadian Biography* (Toronto: University of Toronto Press 1966–76), 2:580–81.

10. See, for example, May 9, 1685, *greffe* of H. Bougine, Archives Nationales de Québec–Montréal (hereafter cited as ANQ-M).

11. See chapter 1. Françoise Le Moyne died in 1687—and so did not live to see her sister assume the leadership of the Congrégation.

12. See the discussion in chapter 1 of Crolo and the early French indentured servants on the farm at La Providence.

13. Jetté, *Dictionnaire généalogique,* 697.

14. See the inventory of Jacques Le Moyne, July 24, 1685, and the subsequent agreement between Le Moyne and Saint-Père, July 26, 1685, [H. Bourgine], ANQ-M.

15. There is a discrepancy here between the two principal genealogies of early Canadian families as to the number of Saint Père's children. Jetté's genealogy states that two of Saint-Père's seven listed children have the same name (Marie-Catherine), indicating that one probably died in infancy. See Jetté, *Dictionnaire généalogique,* 697. Cyprien Tanguay's older genealogy indicates Saint-Père had eight children. See Tanguay, *Dictionnaire généalogique des familles canadiennes* (Québec: Senécal, 1871), 1:370.

16. *Dictionary of Canadian Biography,* 2:581.

17. Ibid. Some of the most important correspondence regarding Saint-Père can be found in the National Archives of Canada, Ottawa. See especially the letters from Compte de Pontchartrain to the Raudots, series c11G, vols. 2–3, reels F-417 and F-418. See also Jacques Raudot's letters to the Paris ministry of October 25 and November 14, 1708, series c11a, vol. 29, National Archives of Canada.

18. The nineteenth-century historian of Wells and Kennebunk Maine, Edward E. Bourne, evidently did not think the young criminal was the same "James Adams" as the adult weaver and war captive. He writes that the kidnapper of the two boys was an adult man who had a feud with the father of the boys, Henry Simpson. However, there is only one "James Adams" recorded as residing at Wells, Maine, in 1679 (the year of the crime) as well as in 1703 (the year of the raid on Wells). The captive is known to have been born in the year 1668. Therefore in 1679 the miscreant, if the same person, would have been about eleven years old. Although it is certainly possible that another James Adams moved into Wells unnoticed by Bourne, the possibility that this was a crime committed by a boy and not an adult man is supported by the particulars of the punishment imposed: a lashing, fine, and temporary banishment from the town. This would have been a remarkably lenient punishment imposed on an adult just convicted of a double attempted murder. The strongest evidence of the juvenile

status of the offender is that James's father, Philip, took responsibility for the fine and assured the court at York that he would take charge of James. See Edward E. Bourne, *History of Wells and Kennebunk* (Portland, Maine: B. Thurston, 1875), 160–61. The original court document, which nowhere indicates that Adams was "a man of bad temper" as Bourne contends, is found in "Extracts from Records in the County of York," in *Collections of the Maine Historical Society,* ed. William Willis (Portland, Maine: Bailey and Noyes, 1865), 1:380–81.

19. For the baptismal record, see Emma Lewis Coleman, *New England Captives Carried to Canada,* 2 vols. (Portland, Maine: The Southworth Press, 1925), 1:401. Coleman lists Agathe Saint-Père as "Agatha de Nere." Coleman's mistake is understandable. Examples of Agathe Saint-Père's signature reveal that "Saint" was abbreviated to "st" which could, as it is written, be mistaken for "de." Further, the *P* in "Père" was written to closely resemble an *N.* For an example of this signature, see the marriage contract of Jacques Le Gardeur de Saint Pierre and Marie-Joseph Guillimin, reproduced in Joseph L. Peyser, trans. and ed., *Jacques Legardeur de Saint-Pierre: Officer, Gentleman* (East Lansing: Michigan State University Press, 1996), 46. However, the transcription of this document on the facing page (47) mistakenly interprets "Saint Père" as "Saint Pierre."

20. The text of the letter reads: "I pray giue my kind loue to Landlord Shelden, and tel Him that I am sorry for all his los. I doe in these few lins showe youe that god has shone yo grat kindness and marcy, In carrying youre Daughter Hanna, and Mary in pertickeler, through so grat an iorney, far beiend my expectation, noing How Lame they war; the Rest of your children are with the Indians, Rememberrance liues near cabect, Hannah also liues with the frenc, Jn in the same house i doe." I am most grateful here to Kevin Sweeney for pointing out an error or mistranscription in Adams's letter. The letters *Jn* suggest that it was John Sheldon's namesake son, John Jr., being held at that time by Saint-Père. In fact, John Sheldon Jr. remained safely in Deerfield—while his brother Ebenezer was being held in Montreal. If this is not a mistranscription, Adams may have been trying to abbreviate a form of "junior"—referring to a son. This letter is reprinted in George Sheldon, *A History of Deerfield, Massachusetts* (Greenfield, Mass.: E. A. Hall, 1895), 1:328. Also, Emma Coleman was mistaken when she placed John's wife Hannah in the same Saint-Père house. The Adams letter clearly indicates that Hannah resided elsewhere; see Coleman, *New England Captives,* 1:400.

21. John Sheldon (Sr.) to Ebenezer (?) Sheldon, April 1, 1705, in Sheldon, *History of Deerfield,* 1:328. The elder John Sheldon writes: "remember my loue to Mr Addams and his wif and iudah writ and all the reste as if named." Also for Wright, see Richard I. Melvoin, *New England Outpost: War and Society in Colonial Deerfield* (New York: W. W. Norton, 1989), 251; Sheldon, *History of Deerfield,* 1:309; Coleman, *New England Captives,* 2:35, 128.

22. On Pendleton Fletcher Jr. as well as his father, see Coleman, *New England Captives,* 2:15–17; for a brief discussion of the *monnaies de cartes,* 2:408–9. Also note that Coleman speculates that the identity of the "weaver" offered to Agathe Sainte-Père in exchange for Warham Williams was perhaps Nathaniel Brooks of Deerfield. In the town records reproduced at various points in George Sheldon's *History of Deerfield,* however, Nathaniel Brooks appears to be a farmer and part-time soldier, not a weaver. See Coleman, *New England Captives,* 2:64 n. 61.

23. See Raymond Boyer, *Les crimes et châtiments au Canada français du XVIIe au XXe siècle* (Ottawa: Le Cercle du Livre de France, 1966), 197.

24. There is a discrepancy here between the New England and the New France sources on the date of return of the New England captives. Fauteux has noted in Saint-Père's writings that the return date for the captives is mentioned as being 1707. One possible explanation is that Adams, Sheldon, and Fletcher returned on the *Marie* in 1706 and the rest returned later. See Fauteux, *Essai sur l'industrie,* 2:467.

25. On baptism in the Congregational church, see, for example, Charles E. Hambrick-

Stowe, *The Practice of Piety: Puritan Devotional Disciplines in Seventeenth-Century New England* (Chapel Hill: University of North Carolina Press, 1982), 123–24.

26. Canadian girls of similar age frequently appear in the baptismal records as godmothers and baptismal sponsors of the children of family friends and relatives. For the Rocbert family see Tanguay, *Dictionnaire généalogique,* 1:524. Coleman, however, mistakenly lists the girl's name as "Marie Elizabeth," perhaps confusing her with her mother, Élisabeth [Duverger] Rocbert. See Coleman, *New England Captives,* 1:401. In another such example, a girl of an extremely prominent noble family, Catherine de Ramezay, earnestly sought out the religious sponsorship of young male captives. When she was ten she served as godmother to her family's own seventeen-year-old captive servant William Taylor. Six years later she signed as the godmother of the twenty-nine-year-old captive Nathaniel Otis. The devoutness underlying these actions is indicated by her choice in 1717 to become an Ursuline sister in Quebec. See Coleman, *New England Captives,* 1:159–60, 368; Jetté, *Dictionnaire généalogique,* 964. (Note that this girl is listed in the genealogy as "Marie-Catherine." A daughter previously born to the Ramezays who apparently died in infancy had been christened "Catherine.")

27. See Jetté, *Dictionnaire généalogique,* 54.

28. For the Pacauds and their captives see Coleman, *New England Captives,* 2:5–8; Jetté, *Dictionnaire généalogique,* 54, 862; *Dictionary of Canadian Biography,* 2:508–9; Marcel Trudel, *Dictionnaire des esclaves et leurs propriétaires au Canada français* (Ville LaSalle, Québec: Éditions Hurtubise, 1990), 58, 394.

29. I am not suggesting that Agathe Saint-Père engaged in a sort of precocious proto-industrial enterprise. To the contrary, Saint-Père's loom-driven factory operated in a quite traditional late-medieval and early-modern mode of production. In fact, the employment of subordinate male artisans by female entrepreneurs seems to have been an established *modus operandi* in the Europe and the Mediterranean frontier in advance of Saint-Père. See Jacques Heers, *Esclaves et domestiques au moyen âge dans le monde méditerranéen* (Paris: Fayard, 1981), 126, 144.

30. On these traditions, see, for example, Adrienne D. Hood, "The Gender Division of Labor in the Production of Textiles in Eighteenth-Century, Rural Pennsylvania (Rethinking the New England Model)," *Journal of Social History,* spring 1994, 537–61. There are also issues surrounding those to whom Saint-Père's New England weavers conveyed their skills. On the basis of Saint-Père's writings, Doyon-Ferland states that the workshop became self-sufficient after the New Englanders departed, thanks to the hiring of (presumably free) Canadian employees. Marcel Trudel's statement that Indian slaves helped in Saint-Père's enterprise is not correct. He misinterprets Agathe's statement that she redeemed New Englanders from the Indians. He states instead that Saint-Père purchased Indian slaves from New Englanders, which is clearly not the case. See Marcel Trudel, *L'esclavage au Canada français* (Québec: Les Presses Universitaires Laval, 1960), 168.

31. For a discussion of this conflict, see Leslie P. Choquette, *Frenchmen into Peasants: Modernity and Tradition in the Peopling of French Canada* (Cambridge: Harvard University Press, 1997), 283.

32. See again Young, "'sauf les perils.'"

33. Sheldon, *History of Deerfield,* 1:328. See also Coleman, *New England Captives,* 1:400.

34. Coleman, *New England Captives,* 2:118.

35. The circumstances of Agathe Saint-Père's life after 1706 as well as those surrounding her death are incomplete—surprising for a *Canadienne* of her social status.

36. Peter Kalm, *Travels in North America* (1770) (New York: Dover, 1987), 403.

37. See Marcel Fournier, *De la Nouvelle-Angleterre à la Nouvelle-France: L'histoire des captifs anglo-américains au Canada entre 1675 et 1760* (Montréal: Société Généalogique Canadienne-Française, 1992), 158; Marc André Bédard, *Les protestants en Nouvelle-France* (Québec: Société Historique de Québec, 1978), 103; Tanguay, *Dictionnaire généalogique,* 4:494, 5:139; Jetté, *Dic-*

tionnaire généalogique, 645; Coleman, *New England Captives,* 2:396. While the lists of the Société Généalogique Canadienne-Française confirm that there was a "Jean L'Anglais" among the Gagnons of Château-Richer who was baptized in 1691, the parish records of Beaupré reveal a 1700 baptism placing a "Jean L'Anglais" in the hands of Jean Baret of Beaupré. This suggests that there were two New England captives with identical names living in the separate parishes. Both Fournier, who writes of the Gagnon captive, and Jetté, who writes of the Baret captive, claim "their" captive went on to marry Anne Raté and, after Raté's death, Thérèse Darde. The evidence suggests Fournier is correct. First, the baptism record of the captive of Jean Baret is listed in the parish of Beaupré, where Baret had moved around 1669. However the marriage records of L'Anglais in 1707, and again in 1710, are recorded in Château-Richer having been performed by the same priest, Jacob, who presided over the Gagnon family ceremonies. Further, the baptism record of the Baret captive lists him as an *"esclave anglais."* This suggests that he was one of the slaves of African descent taken from New England to New France (Anglo-American captives were *not* listed in this way). *Esclave anglais* is better translated as "slave *of* the English" rather than "English slave." It is extremely unlikely that this slave would have been released and then permitted to marry a free French-Canadian woman. Every other record of such captive slaves indicates they were simply re-enslaved in New France. This confusion might have resulted from the fact that Jean Baret had originally been a resident of Château-Richer. For Baret, see Jetté, *Dictionnaire généalogique,* 48.

38. I resume here the convention of referring to married *Canadiennes* by their maiden names. Married women conducting business most often signed documents with their Christian name and original family surname. When a husband's name was invoked in the women's signatures, it was usually his seigneurial title, not his surname. It is possible that French-Canadian women adopted this convention because of the high mortality rate among men and the widows' tendency to remarry quickly. No matter what their current marital status or how often they entered into the sacrament, then, their identity as reflected in their name was continued intact.

39. See Jetté, *Dictionnaire généalogique,* 77. Marie Gagnon died in 1709 at Château Richer as a result of complications from childbirth. She was twenty years old.

40. Louise Dechêne, *Habitants and Merchants in Seventeenth-Century Montreal,* translated by Liana Vardi (Montreal and Kingston: McGill-Queen's University Press, 1992), 255. See also Allan Greer, *Peasant, Lord, and Master* (Toronto: University of Toronto Press, 1985), 10; W. J. Eccles, *The Canadian Frontier, 1534–1760,* rev. ed. (Albuquerque: University of New Mexico Press, 1974), 101. Eccles writes of Canadian boys that they "seized on [military service] eagerly. Youths in their teens were enrolled as cadets and served on campaigns with their fathers and elder brothers to gain experience, then were sent out in command of scouting and small raiding parties for intelligence purposes."

41. See *Dictionary of Canadian Biography,* 2:178–79; Jetté, *Dictionnaire généalogique,* 333.

42. Jetté, *Dictionnaire généalogique,* 1064.

43. Ibid.

44. For an excellent review of child-rearing practices among the Canadian elite generally, see Jan V. Noel, "Women of the New France Noblesse," 26–43, esp. 33–35.

45. See Peter N. Moogk, "Reluctant Exiles: Emigrants from France in Canada before 1760," *William and Mary Quarterly,* 3d ser., 46, 3 (1989): 463–505, esp. 499.

46. The baptismal record from the parish archives of Notre-Dame-de-Montréal, reported by Jetté, uses the word *serviteur* as opposed to *domestique* to describe the position of Kerklass in the Denis household. In ancien régime France, and presumably by extension in Canada, *domestique* was a general term used to identify workers in performing any job related to the greater household, even outdoor or farm labor. *Serviteur,* however, tended to be used specifically to denote a servant employed in personal service to the master or mistress. See the explanation in Jean-Pierre Gutton, *Domestiques et serviteurs dans la France de l'Ancien Régime* (Aubier: Montaigne, 1981), 10–14.

47. Jetté, *Dictionnaire généalogique,* 617.

48. Fournier speculates that Kerklass returned in the truce and prisoner exchange of 1695. This conclusion does recognize the fact that very few deaths in the colony escaped the notice of the vigilant parish priests of French Canada, for this reason alone making it likely Kerklass eventually returned to Corlear. But a 1695 release date is probably not correct. The 1695 prisoner exchange, arranged in the midst of ongoing hostilities, produced an exact list of those English subjects who were released. This list survives, and the name of Kerklass does not appear. That he returned in the general (and relatively undocumented) release at war's end in 1698 is far more likely. See Fournier, *De la Nouvelle-Angleterre,* 154. For the list of the captives returned in 1695 see Coleman, *New England Captives,* 1:72–77.

49. For Goodwin see Coleman, *New England Captives,* 1:185–86; for Willey, 1:255–57.

50. Jan Noel, "New France, les femmes favorisées," *Atlantis* 6, 2 (1981): 82.

51. Laurel Thatcher Ulrich, *Good Wives: Image and Reality in the Lives of Women in Northern New England, 1650–1750* (New York: Vintage, 1982), 95.

52. Jetté, *Dictionnaire généalogique,* 910; Fournier, *De la Nouvelle-Angleterre,* 182–83.

53. Jetté, *Dictionnaire généalogique,* 1125; Fournier, *De la Nouvelle-Angleterre,* 231, c#410.

54. G. Debien, "Liste des engagés pour le Canada au XVIIe siècle," *Revue d'historie de l'Amérique française* 6, 3 (1952): 405.

55. *Greffe* of Gaudron de Chevremont, March 24, 1738, ANQ-M. See also the case mentioned in chapter 2 of the acquisition of the convict Pierre Monet by the Hospital Sisters of Saint Augustine (*greffe* of C.-H. Dulaurant, January 24, 1742, ANQ-M).

56. Jetté, *Dictionnaire généalogique,* 423; Fournier, *De la Nouvelle-Angleterre,* 172.

57. Jetté, *Dictionnaire généalogique;* Fournier, *De la Nouvelle-Angleterre,* 202.

58. Kalm, *Travels in North America,* 403.

59. Ibid., 403, 525.

60. Jan Noel discusses the case of the priest at mass, as well as the visual culture of women's dress generally, in "Les femmes favorisées," 82.

61. Kalm, *Travels in North America,* 403.

62. My translation. See Louis Franquet, *Voyages et mémoirs sur le Canada par Franquet* (1854), (Montréal: Éditions Élysée, 1974), 57.

63. See R.-L. Séguin, "La Canadienne aux XVIIe et XVIIIe siècles," *Revue d'histoire de l'Amerique français* 13 (1960): 493.

64. Ibid.

65. Thomas Brown, "A Plain Narrative of the Uncommon Sufferings and Remarkable Deliverances of Thomas Brown" (c. 1760) in *Captured by the Indians: 15 Firsthand Accounts, 1750–1850,* edited by Frederick Drimmer (New York: Dover, 1985), 69–70. Hereafter cited by page number in the text.

66. See chapter 2 at note 13.

67. Zadock Steele, "The Captivity of Zadock Steele" (c. 1818), in *North Country Captives: Selected Narratives of Indian Captivity from Vermont and New Hampshire,* edited by Colin G. Calloway (Hanover, N.H.: University Press of New England, 1992), 112.

68. Coleman, *New England Captives,* 2:312. The date of Labaree's capture, 1750, and the lack of hesitation with which he was acquired as a "slave" by the Montreal family is an indication that the captivities in fact continued nonstop from the beginning of "King George's War" in 1744 to the fall of Quebec in 1760. The peace between Britain and France lasting from 1748 to 1756 was not always recognized on the northeastern North American frontier.

69. Ibid., 191.

70. Ibid., 272–73.

71. John Crawford, "Narrative of Indian and Tory Depredations in Pennsylvania, 1770–1777," in *Indian Warfare in Western Pennsylvania and North West Virginia at the Time of the American Revolution,* edited by Jared C. Lobdell (Bowie, Md.: Heritage Books, 1992), 29.

72. William Pote Jr., *The Journal of Captain William Pote, Jr. during his Captivity in the French and Indian War from May 1745 to August, 1747*, edited and annotated by Victor H. Paltsits (New York: Dodd, Mead and Company, 1896), 108–9. This journal, probably the longest of all the narratives emerging from the New France captivities, comprises 234 manuscript pages. It was found by chance in Geneva, Switzerland, by an American, John Fletcher Hurst, who purchased it and promptly brought it to the attention of the scholarly community. Dodd, Mead and Company published it in a hard-cover run of 375 copies in 1896. The manuscript currently resides in the Newberry Library.

73. Ibid., xii, 1–80. This edition features a well-drawn map of the party's route.

74. Ibid., 136. This is the only reference I have found in a narrative to extramarital sexual encounters of any kind among Anglo-Americans in captivity. These passages are certainly another form of narrative innovation in the new era. See also Pote's account of Susanah Boillison on page 147.

75. Ibid., 79, 126, 141.

76. "The Journal of a Captive, 1745–1748," in *Colonial Captivities, Marches, and Journeys*, edited by Isabel M. Calder (New York: Macmillan, 1935), 41. No author is named.

77. Interestingly, Pote's passage on the post-fire visit by the Canadian "Ladies" also appears, practically verbatim, in the account by the anonymous author of "Journal of a Captive" on page 58. Evidently, this feeling of animosity was shared by the two men, or the journals shared in part the same author.

78. "Journal of a Captive," 30.

79. A drawing of the prison building, the yard, and the picket fence appears on the frontispiece of the Calder volume. Life in the Quebec prison is the subject of a chapter of an excellent recent master's thesis on the later captivities. See Colleen Gray, "Captives in Canada, 1744–1763" (M.A. thesis, McGill University, 1993), chap. 2.

80. Tanguay, *Dictionnaire généalogique*, 6:311.

81. "Journal of a Captive," 41.

82. See, for example, Margaret DeLacy, *Prison Reform in Lancashire, 1700–1850* (Stanford: Stanford University Press, 1986), 38; and Elizabeth Hooton, letter from Lincoln Castle, undated, reprinted in Emily Manners, *Elizabeth Hooton: First Quaker Woman Preacher, 1600–1672* (London: Headley Brothers, 1914), 14–15.

83. For cooking and laundry see Pote, "Journal," 102.

84. Ibid., 109.

85. Ibid., 99–100, 102.

86. "Journal of a Captive," 36.

87. Pote, "Journal," 102, 128, 144.

88. Ibid., 103; "Journal of a Captive," 36.

89. Pote, "Journal," 103.

90. Ibid., 111, 126.

91. Ibid., 110, 127.

92. Several children were born outside the prison in this way. See, for example, "Journal of a Captive," 48.

93. Ibid., 42–43.

94. Pote, "Journal," 109.

95. George Avery, "George Avery's Journal of the Royalton Raid" (c. 1846) in *North Country Captives: Selected Narratives of Indian Captivity from Vermont and New Hampshire*, edited by Colin G. Calloway (Hanover, N.H.: University Press of New England, 1992), 150.

96. Ibid., 156.

97. Over the years I have managed to follow several promising leads in an effort to find the full names and circumstances of "Lyon" and his wife. As of this writing, however, none of the possible candidates accord closely enough to the circumstances outlined by Avery in his

narrative to mention here. Attempts to conclusively identify these early Jewish settlers are on-going.

98. Avery, "Journal of the Royalton Raid," 156.

99. Ibid., 157.

Afterword

1. I continue here to refer to Esther Sayward by her English name for the sake of continuity and clarity. While at the Congrégation she was probably known by her Catholic baptismal name, Marie-Josèphe Sayer. On business and other official documents she signed after her marriage, however, she used both "Madame Lestage" and "Marie Esther Sayer." Like Lydia Longley, then, the elements of Esther's birth name remained with her through decades of life in French Canada.

2. Emma Lewis Coleman, *New England Captives Carried to Canada,* 2 vols. (Portland, Maine: Southworth Press, 1925), 1:240–42.

3. No historian has yet explicitly connected the sudden dearth of captives in New France to the rise of domestic slavery, but that the numbers of Indian slaves from the Great Lakes region present in the colony rises suddenly and sharply around 1712 and accelerates afterward is at least suggestive. Between 1671 and 1699, only 28 new Indian slaves had arrived in the Saint Lawrence Valley, and an average of just under 6 new slaves each year arrived in the decade between 1699 and 1709. In 1710, as Queen Anne's War wound down, 12 new slaves were brought, followed by 10 in 1711, 20 in 1712, 26 in 1713, and 34 in 1714. For these figures see Marcel Trudel, *L'esclavage au Canada français* (Québec: Les Presses Universitaires Laval, 1960), 84–85. Trudel notes as well that slaves of African descent were numerically insignificant in French Canada until the 1740s (89).

4. Marcel Trudel, *Dictionnaire des esclaves et de leurs propriétaires au Canada français* (Ville LaSalle, Québec: Éditions Hurtubise, 1990), 61, 83, 87, 373. Though the date of purchase is not listed for each slave, the dates of baptism certainly occurred soon after acquisition. It was customary for owners to baptize slaves of all ages and both sexes in order to bring the entire household into the Catholic fold. Note as well that friends and peers of the owners were recruited as godparents.

5. Ibid., 52, 65, 68, 69, 71, 75, 80, 116, 120–21, 373. Other heirs included in the legacy of Pierre Lestage included his niece Marie-Anne Lestage, then Sister Saint-Luc of the Congrégation Notre-Dame, as well the sisters collectively, see *History of the Congrégation Notre-Dame,* 4:73–75, Archives of the Centre Marguerite Bourgeoys, Montreal.

6. Robin Winks discusses the practices in *The Blacks in Canada: A History* (New Haven: Yale University Press, 1971), 9–11.

7. See Trudel, *L'esclavage au Canada français,* 169; Trudel, *Dictionnaire des esclaves,* 120–21.

8. René Jetté, *Dictionnaire généalogique des familles du Québec des origines à 1730* (Montréal: Les Presses de l'Université de Montréal), 725.

9. See chapter 2.

10. *History of the Congrégation Notre-Dame,* 4:435–36, 5:225–26.

11. Trudel, *Dictionnaire des esclaves,* 79.

12. *History of the Congrégation Notre-Dame,* 5:180.

13. The original source on the commission of Pierre Le Ber to execute the portrait of Marguerite Bourgeoys is Charles Glandelet, *The True Spirit of the Institute of the Secular Sisters of the Congregation Notre Dame* (c. 1715) (Montréal: Congrégation Notre-Dame, 1977), 89–90. The story relating to Sister Scott and the painting's restoration is recounted by Patricia Simpson in *Marguerite Bourgeoys and Montreal, 1640–1665* (Montreal and Kingston: McGill-Queen's University Press, 1997), 3.

Index